How Shall We Then Care?

How Shall We Then Care?

A Christian Educator's Guide to Caring for Self, Learners, Colleagues, and Community

Edited by
PAUL SHOTSBERGER
and CATHY FREYTAG

Foreword by
DAVID I. SMITH

WIPF & STOCK · Eugene, Oregon

HOW SHALL WE THEN CARE?
A Christian Educator's Guide to Caring for Self, Learners, Colleagues, and Community

Copyright © 2020 Wipf and Stock Publishers. All rights reserved. Except for brief quotations in critical publications or reviews, no part of this book may be reproduced in any manner without prior written permission from the publisher. Write: Permissions, Wipf and Stock Publishers, 199 W. 8th Ave., Suite 3, Eugene, Oregon 97401.

Wipf & Stock
An Imprint of Wipf and Stock Publishers
199 W. 8th Ave., Suite 3
Eugene, Oregon 97401

www.wipfandstock.com

PAPERBACK ISBN: 978-1-5326-8240-7
HARDCOVER ISBN: 978-1-5326-8241-4
EBOOK ISBN: 978-1-5326-8242-1

Manufactured in the U.S.A.   06/11/20

The contents of some of the chapters of this book are adapted from articles appearing in a special issue of the Journal of the International Community of Christian Teacher Educators. Material from the special issue is used by permission of the editors.

Unless otherwise noted, Scriptures taken from the Holy Bible, New International Version®, NIV®. Copyright © 1973, 1978, 1984, 2011 by Biblica, Inc.™ Used by permission of Zondervan. All rights reserved worldwide. www.zondervan.com The "NIV" and "New International Version" are trademarks registered in the United States Patent and Trademark Office by Biblica, Inc.™

We dedicate this book to teacher educators, current
and future teachers, and all who desire to care for themselves,
their students, their colleagues, and their community
with responsive Christ-like care.

CONTENTS

Contributors | ix
Foreword | xi
Introduction | xiii
   —Paul Shotsberger

Chapter 1
What Can Christians Learn from Care Theory? | 1
   —Sean Schat & Cathy Freytag

Chapter 2
The Successful Communication of Educational Care | 17
   —Sean Schat

Chapter 3
Trauma-Informed School Practices in Response to the Impact of Social-Cultural Trauma | 35
   —Anna Berardi & Brenda Morton

Chapter 4
Game-Based Teaching Methodology and Empathy | 66
   —Angel Krause, Scot Headley, Danielle Bryant, Alicia Watkin, Charity-Mika Woodard, & Sherri Sinicki

Chapter 5
Empathy as a Christian Calling | 99
   —Danielle Bryant

Chapter 6
The Ethic of Care and Inclusive Education | 112
   —David W. Anderson

Chapter 7
Inclusion and the Ethic of Care: Our Responsibility
as Christian Special Educators | 125
—Alicia Watkin

Chapter 8
Dispositions: Real-Time Active Practice | 137
—Michelle C. Hughes

Chapter 9
Self and Soul Care: Spiritual Practices to Sustain Teaching | 159
—Stephanie Talley

Chapter 10
Caring for New Teachers Once They Leave Campus | 174
—Elaine Tinholt

CONTRIBUTORS

David W. Anderson, Founder/President, Crossing Bridges, Inc.; Professor Emeritus of Special Education, Bethel University, St. Paul, Minnesota.

Anna Berardi, Director of the Trauma Response Institute and Professor of Marriage and Family Therapy, Graduate Department of Counseling, George Fox University, Portland, Oregon.

Danielle Bryant, Primary Teacher, Kapa'a Elementary School, Kapa'a, Hawaii.

Cathy Freytag, Associate Dean of the Faculty and Professor of Education, Houghton College, Houghton, New York.

Scot Headley, Professor of Educational Leadership, George Fox University, Newberg, Oregon.

Michelle C. Hughes, Associate Professor and Chair of the Education Department, Westmont College, Santa Barbara, California.

Angel Krause, Assistant Professor of Education, Fresno Pacific University, Fresno, California.

Brenda Morton, Associate Professor of Education, George Fox University, Newberg, Oregon.

Sean Schat, Assistant Professor of Education, Redeemer University College, Ancaster, Ontario.

Paul Shotsberger, Professor of Graduate Studies, Southern Wesleyan University, Central, South Carolina.

Sherri Sinicki, Teacher and Teacher Mentor, Dayton High School, Dayton, Oregon.

Stephanie Talley, Assistant Professor of Education, Abilene Christian University, Abilene, Texas.

Elaine Tinholt, Assistant Professor of Education, Covenant College, Lookout Mountain, Georgia.

Alicia Watkin, Assistant Professor of Special Education, Azusa Pacific University, Azusa, California.

Charity-Mika Woodard, Professor of Art Education, Pittsburg State University, Pittsburg, Kansas.

FOREWORD

It has been my impression that Christian students preparing to be teachers find the idea of an ethic of care as a framework for thinking about education intuitively appealing. The relational focus resonates with the personalistic bent of their faith. There is, on the surface at least, a wholesome simplicity about talk of care, as well as the lure of a quick and easily named connection to Christian intuitions concerning love of neighbor, service, and seeking the wellbeing of the world. The task of articulating why Christian educators might be interested in an educational ethic of care seems to promise a lot less sweat than figuring out how Christian faith might relate to, say, a zone of proximal development or a constructivist learning strategy. For those wrestling with the sometimes alien language of education theory, the idea that a concept as accessible as relational care might be serviceable as a frame for thinking about teaching and learning can seem something of a relief, allowing us to relax back into intuitions directed vaguely toward seeking the good of students, communities, and the wider world about and for which we teach.

    This apparently easy point of contact turns out to be somewhat deceptive. This is not because the promise of care ethics as a fruitful avenue for exploring how faith might relate to teaching is illusory, but because that task is not quite as simple as it seems. An ethic of care is not just an appeal to be nice. It is a careful philosophical proposal with specific roots and contours that quickly open up a range of theological, philosophical, pedagogical, hermeneutical, and practical questions, each calling for further investigation. There is a history of discussion in which proposals have been debated, clarified, tested. The apparent quick fix becomes an invitation to deeper learning in which the need for rigor is, after all, not left behind even as the human experience of relational care (rather than, say, the brain's information processing mechanisms) is placed in the spotlight.

This volume accepts that invitation in the context of Christian reflection on teaching and learning. It sets out to engage with care ethics in a way that stays in conversation with theology. Such an enterprise is valuable not least for its potential to broaden the preoccupations that have tended to frame efforts to understand how faith informs education. Major strands of the faith and learning conversation were long preoccupied with questions about how faith might relate to the bases and processes of knowing. More recently that conversation has diversified considerably, and care ethics, an enterprise that seeks to shift how we think about ethics rather than just solve a dilemma within ethics, offers a different kind of arena for reflection. It invites consideration of how the implicit paradigms within which faith and education have been discussed might have constrained the conversation. It invites engagement with questions not just about how we know, but about how we care, what it means to care, what counts as care, what practices nurture care, and how care is experienced. These are just the questions that the authors of this volume set out to explore. For those seeking to understand how faith, teaching, and learning inform one another, such exploration is welcome.

David I. Smith
Director, Kuyers Institute for Christian Teaching and Learning
Calvin University, Grand Rapids, Michigan

INTRODUCTION

Paul Shotsberger

Why a book for Christian educators on caring? It's a fair question. As one colleague said recently, if we have the gospels, do we really need something else to tell us how others should be treated? We maintain that because of its bidirectional nature and dependence on the unique contribution of women, ethic of care, and particularly a Christian ethic of care, is fundamentally reflective of God's nature. It is not just ethical but also theological: it helps us understand God's love and care for us.

Regarding the bidirectional nature of care, the literature on care theory,[1] especially that of Noddings, tells us that this holds in all situations, including care for someone who is helpless.[2] As Nel Noddings observes, "In contrast to other forms of ethics, a care theory credits the cared-for with a special contribution, one different from a reciprocal response as carer. Infants contribute significantly to the mother-child relation, students to the teacher-student relation . . . "[3] Despite the helplessness, nonetheless the mother receives care from the baby, a fulfillment of a heart's desire, a relationship untainted by selfishness or blind ambition.

And so it is with the educator-student relationship. The unidirectional model of instruction, illustrated in an old cartoon as the teacher lifting a lid on the student's head and pouring in knowledge, is generally recognized to be outmoded. Yet, we also believe it is insufficient simply to adopt a "guide on the side" stance as an instructor rather than a "sage on the stage," because

---

1. I will use the phrase "care theory" (rather than an "ethic of care") when referring to Noddings's research.
2. Noddings, *Educating Moral People*; Noddings, *Philosophy of Education*.
3. Noddings, *Educating Moral People*, 2.

it does not fully recognize the contribution of the student. Yes, in constructivist terms, students must be given the opportunity to build up knowledge and knowledge structures for themselves. But this conception does not close the loop regarding students' active roles in their relationship with an educator: the fulfillment experienced by the educator seeing the student get it, the teacher perhaps being shown a student's solution method to a problem or analysis of a literary passage that is both unexpected and satisfying.

It seems that we can understand God's love for humans in somewhat the same way. His love and care for us precede any thoughts of love we might have for him. However, our love and care also matter to him; in fact, it is something he was willing to send his Son to die for. We were created to worship him, which is an expression of love but also a kind of care. How else can we understand the way in which our free will intertwines with his sovereign will and desires? We are not simply giving in to his plan, treating the gift of salvation as merely fire insurance to avoid judgment, but in a sense we complete the cycle, as an adopted son or daughter, returning praise for blessing.

Besides the bidirectional nature of care, Noddings maintains a unique aspect of care theory is that it is fundamentally reflective of the feminine nature. She says, "In almost all cultures, women seem to develop the capacity to care more often and more deeply than men."[4] Where does this impetus come from? Noddings says it derives from societal expectations, that it is in fact not innate, but we would suggest something deeper.

When God speaks about care for his people in the Bible, often this is done in feminine terms: a bear robbed of her cubs (Hos 13); a mother comforting her child (Isa 66); a woman nursing a baby (Isa 49). Jesus, the second person of the Trinity and equal with God, identifies as a hen trying to gather up and protect her chicks (Matt 23). Protection, comfort, and nurture are all aspects of care, and according to Scripture they are all facets of God's character and heart. A trending view of the Trinity depicts the Holy Spirit as mother, thus completing the nuclear family model of father-child-mother. But this denies the fact that Father God and God the Son both likened themselves not simply to parents, but to caring female beings. Further, if the Bible is to be the pattern for living the life of faith, we must consider seriously these references to care found in its pages.

Thus, from the beginning we have the need to include an ontological consideration of the reality of God and the way in which God sees and values humans. Genesis 1:1 tells us, "In the beginning God . . . " That is, before there was anything or anyone to care for, there was God. Further,

---

4. Noddings, *Educating Moral People*, 19.

Scripture tells us that humans were created in God's image, that God is love, and that we love because he first loved us. By extension, therefore, we care for anything or anyone because God first cared for us. Care is also a command reflective of God's heart. As David W. Anderson notes in his chapter, a pre-fall role given by God to Adam was as caretaker of creation, that is, one who shows care. Thus, caregiving is part of God's perfect design for humans.

One might ask: If care theory captures the essence of God's care for us, why do we need a Christian ethic of care? Because for Noddings, paradoxically, there is no place for God in her theory. As she states, "There is no command to love nor, indeed, any God to make the commandment. Further, I shall reject the notion of universal love, finding it unattainable in any but the most abstract sense and thus a source of distraction."[5] So, from the believer's perspective, there is a *raison d'être* for a Christian ethic of care. However, we must be cognizant of the danger we face of superficially adding God back into Noddings's model, layering love on top like frosting on a cake. It is the ontological realities previously mentioned that help us to avoid putting the ethic of care cart before the scriptural horse. This helps ensure that Christian principles in the Gospels such as the greatest commandment and those found in the good Samaritan story are not merely add-ons to care theory, but rather the bedrock upon which a Christian ethic of care is built. All chapter authors are Christian believers, some working in a specifically Christian context, some in public institutions. Therefore, you will read a mix of overtly Christian ethic of care principles and actions, but others will be more implicit; however, the heart is the same. A Christian ethic of care serves to illuminate our relationship with God while also helping to flesh out what care looks like in various contexts, no matter what that context might be.

In this book, each author or team of authors has made a unique contribution to the ongoing care dialogue.[6] The book begins with a chapter by Sean Schat and Cathy Freytag titled "What Can Christians Learn from Care Theory?" The authors lay a biblical foundation for the Christian love mandate while pursuing the thesis that care theory may help the church to communicate the love and care that the world so desperately needs.

In "The Successful Communication of Educational Care," Sean Schat illuminates key findings from his original research into student perceptions of care in the teacher-student relationship. He notes that while teachers typically hold caring intentions, their attempts to communicate care are

---

5. Noddings, *Caring*, 28–29.

6. Most chapters of the book appeared earlier in article form in the *Journal of the International Community of Christian Teacher Educators* 13.2. The revised articles are used here with permission of the editors.

not always perceived as caring by students. Schat articulates what he has described as a "miscommunication of care," and offers practical considerations for how relational, pedagogical, and interpersonal care can be established and nurtured within caring, responsive teacher-student relationships.

Any robust conversation of care will necessarily address the role of responsive empathy. The chapter by Anna Berardi and Brenda Morton titled "Trauma-Informed School Practices in Response to the Impact of Social-Cultural Trauma" focuses on responding to the effects of relational and sociopolitical trauma within K-12 and higher education settings using their Trauma-Informed School Programming (TISP). The authors maintain that TISP is not only a trauma-informed ethic of care, but central to Christ's call for embrace of the stranger, the foreigner, the marginalized, and the vulnerable.

In "Game-Based Teaching Methodology and Empathy," Angel Krause and colleagues describe the highly-impactful experience they had in a doctoral-level course as their professor utilized a game-based approach to foster empathic care for diverse students and their unique needs. By engaging in a role-playing game (RPG) approach, participants were more highly invested in the course, they were able to carry empathy-building RPG applications into their own contexts, and they reported that the RPG approach helped to foster an enhanced sense of empathy for students in their care.

While Krause et al. describe empathy development on a systems level, Danielle Bryant, author of "Empathy as a Christian Calling," discusses empathy on a more individual level. Taking a narrative inquiry approach, Bryant reflects on empathy research and her own experiences and proposes a model (ACTS: Actively Listen, Communicate Back, Think with Empathy, Speak a Response) for building and enacting empathic care in both K-12 and university classrooms.

While the call to care is universal, David W. Anderson's chapter, "The Ethic of Care and Inclusive Education," and Alicia Watkin's chapter, "Inclusion and the Ethic of Care: Our Responsibility as Christian Special Educators," look more specifically at what it means to care responsively for students within the context of inclusive education. Anderson suggests that a Christian ethic of care in inclusive classrooms should be characterized by compassion, presence, interdependence and hospitality, relationship, authenticity, and service. Watkin maintains that Christian educators have a responsibility to care by listening, showing up, and advocating—not only for their students with special needs, but for parents, colleagues, and any other neighbor we encounter in the inclusive communities we seek to foster.

Those of us who are engaged in the work of preparing preservice teachers realize the profound responsibility we have to equip future educators with resources that will help to sustain them in their practice as caring, nurturing teachers beyond the brief time we have with them in the preparatory phase of their careers. Michelle Hughes continues her work conducting longitudinal research in the area of professional dispositions. In her chapter, "Dispositions: Real-Time Active Practice," she explores the dispositional awareness and practice of program completers as they transition into the K-12 professional teaching context. Her research indicates that there is a dearth of proactive attention given to the ongoing development of dispositions in the professional setting and that it is largely the individual teacher's responsibility to continue to cultivate dispositions that foster sustainable care in the classroom. She suggests ways in which teacher education programs might partner with the profession to ensure that structures are in place to foster the ongoing development of dispositions in beginning teachers.

In "Self and Soul Care: Spiritual Practice to Sustain Teaching," Stephanie Talley poignantly describes the importance of modeling and nurturing faith-informed self-care for our teacher candidates and recent graduates, and proposes creative mechanisms that teacher education programs might employ to foster and sustain these caring, life-giving practices. Similarly, Elaine Tinholt, in her chapter "Caring for New Teachers Once They Leave Campus," emphasizes the need to remain present to our graduates and provide caring, supportive structures for them as they navigate the new challenges they will encounter as beginning teachers.

We trust that you will find each chapter to be timely and informative wherever you might find yourself in this season of your caring vocation.

BIBLIOGRAPHY

Noddings, Nel. *Caring: A Feminine Approach to Ethics and Moral Education*. Berkeley: University of California Press, 1984.
———. *Educating Moral People: A Caring Alternative to Character Education*. New York: Teachers College Press, 2002.
———. *Philosophy of Education*. Cambridge, MA: Westview, 2007.

Chapter 1

WHAT CAN CHRISTIANS LEARN FROM CARE THEORY?

Sean Schat & Cathy Freytag

According to care theory, all human beings have two care-related needs: the need to *care for others*, and the need to *be cared for by others*.[1] Humans are wired for relationship. As Christian researchers engaged in the care theory and ethic of care discourses, this foundational premise resonates deeply with our fundamental beliefs. We believe this is part of the way God made people: human beings need others, we need to love others, and, in turn, we need to be loved by others. This is also part of how we image God, both in being affirmed by love and in seeking to communicate love to others. Human beings were created for relationships and to seek the well-being and flourishing of other image-bearers.

In this introductory chapter, we seek to establish a direct and foundational link between the human need for care and the biblical imperative to love. Drawing on care theory's assertion that care is a relationship,[2] not simply caring intentions and caring actions, we define care as *a relationship between two individuals where the one-caring supports the well-being,*

---

1. Noddings, *Caring: A Feminine Approach*; Noddings, *Caring: A Relational Approach*.

2. Noddings, *Caring: A Feminine Approach*; Noddings, *Caring: A Relational Approach*.

flourishing, and autonomy of the cared-for, and where both relationship partners recognize and assent to what is happening. We believe that care must be successfully communicated in order for love to be recognized and experienced.

PART I—THE LOVE MANDATE: COMMANDED TO LOVE

> Hearing that Jesus had silenced the Sadducees, the Pharisees got together. One of them, an expert in the law, tested him with this question: "Teacher, which is the greatest commandment in the Law?" Jesus replied: "'Love the Lord your God with all your heart and with all your soul and with all your mind.' This is the first and greatest commandment. And the second is like it: 'Love your neighbor as yourself.' All the Law and the Prophets hang on these two commandments." (Matt 22:34–40)

Christ's words in Matthew 22 have often been described as The Love Command, or The Love Mandate. In this crucial passage, Jesus reminds his listeners that the calls to love God and to love others are the two most important commands. Indeed, it is clear from his words that everything else hangs on these two commandments. The body of Christ, his hands and feet and voice in the world, is expected to love God and to love others. The biblical narrative shows us that loving others is one of the most important ways we can show our love for God, while simultaneously obeying his command to love others. As John reminds us, "... Everyone who loves has been born of God and knows God. Whoever does not love does not know God, because God is love" (1 John 4:7–8).

This command to love is clearly picked up by Paul and the other leaders of the first-century church. And then, if the testimony of historians is to be believed, it is so embodied by the members of the early church that the love they communicated changed the world—in Christ's name and on his behalf. History testifies powerfully of the many ways that the embodied love of the early church resulted in the establishment of caring, humanitarian initiatives and institutions that continue to shape the world (e.g., care for the widow and orphan, care for the sick, care for the poor and needy, care for the imprisoned, care for one's enemy, etc.). From the very first days of the embodied church, many Christians have been characterized by their commitment to showing love and care to others through actions that support human well-being and flourishing. Faithful obedience to the love mandate is transformational.

Biblical Foundations

As Christians, we believe that Christ ascended to heaven and sits at the right hand of his Father's throne, interceding for his sinful children. When the time is right, Jesus will return, ushering in the eternal kingdom. God longs for all of his children to join him in his kingdom. But in order to be true to himself, he will not force anyone to join him. God made humans with free will, and humans are, therefore, free to choose to follow him or not. However, God's intention has always been for all of his children to join him in his eternal kingdom. And his unfolding historical plan of redemption and restoration provides the hope that every person will ultimately join him in heaven. Christ's birth, life, death, resurrection, and ascension provided the incarnational potential for all people to be freed from their sins, and to be freed from facing the price of sin: eternal separation from God. Importantly, the outpouring of the Holy Spirit at Pentecost provides the means for reconciliation between God and all of his children. All who hear the message of Christ and respond to his call will have the opportunity to be part of the eternal, already-present-and-constantly-unfolding kingdom.

The complicating factor, however, is that Christ dwells in heaven with his Father, rather than here on earth. And the still-outpouring Holy Spirit can be hard to see, as well as difficult to recognize, even when the Spirit is visible. This is why Christ authorized the church to serve as his hands and feet and voice. Christ needs us to play a role in his unfolding plan. Christians are the primary way for others, who do not yet know Christ, to meet him, and to hear his message of salvation and call on their lives. The primary way for image-bearers who do not yet know whose image they bear to meet Christ is through Christians. And in a sinful and broken world, where sin and brokenness penetrate everything, including our ability to represent Christ and to communicate God's love, our ability to serve as his hands and feet and voice is constantly at risk. Sin has corrupted, distorted, and misdirected everything we are and everything we do. We may be created for love, but just like every other aspect of creation, love can be misdirected, misused, misunderstood, malformed, and incomplete. This demands that Christians be attentive and intentional when it comes to obeying God's command to love. We believe that care theory, with its intentional focus on how others respond to the care that has been offered, can play an important role in helping the church to embody love.

The command to love others is central to our very purpose. Because we love God, we keep his commandments—a response of gratitude, not merely an automatic, unreflective response rooted in fear of the consequences that might flow from disobedience. And we are commanded to love others because they have been made in the image of God, just as we have. As an image-bearer, one is worthy of love. This is the foundation of both love of self and love of others: people are worthy of love because they are made in the image of God. Love is obligated because of their image-bearing. It is one's duty, in response to who God is, what he has done, and what he has commanded us to do.

PART II—HOW THE CHURCH HAS FAILED THE LOVE MANDATE

A closer look at our post-modern, post-Christian context is both sad and revealing. It is not that the world no longer needs their Savior and Lord, of course. The problem is that the church has failed to be the hands and feet and voice of Christ. The world looks at Christians and does not see Christ. As a result, many of the people who need Christ to be their Savior never get a chance to meet him. They do not recognize what Jesus has done for them. They do not hear his call. They completely miss out on what they need most: Christ. And they do not even realize it. To a certain extent, this is the church's fault.

The Harm Christians Have Caused

Both of us have been involved in Christian education for a long time. Recently, I (Sean) had an opportunity to step away from a Christian educational context, entering a local public university in order to attend graduate school. It was at this point that I experienced a significant paradigm shift. I had expected some opposition and hostility because of my Christian faith. I had also expected some hospitality, an openness to diverse belief systems, given the humanistic and pluralistic context of the secular academy. I had expected some mocking. I was not expecting my faith to not be mocked at all. I was not expecting to see my faith overlooked, or seen as a relic. The paradigm shift occurred, however, when I began to realize that I was being granted hospitality, at least in the eyes of some of my colleagues, given the perception they had of Christians. One of the early courses in my program addressed issues of marginalization in Western culture, reviewing the lived experience of different demographic groups that had experienced opposition and marginalization and worse at the hands of Westerners. It took a while for it to dawn on me that I really was being granted hospitality (e.g., by being able to be present, participating in the dialogue), because it soon became very clear that a post-modern, post-Christian review of the history of marginalization in the West clearly and directly connects marginalization and oppression to Christianity and the behavior and actions of Christians.

I would love to be more accurate and instead say that the connection made between Western marginalization and oppression and Christianity was actually described as a link between marginalization and oppression and the terrible behaviors of some misguided, misdirected Christians who were not representing Christ by their actions. As accurate as I believe the latter statement to be, that was certainly not the perception of those participating in our class dialogue (or in the articles we were reading and discussing). And to be fair to the lived experience of the writers and my classmates, their interpretation was legitimate. When looking back at issues of marginalization and oppression in recent Western history, Christians have often been at the forefront, playing a leadership role in the dominant groups that marginalized and oppressed other groups.

Women's Rights

The denigration of women and a deeply rooted denial of women's rights and women's equality often resulted from an interpretation of biblical principles. This interpretation was powerfully articulated and embodied by dominant white, male church leaders, and eagerly followed by many male adherents.

Slavery

Most of the wealthy slaveowners in the nineteenth century were at least nominally Christians, many of whom did not question slavery and sometimes even drew on biblical principles to support their beliefs and behavior, including the fact that they owned other human beings. The same spirit often animates the racism that still remains present in too many communities.

First Nations Residential Schools

Many of the men and women who served at these residential schools, educational institutions that removed First Nations children from their families and communities and sought to integrate them into North American society, were Christians. With big hearts and good intentions, these well-meaning men and women isolated children from their families and disparaged and undermined their culture and traditions (as recently as 1996, when the last school in North America finally closed). We also can't overlook the poor conditions and criminal behaviors that often took place in these schools.

Sexual Identity

In a more current context, opposition to people who identify as LGBTQ+ is often led by Christians, whose judgmentalism and outright hostility clearly comes across as hate-mongering. Christians appear to hate both the sin and the sinner.[3]

As believing Christians, we are confident we could make a compelling case that in these issues of marginalization and oppression, many of the Christians who participated were mistaken, misguided, and misdirected, and did not represent Christ (or even other Christians) in their actions. However, there are two important objections we must raise against our own arguments. First of all, and most centrally, the point is moot, given the lived experience of the victims of marginalization: Christians played a leading role in marginalization and causing harm. Secondly, our arguments, however legitimate, would not be heard.

Christians Played a Leading Role in Issues of Marginalization

Regardless of our legitimate concerns about the behavior of some Christians, reality speaks for itself: Christians played a leading role in issues of marginalization, causing significant harm along the way. This is a historical fact. We could certainly argue that the perpetrators should not be seen to represent Christians, and could probably also argue that for every Christian leading the marginalization, there were probably ten or more who were actively (and quietly and humbly) working to support the marginalized and oppressed. As Christians, living and working in Christian communities, this is an important distinction. But from the outside looking in, this point is moot—it does not matter. The lived experience of the victims and an objective review of history by modern scholars both describe the same reality: terrible things happened, unfortunates were marginalized, oppressed, and harmed, and Christians were heavily involved in leading the process. The conclusion they would draw is accurate: Christians supported marginalization and oppression. Christians participated in and often led the persecution

---

3. Kinnaman and Lyons, *UnChristian*.

and abuse of other human image-bearers. Christians caused harm to others on an epic scale. Some Christians continue to do so today.

In our research into student experiences of the educational care communicated by their teachers, we draw on two important theoretical foundations: care theory[4] and perceptual theory.[5] As a result, we believe we are positioned to make an important, albeit somewhat obvious, point. Perceptual theory draws our attention to the significance of perception. Care theory reminds us that in many of the situations explored above, well-meaning Christians have intended to communicate care, but because their sincere efforts were misguided or misinformed, or because they did not pay sufficient attention to the cared-for, their efforts were not perceived to be caring. Most of the Christians who led the marginalization and oppression were not evil people, seeking to abuse their power and cause harm to others. They were good Christians, seeking to honor God and follow his commands. Indeed, their objective was almost always to (1) make disciples of all nations, and (2) confront sin, and this faith commitment clearly directed their actions. As a Christian community we need to name and own the behavior of our good-hearted brothers and sisters. Their biblically faithful good intentions and the resulting well-intended but sinful actions are our legacy. The church needs to repent. But repentance also implies a change in behavior.

Christians Have Forfeited Their Right to Speak

Despite the objections we may want to voice, in the current milieu, our voice often does not count. In many ways, Christians are seen to have forfeited their right to speak. Christians have had their turn, and their actions have, in the eyes of many, spoken clearly: when Christians had power and influence, they abused their position and harmed others. Now that the voiceless have advocates who are willing to speak for them, or have finally discovered their own voice, the sinful actions of hundreds of thousands of Western Christians have been clearly identified and named.

One of the biggest challenges I (Sean) faced in my graduate program was the irony of the modern dialogue landscape. It is very clear that the marginalized have finally been given a place to speak. This is a good thing. And our collective cultural commitment to pluralism, diversity, and tolerance actively seeks to ensure that anyone who might be marginalized has a place at the table—a place to speak and raise a voice. Except Christians.

---

4. Noddings, *Caring: A Feminine Approach*; Noddings, *Caring: A Relational Approach*.

5. Combs et al., *Perceptual Psychology*; Combs, *Being and Becoming*.

While this is not always the case, I have observed that the Christian voice often has no place at the table. It is not consulted. When a Christian voice is raised, it is almost as if the response is, "You have had your turn to speak, and you abused it. You can't talk anymore." As much as I struggle with this, there is a certain degree of justice and irony. We have had a chance to speak. And we occasionally used it for terrible purposes, causing harm even if we did not intend to do so. Through our actions, we have essentially forfeited our right to speak with authority and influence.

Having worked in Christian communities for more than 20 years, I will also add that this conclusion is not only being drawn by the surrounding secular culture. My own high school and university students have often drawn the same conclusion. I suspect that this issue is directly linked to some of the demographic challenges facing the Western church. Young people and young adults are asking important questions about how we have treated other people, both within and without our Christian communities. And, once again, it is not a stretch to realize that we have often failed to honor God and authentically embody our theoretical beliefs in faithful actions. As David Kinnaman and Gabe Lyons revealed in *UnChristian*, when our own young people and young adults look at Christians, they see the same thing the world sees: too often Christians are hypocritical, judgmental, naïve, and sheltered.[6] We appear to hate those who do not believe what we believe, or act the way we want them to.

As much as we are horrified by the conclusions people draw about Christians, we cannot overlook that the real tragedy of Western marginalization and oppression is the impact on the victims. Lives have been lost. People have been irreparably harmed. Human beings have been demeaned and damaged. Trust has been broken. And many Christians remain unaware and unrepentant. In some cases, Christians continue to cause harm to others. Ironically, when other Christians raise objections, they themselves may face marginalization and oppression.

A Failure to Successfully Communicate Love and Care

While most Christians we have known would never condone the actions carried out by some Christians in either the past or the present, we suspect that many of us have participated in this same failure to successfully communicate love to others. Just like many good-hearted, well-intended Jewish believers who stood at the front of the crowd calling out for Christ to be crucified, firmly believing they had well-rooted scriptural rationale for

---

6. Kinnaman and Lyons, *UnChristian*.

their actions, we suspect that many of us would have gone along with the crowds in supporting slavery, denying the rights of women, encouraging the removal of indigenous children from their own families and communities, and in persecuting people with different beliefs, sexual orientation, and skin color. Indeed, we both recognize that if we had been alive at the time of Christ, we very likely would have been Pharisees. We would have known our Hebrew Bible well. We would have been powerfully aware of Israel's loss of status and power. We would have been conscientiously focused on the injustice of Roman oppression (and the fear of reprisal). And we would have seen Christ as a threat to God's plan for Israel. With all of the fervor we could have mustered, we would have called for and supported his crucifixion. And, to our shame and horror, we would have been wrong, despite our good hearts and good intentions. It is no coincidence that many of the early converts to Christianity were repentant Jews who had seen the error of their ways, were ashamed at what they had done (or what had been done in their name and on their behalf), and were transformed as a result, radically determined to authentically live out their newly awakened faith. It is our hope that we might experience a similar awakening today.

The issue is not that all Christians are hypocritical, judgmental, naïve, sheltered, and hate-mongering. Those from within the Christian community (and hundreds of thousands of those outside of the Christian community who interact regularly with faithful, biblically obedient Christians) know that many Christians are good-hearted, well-intended people who serve God faithfully and whose behaviors are characterized by the love they are commanded to reveal. In today's culture, however, this is not what is most often seen. Instead, because there is ample public evidence to support the conclusion, Christians are too often perceived to be duplicitous, sanctimonious, manipulative, misdirected, and stuck in the past. As ludicrous as the conclusion may seem to some Christians, it is imperative that we realize that perception is reality. The eyes of those outside the church look at the church and see a single body that is not loving. Indeed, from their vantage point, caring is the last word they would use to describe Christians.

Thus we submit that the church has lost the love mandate and failed to love, at least in the eyes of those who should be receiving the love that Christians are commanded to communicate. From the outside looking in, the church has failed to show love, and to claim otherwise perpetuates the problem. When the church denies the wrongs that have been done by Christians, they appear to be struggling with both blindness *and* denial. The real tragedy of the loss of the love mandate is not the bad reputation for Christians, but the fact that people who need Christ never have a chance to encounter him.

PART III—CAN CARE THEORY HELP THE CHURCH SUCCESSFULLY COMMUNICATE LOVE?

This brings us to care theory and a Christian ethic of care. The intentionality, transparency, and authenticity of a caring relationship may be exactly what are needed when it comes to rearticulating and reembodying the love mandate. If the church has failed to embody the Love Command, and has failed to be the hands and feet and voice of Christ in the world, we submit that, when viewed through a biblical lens, care theory and a Christian ethic of care may be the hope of the church. We believe that the simplicity and power of care theory, with its focus on authentic caring relationships, on intentionality and empathy, and on ensuring that care is perceived, received, and experienced, could allow the modern Western church to reengage with the Love Command. When care is recognized and responded to, it changes both perception and behavior. And when people's behavior is characterized by love and care, lives can be transformed. When lives are transformed, the possibility of seeing Christ as the source of love and transformation becomes possible.

Care Theory Foundations

How can the care theory discourse help the Western church to rearticulate and reembody the love mandate? A brief overview of some of the central tenets of care theory may be helpful.

Every Human Being Has Two Care-Related Needs

Foundational to care theory is the recognition that every human being has two care-related needs: the need to care for others and the need to be cared for by others.[7] In the context of the failure of the love mandate, this is a critical starting point. An essential aspect of our humanity is the need to love and be loved. While we may have failed to demonstrate care, and while those we long to care for may appear to be uninterested, or to be rejecting the care we intend to offer, the reality is that all human beings need to be cared for. And, in turn, we need to care for others.

---

7. Groenhout, *Connected Lives*; Noddings, *Caring: A Feminine Approach*; Noddings, *Caring: A Relational Approach*.

Care Is a Relationship

Perhaps the most important element of care theory is the clear declaration that care is a direct personal relationship between the *one-caring* and the *cared-for*.[8] Care is not only caring intentions and caring actions. Relationality is at the core of care. This is something that is far too easily overlooked by Christians, who long to demonstrate care to others, but often fail to recognize that care involves relationship, and this implies that both parties participate. Because people are not only created to be cared for, but also to care for others, there is an element of reciprocity that must be honored. Caring for another individual establishes a relationship between the two people. Both are influenced.

Characteristics of a Caring Relationship

Nel Noddings has identified three primary characteristics of a caring relationship: *engrossment, motivational displacement,* and *response*.[9]

Engrossment focuses on the importance of being receptive or open to others, paying attention to them in order to get to know and understand them. This is an important starting point for Christians, who can appear to be engrossed more with themselves, their intentions, and their mission than with actually being receptive and open to accepting the other person as they are. Christians can too easily enter the relationship with the intention of changing the other person.

What Noddings describes as *motivational displacement* is often referred to as empathy. The care theory literature debates the relationship between these two terms because of the contrast between projective empathy and associative empathy,[10] an important distinction in the context of this chapter. Projective empathy occurs when the one-caring attempts to project themselves onto the cared-for, doing their very best to try to empathize with or understand what the other is going through, or how the other sees things. Associative empathy occurs when the one-caring is much more receptive to the experiences, perceptions, and feelings of the cared-for. In this context, the one-caring comes alongside of the other person, and

---

8. Noddings, *Caring: A Feminine Approach*; Noddings, *Caring: A Relational Approach*.

9. Noddings, *Caring: A Feminine Approach*; Noddings, *Caring: A Relational Approach*.

10. Shen, "Effectiveness of Empathy- Versus Fear-Arousing"; Slote, *Ethics of Care and Empathy*.

earnestly and honestly seeks to see the world through the eyes of the other person. If the one-caring is not intentionally reflective about this, it could be easy to fall into familiar patterns and understandings. Noddings's concept of motivational displacement has potential value because it may challenge people's perceptions and behavior, leading them to focus more on others, thereby making it more likely their intended care will be communicated successfully.

A caring relationship cannot be a one-way relationship. The one-caring must recognize that the cared-for also needs to be able to *respond* to the care. Establishing a caring relationship is always risky because the one-caring may be changed through the experience. The response of the cared-for may be more than the one-caring expects, or even wants. But to deny the relationship or the need (and right) for the cared-for to respond is to prevent the completion of care. Their response ultimately defines the relationship.

Care Must be Completed

And now we get to the heart of the matter. Love is not love if the person who receives the love does not see the love as love, even if the one who is communicating the love is well-intended and earnestly seeks to show love to the other. The distinction between the offering of care and the successful communication of care is a significant one.[11] Care theory identifies the completion of care as fundamental to the successful communication of care. Regardless of the good-hearted, well-intended perceptions and behaviors of the one-caring, care is not care if it has not been perceived, received, and experienced as care by the cared-for. Care must be completed in order to be communicated successfully. This is an essential distinction when it comes to communicating love.

This is far too easy to overlook. Too often the person who intends to communicate care assumes that they have been caring because they intended to be caring and they performed actions that demonstrated their care. To the one-caring, this is often perceived to be sufficient. They are caring, and their intentions and actions testify to this. The problem, of course, is that the cared-for may not necessarily see it this way. And if the cared-for does not recognize and accept the care that was extended, care has not been communicated successfully. The perception of the cared-for defines the communication of care.

11. Schat, "Exploring Adolescent Student Perceptions."

We believe that this gets to the heart of the issue of the failure of the church to communicate love to others. Christians have rested on the laurels of their good intentions and biblically faithful actions. Even a review of some of the worst examples of Christian behaviors can shed light on this issue. Those who worked in First Nations residential schools believed they were helping the natives when they sought to stamp out indigenous cultural practices and traditions, and attempted to indoctrinate students into Western culture. The great explorers and the monarchs who financially supported their voyages were at least partially motivated by their desire to obey both the cultural mandate and the Great Commission (e.g., spread out, discover God's world, tell everyone you meet about Christ). Many of the priests who were present on these famous journeys sought to bring Christ to the "noble savage" and the "infidels." Even today, many good-hearted, well-intended Christians are zealous in their commitment to fight sin and save the sinner. An important distinction needs to be made in this context: biblical obedience and biblical faithfulness are not necessarily the same thing. It is frighteningly possible for Christians to faithfully intend and seek to communicate love to others, but if their love is not received, while they may believe they have been faithful, they actually have not obeyed God's injunction to love. Care theory reminds us that love isn't love if the one you love doesn't see your love as love.

Caring Intentions and Caring Actions Are Not Enough

Using the lens of care theory, particularly Noddings's concept of completion and the three characteristics of a caring relationship, one can better understand why so many non-Christians are skeptical about or suspicious of Christians. Too often what was envisioned as care by good-hearted, well-intended Christians ends up falling far short when held against the touchstone of care theory. Too often, behaviors that were thought to have been caring have been enacted without sufficient attention to the recipient of care. Christians often act on behalf of others without consulting them, or seek to help or even change others without ensuring that the others want (or perceive themselves as needing) the care that is offered. There has been no engrossment, no motivational displacement, and, to the disappointment of so many sincere Christians, no response. There has been no uptake of care because a caring relationship had never been established.

Herein lies the greatest challenge for Christians. In almost all such situations, Christians earnestly want to care for the other person. Perhaps even more importantly, they also want to obey God, who tells them to love others and to spread the news of Christ, to teach others about God's commands, and to combat sin and the forces of darkness in the world. So much of what appears to be care, and is certainly intended to be care, actually does more harm than good due to the absence of a caring relationship. From the inside looking out, Christians believe they are doing good things, and earnestly believe they are exercising their faith and obeying God through their caring actions. But from the outside looking in, such behaviors often ring false. Instead, the actions of Christians often appear to be manipulative, inappropriate, condescending, and arrogant. Christians look as if they think they have the corner on truth and human needs, and look as if they believe they are the arbiters of what others need, and are determined to give it to them, even if they don't want it. From what was said earlier, it is clear that such behavior is, at best, a lack of uptake or a failure to communicate successfully intended care. However, it is also quite likely that others will perceive such care as either malformed or even abusive.

PART IV—FOLLOWING CHRIST

It is, of course, not too late. Throughout the generations, there have been millions of people who have lived out their faith in God through their actions in the world. They have lived faithfully and obediently, and they have exerted a powerfully positive influence on others for the sake of Christ. However, in the West the influence of the church is waning, its numbers declining, its population greying. This influence of the gospel needs to be reclaimed for the sake of Christ, not for the sake of Christians. It will not be reclaimed by rhetoric or proselytizing, nor will it be aided by complaining or bemoaning the current reality, nor by blaming others for actions that have occurred in the past. Christ changed the world through the early church by the church building relationships and by influencing local communities and individual humans, one by one. The church consistently modeled love and hospitality. The failure of the Western church is a failure to love, or, more specifically, to ensure that our well-intended loving actions are recognized as love, and that the One who is the source of love is seen to be the source of our actions.

A Christian ethic of care provides an important touchstone, a lens by which we can examine what has happened in the past, to recognize what has occurred, and to see clearly what needs to be done in response. Care theory could be the hope of the church, insofar as it has the power to challenge faithful followers to ensure that God's love can be seen in the love they communicate to the people around them. To successfully communicate this love in a postmodern, post-Christian setting does not demand that we speak convincingly, but that we act faithfully and obediently. The three characteristics of a caring relationship (engrossment, motivational displacement, and response) are potentially invaluable tools that can challenge Christians to allow Christ to work through them to change the world, one person and one relationship at a time.

At times, we wonder if the failure to communicate love can result from Christians finding themselves caught between the ethic of justice and the ethic of care. On the one hand, Christians are clearly called to confront sin. On the other hand, Christians are clearly commanded to love the sinner. This seems like a simple and clear distinction. But when we look closely at Christ's actions and Paul's words (1 Cor 5:12; Eph 4:17; Col 3:16), the call for believers to confront sin is to confront the sinful behavior of other Christians (as Jesus and his followers often did with the Pharisees and other misdirected religious leaders). In our interactions with unbelievers, building a relationship is much more appropriate than focusing primarily on sinfulness. It seems to us that, far too often, Christians default to confronting the sin, assuming that their good intentions (and the implied love for God and others) will be recognized. The ethic of justice seems to demand that justice and truth take precedence over the human need for care. Therefore, we wonder if these two ethics are too often seen to be in opposition.

In *Justice and Love*, Nicholas Wolterstorff suggests that authentic biblical love requires that if we love someone, we will both seek their well-being or flourishing and seek to ensure that their rights are honored—that they are treated justly. Wolterstorff maintains that the concept of care may best capture this challenging balance, writing,

> Is there a term in present day idiomatic English, in addition to the term "love," for the union of these two kinds of love, love that seeks to enhance a person's well-being or flourishing and love that seeks to secure that a person's rights are honored, that she be treated with due respect for her worth? I think there is. It's the term "care," understood not as caring for someone who needs aid or assistance but as caring about someone.[12]

God commands his followers to love others. We need to do all we can to ensure that we are obedient when it comes to communicating love. Good and caring intentions and actions are essential for offering care, but insufficient for successfully communicating care. The successful communication of care depends on the response of the cared-for. The successful communication of love requires attending to the perceptions and responses of the people with whom we interact. It is too easy to settle for a quick and

---

12. Wolterstorff, *Justice in Love*, 101.

superficial assessment, trusting our hearts and intentions, and assuming that our actions have been recognized.

Care theory has the potential to play an important role in helping the church to embody and articulate love, allowing Christians to be both obedient and faithful. Significantly, this will also position Christians to be used by God to build his kingdom. Care theory's emphasis on relationality, on authentic empathy, and on the importance of paying attention to perceptions (both our own and those of others) have the potential to lead to transformation. People whose lives are transformed by the love they experience are committed to showing love to others. This is the foundation of our Christian faith: once we realize that we have been loved unconditionally by God (even though we don't deserve it), we can only respond by loving others instinctively and automatically, as a response of gratitude. We show our love for God in the ways we show love to others. This is not easy, of course. Sin and human personalities will get in the way. But we must be determined to love, both out of obedience and out of a recognition of the potential power love can display. We believe that a focus on successfully communicating care can help us to reveal God's love to others.

BIBLIOGRAPHY

Combs, Arthur W. *Being and Becoming: A Field Approach to Psychology*. New York: Springer, 1999.

Combs, Arthur W., et al. *Perceptual Psychology: A Humanistic Approach to the Study of Persons*. New York: Harper & Row, 1976.

Groenhout, Ruth E. *Connected Lives: Human Nature and an Ethics of Care*. Lanham, MD: Rowman & Littlefield, 2004.

Kinnaman, David, and Gabe Lyons. *UnChristian: What a New Generation Really Thinks about Christianity. . .And Why it Matters*. Grand Rapids: Baker, 2007.

Noddings, Nel. *Caring: A Feminine Approach to Ethics and Moral Education*. Berkeley: University of California Press, 1984.

———. *Caring: A Relational Approach to Ethics and Moral Education*. 2nd ed. Berkeley: University of California Press, 2013.

Schat, Sean. "Exploring Adolescent Student Perceptions and Experiences of Educational Care." PhD diss., Brock University, 2019.

Shen, Lijiang. "The Effectiveness of Empathy- Versus Fear-Arousing Antismoking PSAs." *Health Communication* 26 (2011) 404–15.

Slote, Michael. *The Ethics of Care and Empathy*. New York: Routledge, 2007.

Wolterstorff, Nicholas. *Justice in Love*. 2nd ed. Grand Rapids: Eerdmans, 2015.

Chapter 2

THE SUCCESSFUL COMMUNICATION OF EDUCATIONAL CARE

Sean Schat

CARE THEORY AND THE LOVE MANDATE

Christian reflections on the nature and communication of care often begin with Christ's words in Matthew 22. When Israel's leaders gathered to challenge Jesus, they asked him which commandment was the greatest:

> Jesus replied, "'Love the Lord your God with all your heart and with all your soul and with all your mind.' This is the first and greatest commandment. And the second is like it: 'Love your neighbor as yourself.'" (Matt 22:37–39)

Most Christians recognize that in this passage Christ commands his followers to love God and others. This is the origin of the *love mandate*: God's command to his children to show their love for him by loving others.

Too often, however, those outside of the church do not perceive Christians as being either loving or caring. Instead, Christians are often seen as negative, judgmental, spiteful, and hypocritical.[1] Sometimes these criticisms

---

1. Kinnaman and Lyons, *UnChristian*.

are legitimate, but sometimes they are not. And sometimes the issue is that good-hearted, well-intended Christians fail to communicate their love and care because they fail to ensure that their intentions are recognized—they fail to develop a relational context in which to offer their criticisms and suggestions. To those they interact with, their actions seem neither loving nor caring.

As noted in the previous chapter, care theory can help the church to better understand how well-intended Christians can fail to communicate God's love to others. A Christian ethic of care, which articulates the principles that cause one to want to communicate care, and provides the impetus to put care in action, establishes an essential foundation for communicating care as a means for obeying God's command to love. Care theory and a Christian ethic of care can help the church to more successfully communicate care and establish caring relationships, thereby providing opportunities for God's love to be experienced and Christ's message and call to be heard.

In this chapter, I focus on the *successful communication of educational care*, the care communicated by teachers to each of their students. It is my hope that an understanding of care theory and its implications for educational care can position teachers to successfully communicate intended care to their students, and that these students, therefore, having experienced more successfully communicated care, will themselves be positioned to successfully communicate care to others. In so doing, Christians may be better positioned to successfully communicate love and care to the world, and care can change the world.

STUDY CONTEXT AND BACKGROUND

The theoretical study of care and the communication of care (often referred to as care theory) emphasizes that care is only communicated successfully if the cared-for recognizes and responds to the care communicated by the one-caring, a process often described as the completion of care.[2] The completion of care leads to the establishment of a caring relationship, positioning the one-caring to have an impact on the cared-for. Based on this central foundation, most explorations of care in education have primarily focused on student perceptions of teacher-caring behaviors, as opposed to focusing on the teacher's perception of the care they have offered to their

---

2. Noddings, *Caring: A Feminine Approach*; Noddings, *Caring: A Relational Approach*.

students. The educational care literature has generated a number of helpful lists of research-affirmed teacher-caring behaviors.[3]

Importantly, the care-related research has also demonstrated the potential value and impact of care on students. When care is communicated successfully, the outcomes are impressive, encompassing a range of some of the most important aspects of education. Care has a marked impact on student motivation,[4] student engagement,[5] student attendance,[6] student preparedness,[7] and is often correlated with student achievement.[8]

The Problem of Care in Education

Unfortunately, despite the powerful evidence concerning the positive impact of educational care and caring teacher-student relationships, too often the communication of intended care is unsuccessful. The literature describes this in a variety of ways: Wilde identified a loss of care in education, observing that there has been a loss of connection between students, teaching communities, and the larger world;[9] Bingham and Sidorkin have described a fog of forgetfulness, observing that too many teachers seem to forget that education is about relationships;[10] Noddings suggested that too many students believe that nobody cares;[11] and the Quaglia Institute national report, a large-scale study of grade 6 to 12 students, determined that only 55 percent of participants believed that their teachers cared about

---

3. Bosworth, "Caring for Others"; Cooper and Miness, "Co-Creation of Caring"; Davis, "Caring Teachers"; Garza et al., "Illuminating Adolescent Voices"; McCollum, "Caring Beliefs and Practices"; McCroskey and Teven, "Relationship of Perceived Teacher Caring"; Wentzel, "Student Motivation in Middle School."

4. Davidson, "Negotiating Social Differences"; Murdock and Miller, "Teachers as Sources"; Phelan et al., "Navigating the Psychosocial Pressures"; Wentzel, "Student Motivation in Middle School."

5. Davidson, "Negotiating Social Differences"; Muller et al., "Investing in Teaching and Learning"; Osterman, "Students' Need for Belonging"; Osterman, "Teacher Practice"; Wentzel, "Student Motivation in Middle School."

6. Cornelius-White, "Learner-Centered Teacher-Student Relationships"; Goodenow, "Classroom Belonging"; Kojima and Miyakawa, "Social Support and School Adjustment"; Sickle and Spector, "Caring Relationships in Science Classrooms."

7. Sanders and Jordan, "Teacher Student Relations."

8. Bryk et al., "High School Organization"; Sanders and Jordan, "Teacher Student Relations"; Shann, "Academics and a Culture of Caring."

9. Wilde, *Care in Education*.

10. Bingham and Sidorkin, "Pedagogy of Relation."

11. Noddings, "Caring in Education."

them as an individual.[12] While it may be true that most teachers intend to care for their students, too often intended care does not result in students experiencing care.[13]

STUDY PURPOSE

This chapter is based on my dissertation research, which explored adolescent student perceptions and experiences of the care offered by their teachers, seeking to identify factors that support or impede the successful communication of educational care.[14] The goal was to better understand and better explain the process of offering care in an educational context, hopefully resulting in the development of a theoretical explanation of the successful communication of educational care. It was my hope that the research results would support student growth and learning by improving and enhancing teacher care capacity and the successful communication of care.

RESEARCH METHODS

Participants

This study involved unstructured interviews[15] with thirteen young adult participants. The participants ranged in age from eighteen to twenty-four, and provided retrospective verbalization,[16] describing their experiences of educational care while they were students in grades 6 to 12. Participant narratives led to the coproduction of rich data concerning teacher actions that influenced the successful and unsuccessful communication of educational care.

---

12. Quaglia Institute for Student Aspirations, "My Voice National Student Report."
13. McLaughlin, "Reconciling Care and Control."
14. Schat, "Exploring Adolescent Student Perceptions."
15. Creswell, *Qualitative Inquiry and Research Design*; Firmin, "Unstructured Interview."
16. Ericsson and Simon, "Verbal Reports as Data."

Data Collection and Analysis

This research design of the study was qualitative, employing a constructivist grounded theory research methodology.[17] Participant interviews ranged from forty-five to 120 minutes, and resulted in the coproduction of data describing teacher actions that contributed to either the successful or unsuccessful communication of educational care. I then employed constructivist grounded theory analysis approaches and processes (e.g., initial, focused, and theoretical coding; memoing; constant comparison; etc.) in order to analyze the resultant data. The initial analysis fragmented the data into over 2,500 individual codes describing teacher actions that influenced the communication of care. Subsequent analysis identified themes and categories, eventually leading to the distillation of what I describe as the thirteen elements and the three primary dimensions of educational care. This, in turn, contributed to the development of a grounded theoretical explanation of the offering of educational care, as well as a theoretical explanation of the successful communication of educational care.

RESULTS

It is beyond the scope of this short chapter to flesh out the analysis processes and to fully describe the claims and results that emerged. Instead, I will highlight the three most significant outcomes that resulted from the review of both the care theory and educational care literature, as well as the research study itself. I will begin by reflecting on the problem of educational care, rearticulating and clarifying the challenges that serve as the context for my research. I will then describe the constructivist grounded theoretical explanation of the offering of educational care that emerged from my research study. This serves as the foundation for the third outcome, a theoretical explanation of the successful communication of educational care.

Clarifying the Problem of Educational Care

As noted, the educational care literature submits that there has been a loss or lack of care in education. Care theory, which serves as the primary theoretical foundation for the study, suggests that every human being has two care-related needs: the need to care for others and the need to be cared

---

17. Charmaz, *Constructing Grounded Theory*.

for by others.[18] In this context, most teachers earnestly desire to offer care to their students, and most students need to receive care from their teachers. The educational care literature, however, also suggests that this has not happened, at least not to the extent that it should. The problem to which this research responds is that educational care is not being communicated successfully or sufficiently. The results of this research study, however, suggest that describing this as a lack or loss of care is not completely accurate. The problem can be better described as a disconnect between teacher caring intentions and the perceptions and experiences of far too many of their students. Teachers want to offer care to their students, and students want to be cared for by their teachers. But too often, intended care fails to translate into experienced care. Most teachers are caring, and believe that they are communicating care successfully. But some of their students do not experience the care the teacher offers.

Although often misunderstood and overlooked, care theory provides a potentially transformational insight: care is a relationship that requires completion.[19] In order to be completed, a student needs to recognize the care offered by their teacher, and they need to accept it and respond to it. If the student does not respond, care is not completed; care was not successfully communicated, and the student does not experience care. Unfortunately, in contrast, people often perceive care as behavior or communication, the unidirectional movement of care from the one-caring to the intended recipient. What is often missing in this conceptualization of care is the actual reception and uptake of care. The potential for care is present in the caring intentions and caring-directed actions of the good-hearted, well-intended teacher (and in the innate care needs of the student). But too often care is not completed, and a caring relationship fails to form. Without completion, care cannot be successfully communicated, even if the teacher believes they have offered care.

A Grounded Theory of the Offering of Educational Care

The participants in the study provided rich and authentic descriptions of teacher actions that, from their perspective, were either successful or unsuccessful in supporting the communication of care. The coproduction of the data resulted in 1528 individual codes describing the successful

---

18. Noddings, *Caring: A Feminine Approach*; Noddings, *Caring: A Relational Approach*.

19. Noddings, *Caring: A Feminine Approach*; Noddings, *Caring: A Relational Approach*.

communication of care, and 1042 codes describing the unsuccessful communication of care. Each code described a specific teacher action that influenced the communication of care.

When I applied constructivist grounded theory approaches and tools (e.g., constant comparison, memoing, revising and grouping codes, the conditional relationship guide, and the reflective coding matrix) as part of the data analysis process, I was able to identify thirteen distinct sub-categories for the codes (elements), which I further divided into three primary categories (dimensions). These thirteen elements and three dimensions could serve as valuable resources for supporting the successful communication of educational care.

The Three Dimensions of Educational Care.

The three dimensions of educational care (see Figure 1) play a central role in this study. Clearly, a list of over 2,500 teacher actions is somewhat unhelpful, even if it is descriptive. A list of thirteen elements could be more valuable because it identifies important categories that teachers could use to assess the offering of their intended care. But even a list of thirteen elements is potentially unwieldy. The study's identification of three dimensions is a potentially significant contribution to the educational care dialogue. The three dimensions articulated by this study include (1) *personal care* (teacher actions that communicate that the teacher cares for the student as a person), (2) *pedagogical care* (teacher actions that communicate that the teacher cares for the student as a learner), and (3) *interpersonal care* (teacher actions that communicate that the teacher cares for the student as a member of the classroom community).

Personal Care	**Pedagogical Care**	**Interpersonal Care**
Teacher actions that communicate that the teacher cares for the student *as a person*	Teacher actions that communicate that the teacher cares for the student *as a learner*	Teacher actions that communicate that the teacher cares for the student *as a member of the classroom community*

The first two dimensions are consistent with the educational care literature.[20] However, the identification of the third dimension, the *interpersonal dimension*, is a unique and compelling aspect of this study. The participants consistently suggested that if a teacher did not ensure that each student was a safe and valued member of a learning community, some students would

---

20. Cooper and Miness, "Co-Creation of Caring"; Cornelius-White, "Learner-Centered Teacher-Student Relationships"; Davis, "Caring Teachers"; Goldstein, *Reclaiming Caring in Teaching*; Murdock and Miller, "Teachers as Sources"; Schussler and Collins, "Empirical Exploration of the Who"; Wentzel, "Student Motivation in Middle School."

not experience educational care, regardless of the teacher's caring intentions and caring actions. What is striking is that there is no clear sequence to the successful communication of educational care. All three dimensions are intertwined, and all three must be present for educational care to be communicated successfully.

The Thirteen Elements of Educational Care.

The Thirteen Elements of Educational Care (see Figure 2) describe categories of teacher actions that influence a teacher's offering of their intended care. Many of the thirteen elements will be familiar to teachers and educational leaders because they refer to very common teacher actions and responsibilities. However, as we will see, each of these elements can either contribute to or obstruct the offering of care. Indeed, everything a teacher does can influence the offering of care. Teachers need to be critically reflective, assessing whether their own practices are likely to support or impede the offering of the care they intend to communicate to their students.

Personal Dimension			Pedagogical Dimension			Interpersonal Dimension						
R1	R2	R3	P1	P2	P3	I1	I2	I3	I4	I5	I6	I7
Teacher-Student Relationships (TSRs)	Knowing	Changing	Helping	Curriculum & Instruction	Assessment & Evaluation	Teacher-Class Relationships (TCRs)	Culture	Management	Communication	Wellbeing	High Expectations	Power Dynamics

The data indicate the existence of three distinct dimensions of educational care. The offering of educational care is the direct result of the offering of care in all three dimensions. A teacher offers educational care to a student through teacher behaviors that indicate that they care for the student as a *person*, as a *learner*, and as a *member of the classroom culture or community*. These dimensions are certainly intertwined, but they are also perceptually distinct. Care is perceptual, and it means different things to different people. Each caring relationship is unique and contextual. Students may have very different care needs depending on their experiences and learning profile. For example, a student who is lonely or feeling alone may need personal care to be communicated first, as might a student who is wired relationally. A student who is struggling with peer culture and social dynamics may need interpersonal care to be demonstrated first, as might an intuitive, socially sensitive student. A student who is struggling in their learning may need pedagogical care first, as will emotionally sensitive students who empathize with those who are struggling with their learning. Every caring relationship is unique, and the offering of care that contributes to the development of a caring relationship must honor this uniqueness. While all three dimensions are needed for care to be successfully communicated, the sequence will vary from student to student and relationship to relationship.

A Theory of the Successful Communication of Educational Care

It is important to stress that describing teacher behaviors associated with the communication of care is only a starting point. The care theory literature is very clear: successful communication of care is not the direct result of offering of care. Care requires the response of the cared-for and the development of a caring relationship. As Noddings observed, there is no recipe for care.[21] The educational care literature contains many great lists of teacher-caring behaviors—things teachers should do in order to communicate care for their students. But these lists of teacher-caring behaviors cannot be used as checklists of the ingredients required for care. Indeed, after the initial empirical studies of student perceptions of care resulted in the generation of lists of teacher-caring behaviors, this is precisely what often happened: well-meaning teachers and teacher leaders focused on what the teachers were doing, considering teacher actions in isolation, rather than focusing on the students' perceptions and experiences.

Instead, lists of teacher-caring behaviors must be recognized as touchstones or guidelines for helping teachers to communicate care successfully. One of my greatest fears is the list of three dimensions and thirteen elements identified by this study could also be misused (by both teachers and their supervisors) as a checklist for assessing teacher care communication. Instead, descriptions of teacher-caring behaviors should be used as essential resources for the dual process of both the offering of care and the establishment of a caring teacher-student relationship—a key factor in the successful communication of care. Care is not unidirectional communication; care is a bidirectional relationship. It may not always be a completely equal relationship, but it certainly involves two parties. A caring relationship can only be established if care is communicated successfully.

The second theory that emerged from my research, the successful communication of educational care, was not subjected to the same grounded theory process that led to the description of the successful and unsuccessful

21. Noddings, *Critical Lessons*.

communication of educational care and the grounded theoretical explanation of the offering of care. Instead, this analysis drew on the words and insights of the participants, as well as a review of the care theory and educational care literature, focusing on an explanation of what happens when the care offered by the teacher is recognized and responded to by the student, resulting in the completion of care and the establishment of a caring relationship. This theory gets to the heart of this research because only when completion occurs can care be experienced by the cared-for. Only then do the caring intentions of the teacher truly intersect with the care needs of their students, resulting in the successful communication of care.

The educational care literature provided an important foundation, contributing both a description of teacher-caring behaviors and a description of the research-affirmed outcomes of educational care. Drawing also on participant narratives and the analysis of the coproduced data, however, I was able to identify the stages involved in the process of successfully communicating care, starting with the students' need for care and the teacher's need to care, flowing through the teacher's caring intentions and intention-directed behaviors, through and beyond the student's recognition and response to the completion of care and the establishment of a caring relationship (see Figure 3).

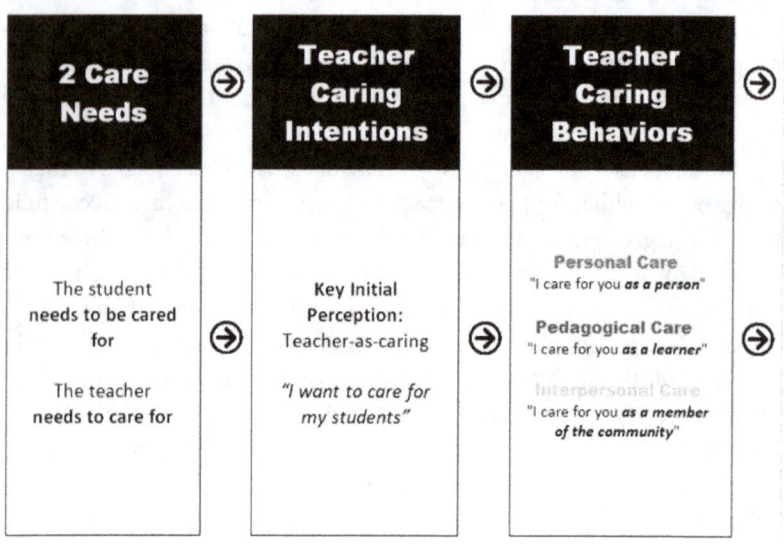

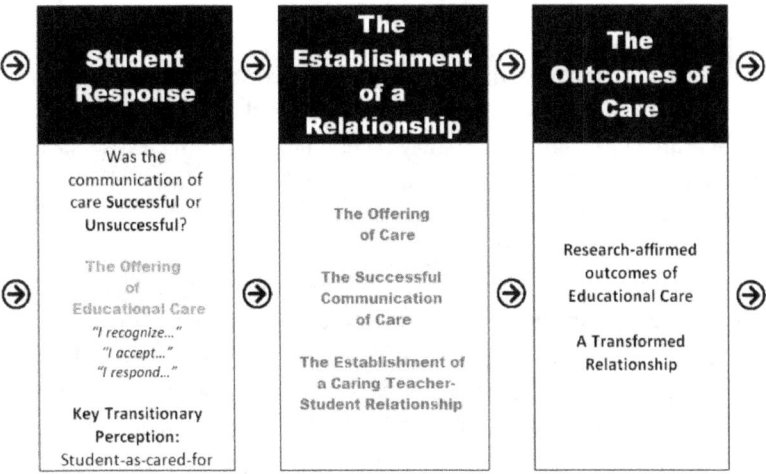

The successful communication of care occurs in six distinct stages: (1) it starts with *two care needs*: the student's need to be cared for and the teacher's need to care; (2) the relationship is initiated, however, by the teacher's *caring intentions*; which then leads to (3) the teacher's *caring behaviors* (drawing on the first theoretical explanation, the offering of care); at this point the onus shifts from the teacher's intentions and behaviors to (4) the *student's response*—Was the teacher's offering of care successful or unsuccessful?; if care was successfully communicated, (5) care is *completed* and a *caring relationship* is formed; and this, finally, is likely to lead to (6) the *outcomes of care*, including the substantial research-affirmed educational outcomes, noted earlier, as well as a transformed teacher-student relationship, positioning the teacher to have influence on the student's growth and learning (e.g., serving as a trusted sounding board, providing critical feedback, etc.).

DISCUSSION

This study has a number of important implications for educators, educational leaders, and educational communities, particularly when it comes to definitions and perceptions of care and the successful communication of care in education. This study has the potential to play an important role in teacher preservice and in-service training. For the purpose of this chapter, I will explore three specific implications: (1) no-fault failure; (2) the vicarious and simultaneous development of multiple caring relationships; and (3) a teacher's care capacity and care communication.

No-Fault Failure

I chose my research topic intentionally, but somewhat reluctantly, recognizing that there will be some who might perceive that I am suggesting that teachers are uncaring, and who may accuse me of attacking teachers. Nothing could be further from the truth. Indeed, I am implicated by my own research. There were many times when my own actions, rooted in what I believed to be a good heart with good and caring intentions, resulted in my students being quite confident that I did not care for them. The same was true for friends and colleagues who were teachers. I knew they were good and caring people, but too often their students did not see them this way. Thus I embarked on a research project that had a double goal: (1) I wanted my study to support students and student learning, but recognized that the only way for this to happen would be to also (2) support teachers and their teaching. I have consistently recognized that teachers have care needs that impact their work with their students, often significantly. Teachers want to care for their students, and want to be cared for by them as well. Too often both needs are unmet. I have also consistently recognized that almost all teachers enter the profession at least partially motivated by an earnest desire to successfully communicate care to their students, sometimes in direct response to the fact that they believed their own teachers did not communicate care for them sufficiently when they were students, and have entered the profession in order to make a difference in the lives of their own students. But care, as we have seen, is a complex, complicated, and messy process. And, too often, intended care does not lead to completed care.

We may believe that teachers are caring, but we also must recognize that sometimes their care is not successfully communicated. Most teachers earnestly want to offer care, and almost all students want to be cared for. But too often there is a disconnect between the teacher's intentions and the students' experiences, and care is not successfully communicated. I don't blame the teachers, and I don't want teachers to be paralyzed by guilt. This is where the concept of no-fault failure may be very helpful, particularly in supporting teacher perceptions of care and in encouraging teachers to participate in addressing the failure of care.[22] When care fails to occur, we can't simply say "Well, we cared!" We need to be able to say, "Well, we tried to communicate care, but we were not successful." We have to recognize failure—care was not communicated successfully—and then take steps to understand the obstacles and what we need to do to make sure the students feel cared for. This could turn out to be a helpful distinction. It may allow

---

22. Noddings, *Philosophy of Education*.

teachers to work toward successfully communicating care when they realize they do not necessarily need to take the blame when care does not happen. If they have good intentions, but recognize care has not been communicated successfully, what do they do? It is too easy to simply move on as if care has been communicated. But it has not, and the teacher knows it. And the student knows it. And the vicarious bystanders know it. The situation requires a strategic recommunication of intended care. In some situations it may not be possible to communicate care successfully. But in most cases, a persistent and perceptive teacher will be able to find a way to ensure their intended care is recognized, received, and responded to.

The Vicarious and Simultaneous Development of Multiple Caring Relationships

One of the complicators from this study is the recognition that teachers need to establish individual caring relationships with each of their students. Because care is a relationship, and if the relationship is established and defined only when the cared-for recognizes the care offered by the one-caring, each caring relationship is unique. This can seem overwhelming and impossible for a busy classroom teacher. However, study participants made an important observation: a teacher can develop more than one caring relationship at a time. Often, the relationship begins to develop vicariously, as the student watches how a teacher interacts with other students. When they observe the offering of care to another student, they recognize that the teacher would likely do the same thing for them as well, particularly when the pattern repeats itself over time (and particularly when the teacher is consistent in offering care even in complex or emotion-laden situations). As a result, the foundations for caring relationships with each student can be established vicariously and simultaneously. That being said, establishing a solid foundation, while an essential starting point, is insufficient on its own. A caring relationship still requires completion, and each individual student still needs to respond to the care that is offered before care is successfully communicated.

A Teacher's Care Capacity and Care Communication

In response to the problem of educational care, I advocate for an important solution: relational reconnection. Too often, students feel disconnected from their teachers. As a result, the students' need for care is unsatisfied, and the teacher's need to care for their students, while very likely present, is also unrealized. I have identified resources and suggested steps that could be taken to develop teacher care capacity and support the offering of care to their students. It is my hope that this study will allow teachers to increase their successful communication of educational care, thereby playing central and formative roles in the establishment of a web of care surrounding each student. These webs, or networks, of caring support extend from the home to the school and into the surrounding community, providing systems of care and pathways to care for every single student, ensuring that no child is left behind.

This study is built upon the premise that every person has the capacity to discover their own best way, provided that they are supported and that obstacles are removed. This has important implications for students and the care they receive from their support networks and systems. But it also has important implications for teachers. Offering care is complex and challenging. But it is essential. It is important to emphasize that care is not an add-on. It is not something else that teachers need to do. Everything a teacher does involves care communication. This research provides resources that can help identify obstacles to the successful communication of care. It also provides resources that can support teachers in communicating the care that they earnestly desire to give to their students. I am confident that if teachers are positioned to respond to the findings of my research, more care will be communicated successfully. And care, as we have seen, can transform people, relationships, and, indeed, local and global communities. Care could change the world.

CONCLUSION—THE REEMERGENCE OF EDUCATIONAL CARE

Care theory emerged in the early 1980s. The initial exploration of care in education reached its zenith in the 1980s and 1990s, when researchers focused the lens of care theory on students and teachers in classrooms. These studies resulted in the production of a number of lists of teacher-caring behaviors.[23] The high hopes of this era, however, were dashed by the apparent practical failure of care. The anticipated increase in student experiences of

---

23. Bosworth, "Caring for Others"; Bulach et al., "Behaviors that Create"; Gray, "Interpretive Analysis"; Hayes et al., "Middle School Child's Perceptions"; McCollum, "Caring Beliefs and Practices"; McCroskey and Teven, "Relationship of Perceived Teacher Caring"; Wentzel, "Student Motivation in Middle School."

care did not occur. Educational care was simply not successfully communicated enough.

A number of more recent educational initiatives, however, have drawn attention to an important emerging focus on affective and relational elements, as well as a significant emerging emphasis on student mental health and well-being (e.g., social and emotional learning, school connectedness, teacher-student relationships, etc.). The successful communication of educational care could be a protective factor that contributes to a proactive emphasis on robust mental health. Central to these initiatives is a clearer understanding of teacher factors that influence student learning, including a reawakened recognition of the importance of relational and affective teacher behaviors.[24] Importantly, such behaviors not only influence student relational and affective outcomes but academic results as well. Educational care is eminently compatible with most of the recent educational initiatives. It could play an important role in supporting and informing their implementation and impact.

In this context, I believe the time is right for a return to a focus on educational care. Affective and relational teacher factors are increasingly recognized for their significant impact on almost all aspects of education. Empirical research into educational care clearly identifies substantial positive outcomes that result when care is successfully communicated. This study suggests that the apparent failure of educational care can be at least partially explained and addressed. If this assertion is correct, educational care has the potential to exert a powerful and transformational impact on student growth and learning, and should, therefore, be a focus for in-service and preservice teacher training.

In this chapter I have focused on educational care, guided by the hope that if more people experience successfully communicated care, they will be better positioned and equipped to successfully communicate care to others. The ultimate goal of care is to perpetuate in others the ability to care effectively.[25] By examining our own care communication, we may also equip the next generation of Christians to succeed where we have not. The church may have failed to successfully communicate love, and therefore may appear to have failed and lost the love mandate. But the mandate still remains in place. Christ still commands that we love others, and the church continues to be the bride of Christ and the hope of the world. Even though we have, in many ways, failed to be the body of Christ, we are still called to

---

24 Cornelius-White, "Learner-Centered Teacher-Student Relationships"; Hattie, *Visible Learning*; Hattie, *Visible Learning for Teachers*.

25. Freytag, "Embodying and Modeling Healthy Self-Care."

be his hands and feet and voice in the world. While people may have failed to encounter Christ, he has not lost his desire to be encountered. The challenge, of course, is that the primary way for others to encounter Christ is to meet him in Christians, and for the Holy Spirit to work in and through the individual Christians who make up the embodied church. Care theory may be an important resource for helping the church to enact a Christian ethic of care and to reembody and rearticulate the Love Command.

BIBLIOGRAPHY

Bingham, Charles, and Alexander M. Sidorkin. "The Pedagogy of Relation: An Introduction." In *No Education without Relation*, edited by Charles Bingham and Alexander M. Sidorkin, 1–4. New York: Peter Lang, 2004.

Bosworth, Kris. "Caring for Others and Being Cared For: Students Talk Caring in Schools." *Phi Delta Kappan* 76 (1995) 686–93.

Bryk, Anthony S., et al. "High School Organization and Its Effects on Teachers and Students: An Interpretive Summary of the Research." In *Choice and Control in American Education: The Theory of Choice and Control in Education, Vol. 1*, edited by William H. Clune and John F. Witte, 135–226. London: Falmer, 1990.

Bulach, Cletus R., et al. "Behaviors that Create a Caring Learning Community." *Journal for a Just and Caring Education* 4 (1998) 441–53.

Charmaz, Kathy. *Constructing Grounded Theory: A Practical Guide through Qualitative Analysis*. Los Angeles: Sage, 2006.

———. *Constructing Grounded Theory*. 2nd ed. Los Angeles: Sage, 2014.

Cooper, Kristy S., and Andrew Miness. "The Co-Creation of Caring Student-Teacher Relationships: Does Teacher Understanding Matter?" *High School Journal* 97 (2014) 264–90.

Cornelius-White, Jeffrey. "Learner-Centered Teacher-Student Relationships are Effective: A Meta-Analysis." *Review of Educational Research* 77 (2007) 113–43.

Creswell, John W. *Qualitative Inquiry and Research Design: Choosing among Five Approaches*. Los Angeles: Sage, 2012.

Davidson, Ann L. "Negotiating Social Differences: Youths' Assessment of Educators' Strategies." *Urban Education* 34 (1999) 338–69.

Davis, Heather A. "Caring Teachers." In *Psychology of Classroom Learning: An Encyclopedia*, edited by Eric M. Anderman and Lynley H. Anderman, 138–41. Detroit: Macmillan, 2009.

Ericsson, K. Anders, and Herbert A. Simon. "Verbal Reports as Data." *Psychological Review* 87 (1980) 215–51.

Firmin, Michael W. "Unstructured Interview." In *The Sage Encyclopedia of Qualitative Research Methods*, edited by Lisa M. Given, 907. Los Angeles: Sage, 2008.

Freytag, Cathy E. "Embodying and Modeling Healthy Self-Care in Teacher Education." *International Christian Community of Teacher Educators Journal* 11.1 (2016) https://digitalcommons.georgefox.edu/icctej/vol11/iss1/3.

Garza, Ruben, et al. "Illuminating Adolescent Voices: Identifying High School Students' Perceptions of Teacher Caring." *Academic Leadership Journal* 7 (2009) 1–19.

Goldstein, Lisa S. *Reclaiming Caring in Teaching and Teacher Education*. New York: Peter Lang, 2002.

Goodenow, Carol. "Classroom Belonging among Early Adolescent Students: Relationships to Motivation and Achievement." *Journal of Early Adolescence* 13 (1993) 21–43.

Gray, Mary A. C. "An Interpretive Analysis of Elementary Teachers' Conceptions of Caring." PhD diss., The University of North Carolina at Greensboro, 1986.

Hattie, John. *Visible Learning: A Synthesis of over 800 Meta-Analyses Relating to Achievement*. New York: Routledge, 2009.

———. *Visible Learning for Teachers: Maximizing Impact on Learning*. London: Routledge, 2011.

Hayes, Charles B., et al. "The Middle School Child's Perceptions of Caring Teachers." *American Journal of Education* 103 (1994) 1–19.

Kinnaman, David, and Gabe Lyons. *UnChristian: What a New Generation Really Thinks about Christianity. . .And Why it Matters*. Grand Rapids: Baker, 2007.

Kojima, Hideo, and Juji Miyakawa. "Social Support and School Adjustment in Japanese Elementary School Children." Paper presented at the biennial meeting of the Society for Research in Child Development, New Orleans, Louisiana, April, 1993.

McCollum, Barbara D. "The Caring Beliefs and Practices of Effective Teachers." *Electronic Theses & Dissertations*, Paper 1186 (2014) 1–226.

McCroskey, James C., and Jason J. Teven, "The Relationship of Perceived Teacher Caring with Student Learning and Teacher Evaluation." *Communication Education* 46 (1997) 1–9.

McLaughlin, H. James. "Reconciling Care and Control: Authority in Classroom Relationships." *Journal of Teacher Education* 42 (1991) 182–95.

Muller, Chandra, et al. "Investing in Teaching and Learning: Dynamics of the Teacher-Student Relationship from Each Actor's Perspective." *Urban Education* 34 (1999) 292–337.

Murdock, Tamera B., and Angela Miller. "Teachers as Sources of Middle School Students' Motivational Identity: Variable-Centered and Person-Centered Analytic Approaches." *The Elementary School Journal* 103 (2003) 383–99.

Noddings, Nel. *Caring: A Feminine Approach to Ethics and Moral Education*. Berkeley: University of California Press, 1984.

———. *Caring: A Relational Approach to Ethics and Moral Education*. 2nd ed. Berkeley: University of California Press, 2013.

———. "Caring in Education." In *The Encyclopedia of Informal Education* (2005). www.infed.org/biblio/noddings_caring_in_education.htm.

———. *The Challenge to Care in Schools: An Alternative Approach to Education*. New York: Columbia University Press, 1992.

———. *Critical Lessons: What Our Schools Should Teach*. New York: Cambridge University Press, 2006.

———. *Philosophy of Education*. Oxford: Westview, 1998.

Osterman, Karen F. "Students' Need for Belonging in the School Community." *Review of Educational Research* 70 (2000) 323–67.

———. "Teacher Practice and Students' Sense of Belonging." In *International Research Handbook on Values Education and Student Well-being*, edited by Terence Lovat et al., 239–60. New York: Springer Science 1 Business Media, 2010.

Phelan, Patricia, et al. "Navigating the Psychosocial Pressures of Adolescence: The Voices and Experiences of High School Youth." *American Educational Research Journal* 31 (1994) 415–47.

Quaglia Institute for Student Aspirations. "My Voice National Student Report 2014, Grades 6–12." http://quagliainstitute.org/qisa/library/view.do?id=459.

Sanders, Mavis G., and Will J. Jordan. "Teacher Student Relations and Academic Achievement in High School." In *Schooling Students Placed At-Risk: Research*, edited by Mavis G. Sanders, 65–82. Mahwah, NJ: Lawrence Erlbaum, 2000.

Schat, Sean. "Exploring Adolescent Student Perceptions and Experiences of Educational Care." PhD diss., Brock University, 2019.

Schussler, Deborah, and Angelo Collins. "An Empirical Exploration of the Who, What, and How of School Care." *Teachers College Record* 108 (2006) 1460–95.

Shann, Mary H. "Academics and a Culture of Caring: The Relationship between School Achievement and Prosocial and Antisocial Behaviors in Four Urban Middle Schools." *School Effectiveness and School Improvement* 10 (1999) 390–413.

Sickle, Meta V., and Barbara Spector. "Caring Relationships in Science Classrooms: A Symbolic Interaction Study." *Journal of Research in Science Teaching* 33 (1996) 433–53.

Wentzel, Kathryn R. "Student Motivation in Middle School: The Role of Perceived Pedagogical Caring." *Journal of Educational Psychology* 89 (1997) 411–19.

Wilde, Sandra. *Care in Education: Teaching with Understanding and Compassion*. New York: Routledge, 2013.

Chapter 3

TRAUMA-INFORMED SCHOOL PRACTICES IN RESPONSE TO THE IMPACT OF SOCIAL-CULTURAL TRAUMA

Anna Berardi & Brenda Morton

IN THIS CHAPTER WE present a model for addressing the academic and behavioral challenges of students impacted by unmitigated stress and trauma. Typically, trauma-informed school literature addresses trauma resulting from abusive or neglectful behaviors that occur in the home.[1] Here, the type of trauma we are addressing is threats to the physical and emotional health of students due to social and cultural factors. Perhaps most detrimental and deadly is trauma resulting from war, economic collapse, civil unrest, and social-political attitudes, laws, and customs that exclude, marginalize, exploit, or subjugate an identified vulnerable population. Like members of a family in which chronic conflict and abuse occur, this type of violence involves all of us, whether we are direct recipients of abuse, observers of those supporting such abuse (oftentimes people we love), or searching for ways to effectively intervene on behalf of the victims. We cannot stay in a merely objective observer position as all of us are stressed by events happen-

---

1. Bailey, *Conscious Discipline*; Craig, *Trauma-Sensitive Schools*; Massachusetts Advocates for Children, *Helping Traumatized Children Learn*; Souers and Hall, *Fostering Resilient Learners*.

ing across the globe, and emotionally, socially, and perhaps economically impacted by events occurring within our own communities.

Further complicating social-cultural abuse is the co-opting of a religious system to legitimize inhumane and abusive actions. Political responses referring to laws and practices enacted by elected leaders that reflect constituent attitudes as well as shape public sentiment often use religious metaphors and distorted theology to both justify and rally support. This tactic has been used throughout history to garner a collective energy to fight a perceived threat, oftentimes for less than obvious ulterior motives.[2] It is an element that makes social-cultural abuse so heinous, as the perpetrators are fomenting hate and violence with a morally superior claim that God is on their side in this battle of good versus evil.

As global populations shift with mass migrations due to violence, war, and the collapse of economic and civil infrastructures required for sustaining life, every country is faced with the intensifying dilemma of: How shall we then respond?[3] Nationalism and classifying immigrants as lawbreakers bent on crime and as being infested with disease are common rallying cries aimed to exclude and protect self-interests.[4] Upon touring a holding facility crammed with immigrants, adults, and children separated from one another and denied proper care for weeks, a prominent religious leader claimed he saw a room of disease-ridden, dangerous, uneducated, and undeserving persons who have no business seeking shelter in the United States.[5] His words reinforce the attitudes of many of his constituents who adopt the mindset Scripture speaks against, wherein human fear and greed allow us to trade a truth for a lie, to spit upon or ignore the beggar on the side of the road, or deny embrace of those who, according to our human logic, have not earned it.

The story of the prodigal son (Luke 15:11–32) is a glimpse into how all of us, regardless of our current response to the needs of those on the losing end of global politics and markets, are vulnerable to not responding to the cries of those suffering social-cultural-sponsored abuse. The parable leaves no doubt as to the sloth, greed, or carelessness of the younger son as he flits away his inheritance, leaving him destitute and reduced to barely subsisting as he lives among the swine. Unlike those seeking to immigrate

---

2. Kippenberg, "Social Matrix of the Attack"; Longman, *Christianity and Genocide in Rwanda*; McDurmon, *Problem of Slavery*; Woodley, "Fullness Thereof."

3. Arvanitis, "Refugees' Narratives."

4. Fea, *Believe Me*; Fea, "Why Do White Evangelicals?"; Hunter, *To Change the World*; Woodley, "Fullness Thereof."

5. Dobson, "Dr. Dobson's Visit"; Massey, "James Dobson's Anti-Immigrant Rhetoric."

who are most often victims of powers and principalities, Christ drives the point home as to what constitutes care by using a case example of one who we might conclude does not deserve anything more. Upon the son's return home, as his father prepares to honor and embrace him with the ultimate community celebration, the older brother is appalled that unearned honor in attitude (love and care) and action (sharing of remaining resources) is bestowed upon such an undeserving creature.

Who among us has not felt that way, using natural and logical consequence reasoning to justify our position? We are all the older brother. But with a renewing of our hearts and minds, we are capable of following the dad's lead, and tapping into our own storehouses of goodwill and resources whether the persons in need have what we perceive to be a legitimate claim to our help or not.

Our internal attitudes do not always stem from mere jealousy and resentment of someone getting something they did not earn. In the news example above, a man of financial power and religious influence could not look into the face of human pain and suffering and see Christ; he could not see the face of those marginalized by some of the same forces that allowed him to succeed, those qualities of privilege that always include unmerited winners and losers. Scripture and psychology might call his defensive reaction shame. When we feel immense disdain or judgment towards a hurting person, we are encountering a series of convoluted internal thoughts and feelings that are difficult to identify. Ultimately it reflects or activates feelings of resentment, guilt, and shame, and our first instinct is to defend against it and make the innocent victim the guilty party. This is often the internal dynamic operating in persons who intentionally hurt children and animals; the innocence and vulnerability seen in others causes this internal discomfort. It contorts into hate and a drive to destroy or banish it from sight. We see this in Cain's impulse to kill his brother, despite God's voice on his shoulder warning him to harness these deep, intensely distorted convolutions in thoughts and feelings that led to deadly actions (Gen 4).

In the pages ahead we unpack the nature of social-cultural trauma, along with a trauma-informed school method of responding to students whose growth and development are deeply impacted by these experiences. We do not know how to arrive at solutions to create more equitable and sustainable communities to stem the tide of migrants. It is beyond our scope of practice and competence to figure out how to garner the financial resources to respond to social-cultural trauma victims. But we do have a vision, grounded in social science research and our Christian faith, for how to create communities of care that can make a difference in the lives of all children and their families.

Trauma-Informed School Practices (TISP)[6] proposes a rationale and method for extending care to all based on the fundamental building blocks of what each of us need to become healthy, contributing members of society. To enact TISP, we emphasize that it is not about a series of techniques, but a shift in mindset in which we encounter each student—whether a victim of abuse or a bully, or a seemingly well-adjusted emotionally grounded child—and see their preciousness and vulnerability in need of our care on behalf of their current and emerging developmental needs. Such encounters with the stories and experiences of others change us, soften our hearts, sharpen our eyesight, and strengthen our resolve. We hope that learning more about TISP contributes to this process.

THE NATURE AND IMPACT OF SOCIAL-CULTURAL TRAUMA

All forms of abuse, whether between family members or enacted by social-cultural forces, impair development and hence the ability to engage in age-appropriate academic and social tasks.[7] And most, if not all, interpersonal dysregulation between parent and child has a social-cultural context influencing that parent's ability to respond to the attachment needs of the child. This chapter focuses on traumatic events and practices that are a direct reflection of cultural values and mores that put in motion distinct beliefs and practices endorsed and enacted by a community and its members. It is never a simple matter of a current predicament being the result of a political party; generational attitudes and relational patterns have created fertile ground for an astonishing manifestation of human violence or evil.

---

6. Berardi and Morton, *Trauma-Informed School Practices*.

7. Berardi and Morton, *Trauma-Informed School Practices*; Blaustein, "Childhood Trauma"; Bremner, *Does Stress Damage the Brain?*; Carrion and Wong, "Can Traumatic Stress Alter the Brain?"; Cozolino, *Neuroscience of Human Relationships*; Everly and Lating, *Clinical Guide to the Treatment*; Morton, "Grip of Trauma"; Morton and Berardi, "Creating a Trauma-Informed Rural Community"; van der Kolk, *Body Keeps the Score*.

Factors Contributing to Stress, Trauma, and Resilience

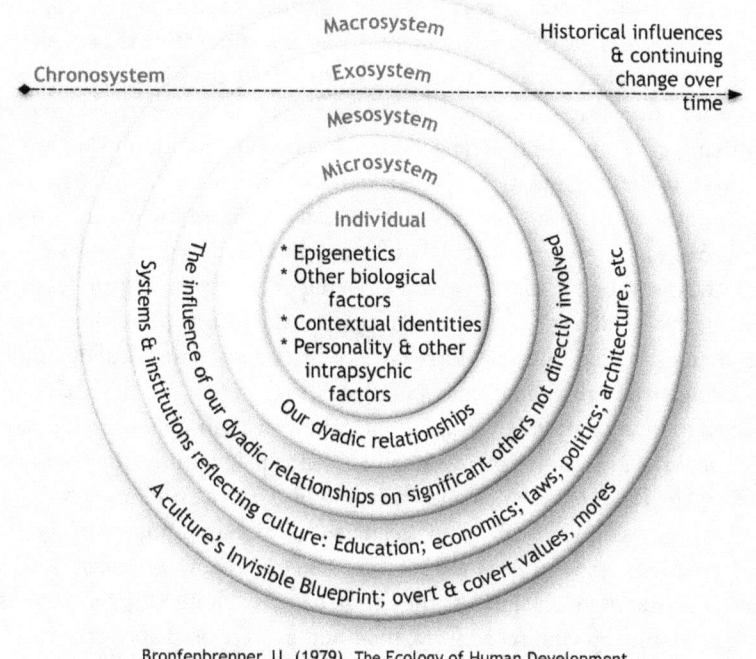

Bronfenbrenner, U. (1979). The Ecology of Human Development.
Amended for use in Berardi, A. (2010), *GCEP 510 Human Growth & Development*.
Graduate School of Counseling; George Fox University - Portland, OR.

Figure 1 recalls Bronfenbrenner's ecosystemic model of human growth and development[8] as a visible reminder of the complexity of social-cultural factors contributing to how abusive trends are set in motion with full endorsement of wide segments of a given population. Later in this chapter we will discuss the role of attachment theory in understanding and mitigating the impact of stress and trauma. But it is helpful to remember the power and influence of cultural attitudes that shape how we view self and other, which also then shape our social behaviors and attachment relationships. Hence, the macrosystem is identified as the most powerful influencer shaping our individual and corporate identities and behaviors, earning the title *invisible blueprint*.

While all of us are vulnerable to secondary trauma when we walk with others through their trauma recovery process, the nature of social-cultural trauma personally involves and impacts all of us. Persons throughout the

8. Bronfenbrenner, *Ecology of Human Development*.

world are on alert as mass migrations are revealing larger pockets of unsustainable communities; the reality of mass migration and the changes this brings to the places we call home is here to stay for the foreseeable future.[9] In North America, many are appalled by the government's actions towards immigrants, and even more traumatized by the endorsement of such behaviors by religious leaders. We are observing their constituents energized by what they believe to be a holy war against all things wrong and immoral, justifying cruel and inhumane actions.[10] This is our family, and we are all involved in these traumatic global atrocities whether we want to be or not.

Most persons born and raised in a Western culture such as the United States can easily grasp what social-culture trauma involves. In our own history, the institution of slavery and the seizing of Native American lives and land, both of which were practices enacted in establishing the United States, are vivid examples. The very formation of this country was founded upon declaring certain marginalized populations less than human who had no divine right to their land, government, or culture.[11] Their lives were inconsequential to the invading, and eventually established, culture. The seizing of Native American homelands and enslaving of African Americans for generations seems otherworldly, as if an ancient version of humans engaged in such practices. As we try to imagine the lives of Native and African Americans, it is incomprehensible. As they were being exploited for generations, their humanity was not recognized; their bodies were used and tossed aside while the perpetrators sang hymns of praise to God. All of us still suffer the consequences of these social-cultural traumas from generations ago.

Social-cultural trauma includes horrendous ordeals on a daily basis originating within our home communities, magnified by many of the atrocities being endorsed by a majority culture. On television, we see seemingly healthy people, with the stamina to walk across deserts, who merely look foreign and out of compliance with human-made laws. Our rejection, our abusive tactics, and our rationalizations make us culpable in adding to their pain and suffering. The poet Warsan Shire captures the unspeakable truths of those who find themselves fleeing their homelands in her poem "Home." We share an excerpt below, and encourage you to read it in full:

> no one leaves home unless
> home is the mouth of a shark
> you only run for the border

---

9. Arvanitis, "Refugees' Narratives."
10. Fea, "Why Do White Evangelicals?"; Hunter, *To Change the World*.
11. Woodley, "Fullness Thereof."

when you see the whole city running as well[12]

If you have taken the time to read her words in full, or the stories of other migrants, perhaps as captured in autobiographies or novels,[13] Shire is not exaggerating. Seeking a life—not just a better life—is not a moral choice but a parent's mandate. But when those of us in privileged spaces use God and country as justification to deny access, we add to their abuse.

As illustrated in Shire's words, families who have been forced to leave their home communities, whether fitting the legal definition of migrant or refugee, have endured traumatic events making the risks and uncertainty a far better option than staying.[14] Tragically, they often experience abuse and violence along the path to an uncertain final destination. The situation that prompted their decision to flee, and the experiences they encountered seeking safety, such as detention facilities, separation of parents and children, and potential deportation, have long-lasting implications to their physical and mental health. In their 2019 study, Muniz de la Pena, Pineda, and Punsky found family separations to be "one of the most significant sources of distress among refugees and migrants."[15] It is no surprise that research indicates that children who have been separated from their primary attachment relationships, or who faced significant unmitigated challenges or adversity, were at increased risk for both general and mental health issues.[16]

Most citizens of a dominant culture are oblivious to the day-to-day lives of marginalized groups who are under siege. In the United States, those of Central and South American ancestry are aware that there are two parallel worlds: a seemingly safe society where each individual merely goes about their daily business earning a living and providing for their families; and others who know that the safety is but a veil and exists only for those of a dominant group, and they are not a part of that group.

This is what our students from marginalized populations bring into the classroom. They suffer the consequences of losing their homeland, their cultural identity, their place in society, with parents who lost any semblance of being able to promise ongoing safety while secretly carrying the pain of atrocities committed against them. They enter communities where their peers are taught through their homes or media that immigrants are law-breakers and dangerous, raising up the next generation of adults who will

---

12. Shire, "Home," lines 1–4.
13. McCall Garcia, *All the Stars Denied*.
14. Ballard et al., *Immigrant and Refugee Families*.
15. Muniz de la Pena et al., "Working with Parents and Children," 156.
16. Levers and Hyatt-Burkhart, "Immigration Reform"; Muniz de la Pena et al., "Working with Parents and Children."

not be able to see the full context that stands before them, blind to human pain and suffering.

In *Trauma-Informed School Practices*,[17] we introduce Ben, a student who represents a composite sketch of our very neighbors who wake up each day knowing they are living in a dangerous community, with armed Immigration and Customs Enforcement (ICE) agents who could appear at his door or school at any moment and threaten to take his parents and him away. Ben is no stranger to the physical and emotional toll of uprootedness as his family has moved frequently due to his parents seeking economic and social safety for the family. On a daily basis his parents prepare Ben for the possibility that mom or dad may be arrested, detained, and deported. The children are taught how to survive, how to respond if they too are ever questioned or detained. All family members, children alike, carry proof of their identity and legal status. Ben knows how to spot whether you are a safe and aware advocate, or are someone to be avoided. He can walk into his school on any given day, and see through visual images such as peer clothing and overheard conversations, whether or not this is a safe refuge or a continuation of the danger that exists outside the school's doors.

Similar preparedness processes unfold for African American families as parents need to teach their children about the legacy of racism still present within the fabric of our society, and as a result, how to manage social interactions with those in authority, such as an encounter with law enforcement should they be pulled over for a traffic stop.[18] Those most vulnerable to social-cultural trauma are most aware of this parallel world that many dominant culture members are often unaware of or unmoved by, inspired by social lenses we use to make sense of the world.[19]

Given the current climate of raids, arrests, family separations, and threats of more to come, children are at risk for traumatic distress.[20] Adverse Childhood Experiences (ACE) survey data[21] have sounded the alarm to the level of distress most children bring into our classrooms on a daily basis and the devastating impact unmitigated stress and trauma wreak in the lives of these students across the lifespan. In fact, ACE data have, in large part, inspired the trauma-informed school movement.[22] Add to this the devastating

17. Berardi and Morton, *Trauma-Informed School Practices*.
18. Coates, *Between the World and Me*.
19. Harari, *Sapiens*.
20. Levers and Hyatt-Burkhart, "Immigration Reform."
21. Anda et al., "Enduring Effects of Abuse"; Centers for Disease Control and Prevention, *ACE Study*; Centers for Disease Control and Prevention, *About the CDC-Kaiser ACE Study*; Felitti et al., "Relationship of Childhood Abuse."
22. Berardi and Morton, *Trauma-Informed School Practices*; Craig, *Trauma-Sensitive*

implications of social-cultural trauma, perhaps best captured in the ACE International Questionnaire,[23] and we know our classrooms are complex communities with children who need us to see their hurt and pain in all its causes and manifestations.

CALL FOR AN ETHIC OF CARE

The traumatic experiences of children and families call for a different model of educating children and interacting with parents and community. We explore this need through the lens of an ethic of care. When educators hear the term "ethic of care," many will immediately recall the work of Nel Noddings, who suggests that caring is ". . . both a moral orientation to teaching and an aim of moral education."[24]

Care is fundamental to the human experience. Noddings posits that teachers and students need to be in intentional relationship with one another. She identifies the complexities of these dyadic relationships as including " . . . love or hate, anger or sorrow, admiration or envy; or, of course, they may reveal mixed affects—one party feeling, say, love and the other revulsion."[25] Noddings identifies how each member of the teacher-student dyad has differing roles. The caregiver (teacher) attends to the needs or desires of the relational other (student), while the care receiver is expected to respond in acknowledgment. She calls out our preconceived notions that students should just obey our lead: "If, without knowing a student—what he loves, strives for, fears, hopes—I merely expect him to do uniformly well in everything I present to him, I treat him like an unreflective animal."[26] Martin Buber refers to this as I-It relating, whereby the essence of intimacy, of seeing the wholeness of our relational other as much as we allow ourselves to be seen, is inaccessible, prohibiting I-Thou relating captured in God's relational movement with his creation.[27]

In our *TISP Tri-Phasic Model*, we acknowledge the work of Noddings, and respectfully add to it through a trauma-informed lens. To that end, we posit that, "Trauma-informed practice is ultimately a commitment to being

---

Schools; Massachusetts Advocates for Children, *Helping Traumatized Children Learn*; Morton, "Grip of Trauma"; Morton and Berardi, "Creating a Trauma-Informed Rural Community"; Souers and Hall, *Fostering Resilient Learners*.

23. World Health Organization, "Adverse Childhood Experiences."
24. Noddings, "Ethic of Caring," 215.
25. Noddings, "Ethic of Caring," 218.
26. Noddings, "Ethic of Caring," 224.
27. Buber, *I and Thou*.

in community in a manner that provides a welcome and inclusive environment fostering relational safety and well-being, the basic ingredients we all need to thrive throughout the lifespan."[28] This ethic of care is not just teacher to student, as Noddings encouraged, but ". . . a consistent ethic of care means that the relational values educators extend to students are offered to each other as well,"[29] including co-workers, parents/guardians of students we serve, and the larger community. "Caring about educator well-being is a central value as expressed in *Person of the Educator* practices, in recognition that attuned and supportive interpersonal relationships nurture resilience and well-being amidst the challenges of educating highly stressed students."[30] Reflecting an ethic of care, TISP acknowledges the vulnerability of educators to secondary trauma as a result of our working with trauma-impacted students, even as we may be experiencing our own unmitigated stress and trauma. In essence, a Christian ethic of care is I-Thou relating, mirroring the title of Parker Palmer's 1993 work.[31]

THEORETICAL CONSTRUCTS INFORMING TISP

We have offered a quick glimpse into the world of students who have experienced social-cultural trauma as a result of social unrest and upheaval that threaten their safety and belonging. These students join the chorus of children and young adults filling our classrooms who bring the side effects of unmitigated stress and trauma with them, expressed in a wide range of behaviors that undermine their academic and social functioning. In order to understand how TISP serves all of these students, the following offers a quick overview of major conceptual elements informing the model.

Attachment Theory

Advances in a neurobiological understanding of what happens when we encounter stress and trauma, and the impact of consistent versus inadequate care in response, has led to a confirmation of several attachment theory hypotheses that the social-behavioral sciences have long trusted, as well as provided a foundation upon which to design effective responses. Attachment theory has long proposed that attuned and mentoring relationships

---

28. Berardi and Morton, *Trauma-Informed School Practices*, 120.
29. Berardi and Morton, *Trauma-Informed School Practices*, 120.
30. Berardi and Morton, *Trauma-Informed School Practices*, 120.
31. Palmer, *To Know as We are Known*.

are key to psychosocial growth and development across the lifespan. Its primary hypothesis is that when you and I get "good-enough" (consistent attunement and mentoring, not perfection) parenting by at least one stable caretaker, preferably more, throughout our first eighteen years of life, we will have a better chance of managing anxiety, which is an inevitable companion for all living creatures as long as we have breath.[32] This concept resonates with Scripture, wherein we see illustrated repeatedly that life is full of hardships, dangers, and uncertainty; but we also see God as Refuge, as the One who is always with us, the Rock who offers us assurance that whatever comes our way (even if it costs us our lives) is doable and manageable. We can face hardship, we can even face our own death, taking great comfort in knowing we are loved and not alone.

This is made most real when we speak of the love and care of our parents reflecting the first tangible signs of God's love, designed to create in us lifelong anchoring schemas that we matter and we can find our way through whatever challenges life throws our way. Strong, consistent attachment is the neurological and psychosocial key to containing and managing lifelong encounters with anxiety, and is the wellspring of resilience in the face of challenge.

When children do not get good-enough parental attunement and mentoring during their formative years, they experience an overabundance of anxiety, and they often fail to develop the cognitive and behavioral skills and ability to contain or manage that anxiety.[33] A similar process unfolds when we sense the world outside our home disdains us and threatens our very physical safety. We develop distortions regarding our worth, abilities, the trustworthiness of others, and the value and purpose of living. Anxiety and the factors contributing to its overabundance set off a unique tumbling effect in each of us. For educators developing trauma-informed competencies, once they revisit the attachment literature and examine the myriad of ways mistuned attachment impacts thoughts, feelings, and actions, they can quickly identify children whose dysregulated behavior (whether displayed through acting out or withdrawal) likely reflects signs of unmitigated stress and trauma, regardless of its source.[34]

---

32. Berardi and Morton, *Trauma-Informed School Practices*; Bowlby, *Secure Base*; Bowlby and Golding, "Attachment"; Cozolino, *Neuroscience of Human Relationships*; Karen, "Becoming Attached"; Levine and Heller, *Attached*; Siegel, *Developing Mind*.

33. Scaer, *Trauma Spectrum*; Schore, *Affect Dysregulation*; Siegel, *Developing Mind*.

34. Bailey, *Conscious Discipline*; Berardi and Morton, *Trauma-Informed School Practices*; Craig, *Trauma-Sensitive Schools*; Morton, "Grip of Trauma"; Morton and Berardi, "Creating a Trauma-Informed Rural Community."

While attachment theory focuses on the relationships between a caretaker and a dependent child, a foundational principle is that we all need attachment relationships throughout our lives.[35] Stress and coping theory,[36] as discussed below, as well as attachment theory, propose that the stronger our formative attachment relationships are, the more resilient we are to relational failures and disappointments we may experience outside the home. But there is a tipping point. The old saying about "sticks and stones" is only true to the degree that our inner strength can withstand the intensity of the verbal or attitudinal attack. Because we are relational beings dependent on needing loving and affirming relationships, if a community identifies our essence as wrong or unworthy, this is not merely name calling; this is psychological warfare. If public sentiment results in laws and practices that exclude or threaten to take away a person's capacity to establish a safe and equitable life without socially sanctioned ridicule and acts of exclusion, that is the equivalent of a spear, not merely sticks and stones.

Advances in neurobiology have allowed us to physically observe changes in the brain when we are in an attuned state versus when we are not.[37] Cognitive psychology and cognitive developmental theories have long proposed that our thinking and affective states are influenced by internal schemas that help us decode and make sense of environmental stimuli. We now understand the neurochemicals and the regions of the brain comprising the formation, storing, and accessing of these schemas developed through our attachment relationships.[38] The movie *Inside Out* illustrates these advancements.[39]

The Neurobiology of Unmitigated Stress and Trauma

If consistent attachment over time is the catalyst that promotes brain development, then what occurs when we do not receive the stress-mediating benefits of attuned and mentoring relationships during our primary

---

35. Ainsworth et al., *Patterns of Attachment*; Berardi, "Fear of Being Alone"; Berardi, "Margaret Mahler"; Bowlby and Golding, "Attachment."

36. Boss, *Family Stress Management*; McCleary and Figley, "Special Issue on Resilience"; McCubbin and Patterson, "Family Stress Process."

37. Schore, *Affect Dysregulation*; Shapiro, *Eye Movement Desensitization*; Siegel, *Developing Mind*.

38. Everly and Lating, *Clinical Guide to the Treatment*; Perry, "Fear and Learning"; Perry, "Examining Child Maltreatment"; Porges, *Polyvagal Theory*; Porges and Furman, "Early Development"; Siegel, *Developing Mind*; Vermetten and Bremner, "Circuits and Systems in Stress."

39. Docter, *Inside Out*.

developmental years? Attunement and mentoring allow us repeated experiences with having our encounters with the world validated, whether interactions with others or our own internal challenges. This validation allows us to feel loved, seen, and understood. Parental mirroring[40] helps us put language to our experience, thereby increasing our ability to engage in abstract reasoning as we continue to grapple with life challenges. The more we feel safe to explore our world both physically and emotionally, the more confidence we gain that we can survive such challenges. Likewise, the more we experience the micro disappointments in trusting relationships—that people we love and trust will disappoint us, as we will them, but we can work through these breaks—the more the developing child can tolerate relational distress even as they strive to figure out solutions. All of these social-emotional processes coexist with meaning-making schemas built through verbal and nonverbal, overt, and covert teachings the child is picking up from their primary attachments as well as the broader relational community.

A child denied such consistency in attunement and mentoring will not experience a strengthening of neurostructures required to make sense of internal need states or the complex messages received from social interactions. Coupled with distortions about their own worth and the trustworthiness of others, various domains of neural functioning fail to develop, causing a cascade of social-emotional vulnerabilities. For many, this is accompanied by difficulties focusing on a task, encoding short- and long-term memories, and being able to delay gratification while tolerating frustration, all executive functioning skills needed to be academically successful.[41]

A quick way to understand the interconnection between neurological functions and behavior is to examine what happens to our stress response systems when impacted by unmitigated stress and trauma. Under typical circumstances, when faced with a stressor or trauma, norepinephrine is released to aid us in response as we determine whether we need to fight, flee, or freeze. This coincides with the release of cortisol, a hormone that helps us continue responding to the trauma as norepinephrine is designed to just get us out of immediate danger. When our responses are effective, and/or we receive the safety and validation we need from our relational community, our body returns to its original state of homeostasis. Crisis averted; lessons learned.

But when we are in a constant state of alarm, and those we love and trust the most are either perpetuating or are unable to stop the stress, our

40 Mirroring is when one acts like others (wording, mannerisms, etc.) in their presence.

41. Berardi and Morton, "Maximizing Academic Success"; Berardi and Morton, *Trauma-Informed School Practices*.

brain's capacity to self-regulate states of alarm and calm become impaired.[42] This mirrors glitches in the formation of internalized schemas regarding self-worth and abilities, as well as the goodness or trustworthiness of others. Cognitive distortions and impulsive behavioral choices are often indicators of these faulty processes.[43] Students unable to regulate their stress response systems are now consumed with survival, whether they know this overtly or not. Academic and social behavioral expectations are the least of their worries, although struggles in these arenas further compound negative internalized beliefs.[44]

Therefore, when children struggle to function successfully in the classroom, their behaviors and dispositions are communicating a struggle with a variety of negative neural networks intensified as a result of unmitigated stress and trauma. In response, the developing child needs educators to understand the nature and variation of how these negative neural networks are operating, and how they can be counterbalanced with distinct rituals, routines, and practices that promote the creation of positive neural networks in response.[45]

Stress and Coping Theory

Stress and coping theory[46] hypothesizes that we have the greatest chance of being resilient in the face of traumatic experiences when we have access to external (for example, financial support or medical care) and internal (for example, a sense of humor or the capacity to be flexible) resources, combined with a *sense of coherence* that allows access to additional internal and external resources.[47] One's sense of coherence is most synonymous with an internalized worldview that allows us to a) make sense of what is challenging us, congruent with and supported by dominant cultural values and

---

42. Berardi and Morton, *Trauma-Informed School Practices*; Briere and Scott, *Principles of Trauma Therapy*; Morton and Berardi, "Creating a Trauma-Informed Rural Community"; Vermetten and Bremner, "Circuits and Systems in Stress."

43. Berardi and Morton, *Trauma-Informed School Practices*.

44. Berardi and Morton, *Trauma-Informed School Practices*; Craig, *Trauma-Sensitive Schools*; Massachusetts Advocates for Children, *Helping Traumatized Children Learn*; Morton, "Grip of Trauma"; Morton and Berardi, "Trauma-Informed School Programming"; Morton and Berardi, "Creating a Trauma-Informed Rural Community"; Souers and Hall, *Fostering Resilient Learners*.

45. Berardi and Morton, *Trauma-Informed School Practices*.

46. Boss, *Family Stress Management*; McCubbin and Patterson, "Family Stress Process"; Rosino, "ABC-X Model."

47. Antonovsky, *Unraveling the Mystery of Health*.

practices; b) find meaning in life that inspires coping efforts; and c) access coping resources endorsed and made available by one's community. These researchers identify our sense of coherence as having the greatest level of influence over whether or not we stand a chance of successful coping.[48]

This is of primary relevance when responding to victims of social-cultural exclusion and violence. When besieged by a group of persons legally having the right to exclude or threaten the safety of another based on some aspect of their contextual identity, victims of such actions will not find the dominant culture acknowledging, let alone caring about, their pain and suffering. Examples of these contextual identities include national origin, residency status, race, ethnicity, religion, sexual orientation, gender identity, socioeconomics, appearance, ability, or any other aspect of one's identity that the dominant culture may enact laws and practices to disempower. These acts of social exclusion add to trauma injuries. And finally, access to external resources is consequently found to be limited to nonexistent since the dominant culture is not empathically moved by the trauma they are causing, and part of the weaponry is denying victims coping resources.[49]

For educators serving displaced students and their families, it is important to recognize that these parents bring their children to school wondering if this is one more place where their experience will be ignored, their presence disdained, and whether their child needs to prepare for adults and students who will perpetuate their trauma through words, actions, or attitudes, whether in overt or covert ways. If a school or place of worship can do only one thing, this is it: examine closely what it means to provide a safe space, a space that says "I am so glad you are here. . .welcome!" A space that calls out and stops all forms of bullying, even while teaching all of its members about the importance to stop abuse, stop trauma, and promote healing within caring relationships. Then listen to the stories of newcomers, and search for ways to include them in the life of the community even while providing them with much-needed tangible resources. This is trauma-informed response, whether enacted within a school or faith community.

THE TISP TRI-PHASIC MODEL AS RESPONSE

Advances in the fields of traumatology and neurobiology have allowed mental health professionals to evaluate and redesign treatment approaches congruent with these advancements. But what has been most exciting is an awareness that the basic blueprint of a best practice response to those

---

48. Antonovsky, *Unraveling the Mystery of Health*; Rosino, "ABC-X Model."
49. Samuels, "People Want to Donate Diapers."

impacted by unmitigated stress and trauma is appropriate for use by all persons caring for others, applied according to one's role and context.

Further inspiring the application of best-practice trauma-informed models of care beyond mental health service settings is the sobering data gleaned from the ACE survey.[50] Without intervention, cycles of trauma are guaranteed to impact future generations as well, whether through multigenerational relational patterns or actual biological vulnerabilities due to the unresolved trauma of their ancestors.[51]

This best-practice blueprint is commonly called the tri-phasic model of recovery.[52] While each mental health practitioner may alter the language and tasks of each phase, it generally consists of the following themes most clearly articulated by Herman.[53] The first phase, *safety and stabilization*, recognizes that when we are in a state of panic or alarm, whether that has led to severe anxiety, deep depression, addictions, poor choices, compulsive behaviors, or is simply masked through acting out or avoidance behaviors, we cannot begin to make sense of what has happened to us, how we are responding, and how we need to change (problem-solve), until we first establish a sense of emotional and/or physical safety, including the ability to self-regulate.

This acknowledgment is grounded in our greater understanding of how our stress response systems operate, and what occurs when these systems can no longer work properly, whether they are over- or under-responding to perceived or actual threats. When our bodies cannot self-regulate in response to our internal need states or the relational demands in the environment, we feel a lack of control, adding to a sense of fear. We cannot access higher-order thinking process (executive functions) needed to sort our way through the precipitating issues. Learning about fear and anxiety circuits and how to calm physiological processes is the first step to being able to effectively respond to the need or issue driving the fear.

50. Centers for Disease Control and Prevention, *ACE Study*; Centers for Disease Control and Prevention, *About the CDC-Kaiser ACE Study*; World Health Organization, "Adverse Childhood Experiences International Questionnaire."

51. Centers for Disease Control and Prevention, *ACE Study*; Centers for Disease Control and Prevention, *About the CDC-Kaiser ACE Study*; DeSocio, "Epigenetics, Maternal Prenatal Psychosocial Stress"; Hurley, "Grandma's Experiences Leave a Mark"; Ptak and Petronis, "Epigenetic Approaches to Psychiatric Disorders."

52. Baranowsky et al., *Trauma Practice*; Blaustein and Kinniburgh, *Treating Traumatic Stress*; Bloom, "Sanctuary Model"; Briere and Scott, *Principles of Trauma Therapy*; Herman, *Trauma and Recovery*; Kinniburgh et al., "Attachment, Self-Regulation, Competency"; Shapiro, *Eye Movement Desensitization*; Van Der Hart et al., "Pierre Janet's Treatment."

53. Herman, *Trauma and Recovery*.

The second phase of the tri-phasic recovery model, commonly referred to as *remembrance and mourning*, is the hard work of taking inventory of the trauma and its impact. Traumatic events or ongoing relational sequences, especially when not adequately responded to by those who know and care for us, undermine our sense of self, leading to a variety of possible side effects. This is often understood to be the heart of therapy, and the path through this process is unique for each person.

The final phase, often called *reengagement* or *reentry*, is determined by the person's ability to reengage in life with a renewed sense of comfort and purpose. For some, it means envisioning a new sense of one's identify. For others, it is about discovering a new way of listening to what is most important in their life now along with changes they would like to pursue. As with phase two, this process is unique to each person.

This tri-phasic blueprint is embedded within most trauma-informed models, shaping best practice approaches when working in clinical mental health as well as disaster response settings.[54] Its principles apply to trauma-informed school applications, but not in a manner easily discerned for school professionals. Hence, we identified how the tri-phasic model applies to schools and developed the *Trauma-Informed School Practices Tri-Phasic Model* (Figure 2) as will be described below.

---

54. Brymer et al., *Psychological First Aid*.

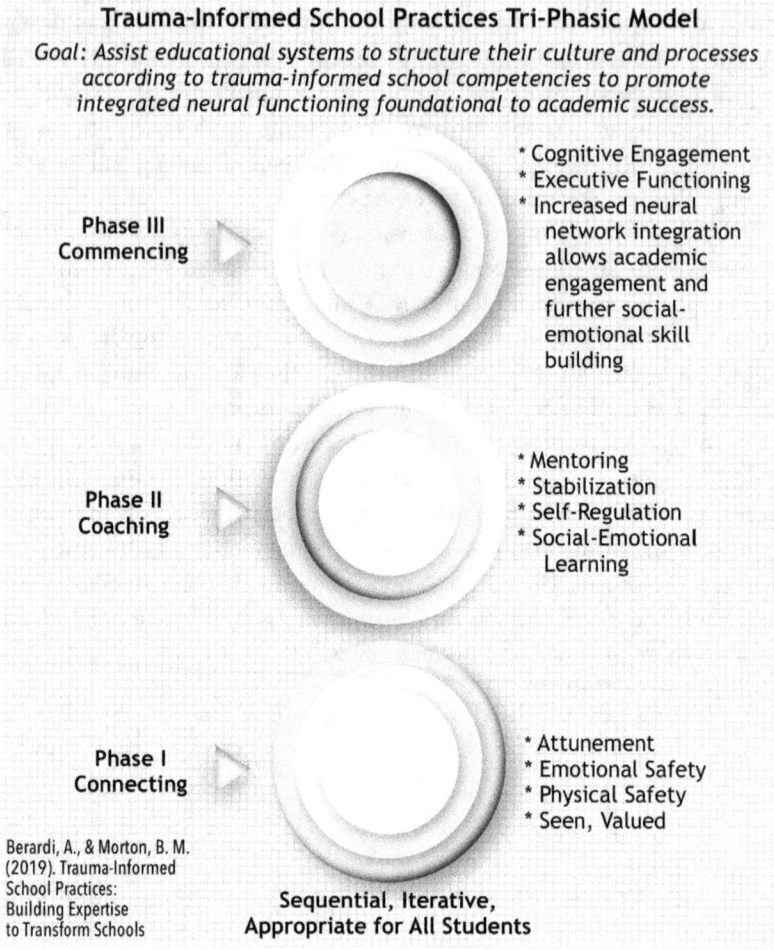

The *TISP Tri-Phasic Model* includes language and practices congruent with the tasks expected of teachers and school professionals, extending the principles of the tri-phasic model of recovery to the school setting. As noted in Figure 2 above, we identified three specific elements essential to TISP: *connecting, coaching,* and *commencing.*

Congruent with all trauma-informed tri-phasic models, *connecting* recognizes that children cannot learn until they feel safe. Berardi and Morton state:

> *Connecting* addresses the primary need of students to experience adults attuning to their affective states, current needs, and successes in order to feel both emotionally and physically safe

and welcome in the school environment. It reflects the recognition that until we feel seen, heard, and valued, key indicators of secure attachment leading to the thoughts, feelings, and sensations related to safety, we cannot self-regulate (stabilize). And until we establish a sense of safety and stabilization, we cannot resume growth or daily tasks, all of which require higher-order executive functioning.[55]

Connecting describes the method through which we help students learn about how stress and anxiety are hijacking their brain, while finding ways to regain a sense of safety and stabilization. It includes examining how educators, school administrators, and district leaders stand in relationship with each other, students, and their families (whose specific needs are addressed in the *community* element of system change). By connecting with our students and community, we are practicing an ethic of care. This ethic of care includes creating rituals and routines essential to modeling and embodying that each person is seen and valued. Daily, weekly, and seasonal rituals and routines in the classroom foster connection by creating predictability, inviting the student to relax into the school environment. By connecting with our students and families, we are welcoming them into the educational setting and partnering with parents and guardians, thus earning the privilege to speak into the growth and development of their child through *coaching*.[56]

Coaching is most synonymous with social-emotional skill building but its methods are informed by trauma-informed research and best practices. This element of the tri-phasic model has been contextualized to educators who work with students' trauma, not through direct memory processing, but through a recursive attunement and mentoring process as they face academic and social challenges. Educators are helping students integrate various domains of neural functioning that have been impaired by unmitigated stress and trauma. Through connecting and coaching, the impact of trauma is discovered and worked through in the context of academic and social challenges.

Coaching is essential to executive functioning growth and development. Coaching includes teaching social-emotional self-regulation skills to students for use in all types of educational settings including small and large groups, and one-on-one interactions with peers. Educators teach the skills, provide opportunities for practice throughout the school day, and provide coaching through feedback and support as necessary when interactions

---

55. Berardi and Morton, *Trauma-Informed School Practices*, 134 (italics original).
56. Berardi and Morton, *Trauma-Informed School Practices*.

with peers and others do not go as hoped. Throughout this process, the teacher continues to *connect* with students, assuring them that they are seen and valued, and that when they struggle, as they inevitably will, they will be "caught" by the safety net of the connection, and coached through the difficulties. Realizing that they are no longer alone in the classroom setting, they are able to increase their window of tolerance for the anxieties associated with school-based tasks, and resume growth and development through *commencement*.[57]

Commencing is evident when a student is able to engage in academic activities and more easily navigate social-emotional relational challenges. As a result of feeling a greater sense of competence in managing anxiety due to connecting and coaching, the student is now in a position to access higher-order executive functions needed to learn and problem solve. This is not to say that the student won't continue to face challenges or even encounter day-to-day struggles, but school has now become a safe and secure place where they can face their fears, and meet new challenges, knowing they are seen and cared for. This builds confidence that it is okay to risk—and to fail—even as they experience successes. The daily rituals and routines of the trauma-informed classroom environment continue to strengthen the internal neural structures required to face the next step of academic and social developmental demands.[58]

As illustrated above, the *TISP Tri-Phasic Model* has distinct knowledge, skills, and dispositions for each phase. And while initially the stages may be implemented sequentially, ongoing implementation is iterative, and appropriate for all students. The model does not place attachment as more important than academic achievement; rather, it reflects a sober encounter with data that illustrates learning must take place within the context of attuned and mentoring relationship. This also indicates why TISP is a system-wide change process: to maximize the benefits of a trauma-informed school approach, each child needs a continuity of TISP classroom and school methods throughout their school career.

Fundamentals of Preparing to Implement TISP

Many educators quickly grasp the logic of TISP given the academic and social challenges of an increasing number of students, not just those severely impacted by social-cultural hostilities. Given the high risk all students have of experiencing the negative impact of unalleviated stress and trauma, a

---

57. Berardi and Morton, *Trauma-Informed School Practices*.
58. Berardi and Morton, *Trauma-Informed School Practices*.

school environment informed by traumatology and the role of attachment-focused relational processes makes sense as an effective approach to promoting the neural integration that is prerequisite to executive functioning.

But TISP emphasizes the importance of understanding that while the concepts are logical and have an inherent simplicity (it is all about attunement and mentoring), implementation requires intentional planning and a commitment to acquire the knowledge, skills, and dispositions of a new content domain. It is not implemented through a series of quick strategies.

But, take heart that changes in our teaching and administrative practices can begin immediately. And while most of us want immediate change, it is also comforting to accept that the change process is developmental in nature and does take time. We can begin transferring to a trauma-informed school system even while we are developing the competencies.

The following provides a brief outline of what lies ahead should your system decide to adopt a TISP framework. This overview is intended to inspire you to dig deeper into your TISP specialty training as well as provide insight into what such a commitment might require of you. Our primary concern is that TISP be properly understood and implemented in order that students and staff thrive and benefit from the approach. Misperceptions and improper training create the potential for frustration, disillusionment, and ineffective results due to improper application of concepts.

Preliminary Guiding Principles

TISP is not creating educators who are mental health professionals, but it is requiring educators to become trauma-informed education experts. This includes understanding the role of social-emotional processes that influence brain development, and hence the student's capacity to engage in academic and social learning. It also requires educators to understand the traumatology and neurobiology literature that has confirmed best practices in our relational response to those whose academic and social-emotional development is impacted by unmitigated stress and trauma. Negative experiences or results could occur due to educators fearing they are expected to acquire mental health competencies, thus avoiding the training necessary to become trauma-informed educators; misunderstanding the role of attunement (*connecting*) as an ongoing mindset, not a once-and-done stage; or not understanding the scaffolded process of helping students increase domains of self-regulation that concurrently occurs with academic learning processes (*coaching and commencing*). These potential misunderstandings and frustrations are clarified and minimized all along the TISP training process, even while implementing TISP in the school setting.

But perhaps three of the most significant principles that can make or break your system's success in adopting a trauma-informed framework are as follows:

1. *TISP is about changing the educator*: Becoming a trauma-informed educator is not so much about acquiring strategies to change the student, but a shift in worldview that changes the educator. Armed with trauma-informed knowledge, such as the nature and impact of social-cultural trauma, the educator is then able to make perceptual and conceptual sense of what they are observing in the classroom, and then make informed decisions on how to act. Prescribed strategies then serve as a resource to inspire their own brainstorming of how best to implement TISP concepts.

2. *TISP requires education system change*: While a single educator can implement TISP in their classroom, classroom teachers are not the ones primarily responsible for creating a trauma-informed school environment. To expect a teacher to attend a seminar and then return to the classroom as a trauma-informed educator is misleading at best, and abusive at worst. It places an inappropriate expectation on that educator who is then at high risk of failing to produce the desired results, or negating the merit of the approach before it is fully understood.

3. *TISP implementation must proceed with titrated intentionality*: Titration provides an image of pacing or regulating the speed of change congruent with the needs of your setting. Intentionality requires us to have eyes wide open as to how best to accomplish system change. Successful implementation requires educators from all roles to commit to learning a new content domain. It also requires deep conversation and collaboration with colleagues. And while immediate benefits will be observed, changes in desired outcomes indicating student success in academic and social functioning will take a few years to fully manifest in some statistically significant way. Move too fast, expect too much, or proceed without educator support at all levels of the system and TISP may become another passing fad. Building multilateral interest, charting a course of growth that feels "doable" given current time demands, and catching a vision for the developmental process of an education community change process offers the best chance for inspiring successful TISP adoption.

Recognize TISP Requires Education System Change

This chapter intends to begin building educator interest in a trauma-informed approach to learning as suggested in item #1 above in *Preliminary Guiding Principles*. But what do we mean by TISP requiring education systems to undergo a change process, and why do we caution against assuming TISP is merely about requiring classroom teachers to change?

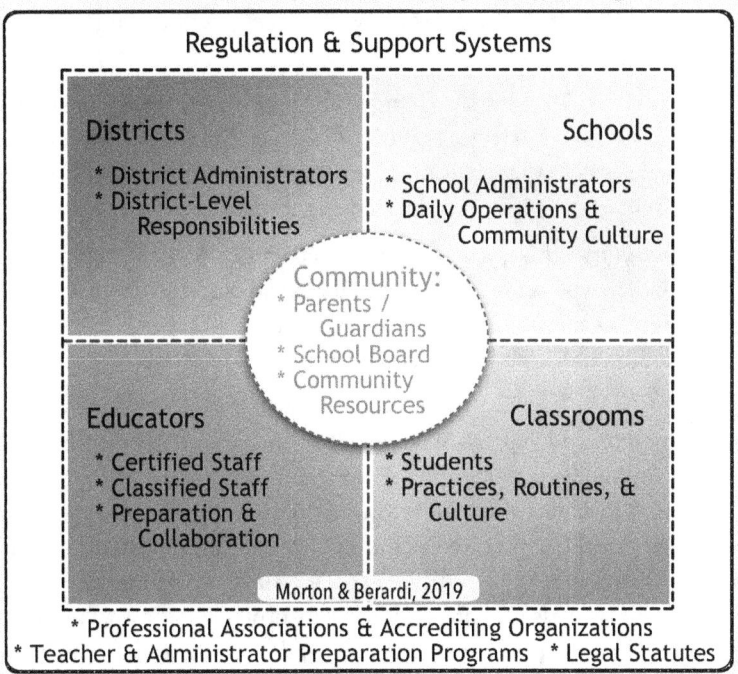

Figure 3 illustrates six elements or subsystems of a K-12 education system. When an educator commits to implementing TISP, the brief descriptions of each element's role in the change process provides insight into items addressed in further training:

1. *Districts*: This system element identifies the role of a superintendent and other district leaders as responsible for not only supporting TISP but participating in training and implementation processes as well. A District Strategic Planning Team is crucial to giving structure to a process that can feel overwhelming whenever a system undergoes a major change.

2. *Schools*: TISP will require changes in school routines, practices, and ethos. In addition to school administrators also needing to participate in training and implementation activities, a School Strategic Planning Team needs to plan ahead for a variety of tasks including how to navigate evaluation and possible changes to preexisting systems that are no longer congruent with trauma-informed practice.

3. *Educators*: All personnel who serve students are viewed as educators, from board members to bus drivers. However, this system element places great emphasis on the tasks and needs of classroom teachers who carry primary responsibility for directly serving large groups of students on a daily basis.

4. *Classrooms*: This system element examines the changes in teaching and classroom strategies that occur between the educator and the student, as well as the inclusion of students as partners with educators in creating trauma-informed learning communities.

5. *Community*: This system element recognizes key stakeholders and providers who serve our schools: parents, board members, and community agencies. Community member support and involvement, including participation in TISP training, are crucial to the success of TISP.

6. *Regulation and Support Systems*: TISP represents a shift in the way we understand how students learn best in the face of pressures that have eroded their historic ability to function in academic settings. These shifting realities require education systems to reevaluate the knowledge, skills, and dispositions expected of an educator. This system element addresses changes needed in professional associations and accrediting organizations, teacher and administrative preparation programs, and legal statutes responsible for establishing competency expectations. In the absence of infrastructure change within the education profession, districts and their schools will constantly be required to retrain new hires, draining human and financial resources.

Form a Strategic Planning Team

School-based and district-wide strategic planning teams are crucial to successful TISP implementation. These teams should be diverse; choose your team from a range of administrators, teachers, instructional assistants, school-based personnel, and community members, as change requires a "board to bus" approach. We encourage you to choose wisely as this is not a committee for those who wish to avoid change and maintain the status quo. Identify key people—those who are your teacher leaders, or those whom others look to within your school. Choosing good ambassadors who will keep their colleagues informed as to how their school is transitioning to TISP can often sway others to willingly join the process. Look for participants you believe would be willing to commit to deep TISP professional development, including continued education, professional readings, and conferences. Create space for this work to take place so that those on the team are not unduly burdened by an increased workload, and set clear expectations up front regarding expected time commitments and length of service.[59]

Commit to Learning a New Content Domain

Perhaps most daunting at first is the realization that to become a trauma-informed educator, each professional must commit to mastering a new content domain of knowledge, skills, and dispositions. This includes absorbing the professional traumatology literature (not just literature related to the application of trauma-informed practices within the school setting) as well as attending trainings regarding the specific application of trauma-informed practices within school and classroom settings. These activities will deepen your knowledge and create the mind shift necessary for this work. If you are an administrator, institute a peer-sharing or mentoring process whereby those who have received training can then share their learning with others.[60]

Don't Expect Changes Overnight

As you begin to implement trauma-informed practices in your classroom, school, or teaching practice, recognize that you will have good days and days when things just didn't come together as you had hoped. This is a normal part of the transition process. You may see progress and a glimmer of hope with a student, only to find that student reverting back to previous behaviors or dispositions. Stay the course. Demonstrating consistency, creating trauma-informed rituals and routines, and continuously connecting with your students will bear fruit. Celebrate the small victories along the way.[61]

59. Berardi and Morton, *Trauma-Informed School Practices*.
60. Berardi and Morton, *Trauma-Informed School Practices*.
61. Berardi and Morton, *Trauma-Informed School Practices*.

Engage in the Change Process Together with Others

Do not go it alone. Join with your colleagues for book clubs, strategic goal-setting, and mutual support. Recognize your limits and consult with trauma-informed education and mental health professionals. Be sure these individuals have proven experience in the application of trauma-informed principles within school settings. Rely on them for strategic planning advice and TISP trainings. Talk with other teachers and administrators from other districts about how they navigated the change process; they are full of wisdom and rich ideas. TISP is still relatively new; we are pioneers and benefit most from engaging in this journey with others committed to the same.

FINAL THOUGHTS

This chapter provided insight into the rationale and process for transforming schools into trauma-informed learning communities. The source of human distress inviting this examination reflects current events for much of the world's population impacted by war, social upheaval, and unsustainable communities forcing mass migration. Our additional lens of examining just what a Christian ethic of care requires invites us to ponder how our own faith communities might have a deep encounter with the cost of care. TISP offers a process for inviting all of us into the world of trauma, as well as the awareness that overt acts of love and care truly are the first steps in a long, complicated recovery process.

We began our chapter with an acknowledgment that the trauma we are addressing here is one in which we are participants; all of us are impacted, not just students whose classrooms, at any given moment, represent a meeting place of social-cultural wars. We cannot approach the needs of our students from an abstract, conceptual level, but as participant-observers. This requires us to examine our own mindset, and the role our faith communities play in either guiding us to sit in our human tendencies to be protectionist and merit-based like the older brother in Christ's parable of the prodigal son, or open to a renewed understanding and embrace of what care requires and looks like as exemplified in the prodigal's father. We reflected on how encounter with the needs and vulnerabilities of others is a crucial step in being able to realize the gospel message and its embodiment of care.

TISP practices then have the potential of helping lift the veil from our own eyes, and, dare we say, invite a clearing of the temple in our own hearts and minds (John 2:13–17).

We close with this image: Christ walking into the temple, the place where the children of God come to worship their Creator with a humility of spirit in order to lay open places where they need a renewing by God's Spirit, resulting in a changed perspective and a radical new way of discerning how to respond to the needs of self and other. We see a rage let loose in Jesus as he absorbs how this sacred space has become consumed with the values and practices characteristic of the world. What Jesus witnessed was not merely misguided brainstorming that led to a poor decision regarding how to solve the temple's financial problems or aspirations. It was a systemic, cultural failure on the part of those professing faith in Yahweh to preserve the sanctuary. The persons responsible for allowing the temple to play host to a marketplace had lost sight of who God is and what he requires of us, and instead traded the truth for a lie, a god fashioned in their own image and logic. Jesus' outrage was appropriate and logical, as any of us might respond if we were to walk into our home and witness our children being exploited and coerced into doing something heinous and harmful.

Christ cleared the temple with strength and conviction grounded in the passion of love and the pain of grief. So too do we need to clear our temples—both our faith institutions and our own inner sanctuaries. Clearing our inner temples takes courage and conviction of spirit born from compassion, with the ultimate goal to live in the fullness of the word of God as love, and Christ as Word made flesh.

BIBLIOGRAPHY

Ainsworth, Mary D., et al. *Patterns of Attachment: A Psychological Study of the Strange Situation*. New York: Taylor & Francis, 2015.

Anda, Robert F., et al. "The Enduring Effects of Abuse and Related Adverse Experiences in Childhood." *European Archives of Psychiatry and Clinical Neuroscience* 256 (2006) 174–86.

Antonovsky, Aaron. *Unraveling the Mystery of Health: How People Manage Stress and Stay Well*. San Francisco: Jossey-Bass, 1987.

Arvanitis, Eugenia. "Refugees' Narratives: Liminality and Home Construction." Plenary address. The 19th Annual Diversity Conference: Border Crossing Narratives: Learning from the Refugee Experience, at the University of Patras, in Patras, Greece, June, 2019.

Bailey, Becky A. *Conscious Discipline: Building Resilient Classrooms*. Oviedo, FL: Loving Guidance, 2015.

Ballard, Jaime, et al. *Immigrant and Refugee Families: Global Perspectives on Displacement and Resettlement Experiences*. Minneapolis: University of Minnesota Libraries, 2016. doi.org/10.24926/8668.0901.

Baranowsky, Anna B., et al. *Trauma Practice: Tools for Stabilization and Recovery*. Ashland, OH: Hogrefe & Huber, 2005.

Berardi, Anna. "Fear of Being Alone." In *Cultural Sociology of Divorce: An Encyclopedia*, edited by Robert E. Emery, 70–71. Thousand Oaks, CA: SAGE, 2012.

———. "Margaret Mahler." In *The SAGE Encyclopedia of Theory in Counseling and Therapy*, edited by Edward S. Neukrug, 624–26. Thousand Oaks, CA: SAGE, 2015.

Berardi, Anna, and Barbara Morton. "Maximizing Academic Success for Foster Care Students: A Trauma-Informed Approach." *The Journal of At-Risk Issues* 20 (2017) 10–16.

———. *Trauma-Informed School Practices: Building Expertise to Transform Schools*. Newberg, OR: Pennington, 2019.

Blaustein, Margaret E. "Childhood Trauma and a Framework for Intervention." In *Supporting and Educating Traumatized Students: A Guide for School-Based Professionals*, edited by Eric Rossen and Robert Hull, 3–21. New York: Oxford University Press, 2013.

Blaustein, Margaret E., and Kristine M. Kinniburgh. *Treating Traumatic Stress in Children and Adolescents: How to Foster Resilience Through Attachment, Self-Regulation, and Competency*. New York: Guilford, 2019.

Bloom, Sandra L. "The Sanctuary Model: Changing Habits and Transforming the Organizational Operating System." In *Treating Complex Traumatic Stress Disorders in Childhood and Adolescence*, edited by Julian D. Ford and Christine A. Courtois, 277–94. New York: Guilford, 2013.

Boss, Pauline. *Family Stress Management: A Contextual Approach*. 2nd ed. Thousand Oaks, CA: SAGE, 2002.

Bowlby, John. *A Secure Base: Parent-Child Attachment and Healthy Human Development*. New York: Basic, 1988.

Bowlby, Richard, and Kim S. Golding. "Attachment: Theory into Practice, An Overview." In *Attachment Theory into Practice: Briefing Paper*, edited by Kim S. Golding, 9–30. Leicester, UK: British Psychological Society, 2007.

Bremner, J. Douglas. *Does Stress Damage the Brain?: Understanding Trauma-Related Disorders from a Neurological Perspective*. New York: W. W. Norton, 2002.

Briere, John N., and Catherine Scott. *Principles of Trauma Therapy: A Guide to Symptoms, Evaluation, and Treatment*. Thousand Oaks, CA: SAGE, 2006.

Bronfenbrenner, Urie. *The Ecology of Human Development*. Cambridge, MA: Harvard University Press, 1979.

Brymer, Melissa, et al. *Psychological First Aid: Field Operations Guide*. 2nd ed. Los Angeles: National Child Traumatic Stress Network, 2006.

Buber, Martin. *I and Thou*. New York: Touchstone, 1971.

Carrion, Victor G., and Shane S. Wong. "Can Traumatic Stress Alter the Brain? Understanding the Implications of Early Trauma on Brain Development and Learning." *Journal of Adolescent Health* 51 (2012) S23–S28.

Centers for Disease Control and Prevention. *About the CDC-Kaiser ACE Study*, 2019. https://www.cdc.gov/violenceprevention/childabuseandneglect/acestudy/about.html.

———. *ACE Study: Major Findings*, 2015. http://www.cdc.gov/violenceprevention/acestudy/findings.html.

Coates, Ta-Nehisi. *Between the World and Me*. New York: Spiegel & Grau, 2015.

Cozolino, Louis. *The Neuroscience of Human Relationships: Attachment and the Developing Social Brain*. 2nd ed. New York: W. W. Norton, 2014.

Craig, Susan E. *Trauma-Sensitive Schools: Learning Communities Transforming Children's Lives, K–5*. New York: Teachers College Press, 2016.
DeSocio, Janiece E. "Epigenetics, Maternal Prenatal Psychosocial Stress, and Infant Mental Health." *Archives of Psychiatric Nursing* 32 (2018) 901–6.
Dobson, James "Dr. Dobson's Visit to the Border: An Open Letter." https://stream.org/dr-dobsons-visit-to-the-border-an-open-letter/.
Docter, Pete, dir. *Inside Out*. 2015; Los Angeles: Walt Disney Studios, 2015.
Everly, George S., and Jeffrey M. Lating. *A Clinical Guide to the Treatment of the Human Stress Response*. New York: Springer, 2012.
Fea, John. *Believe Me: The Evangelical Road to Donald Trump*. Grand Rapids: Eerdmans, 2018.
———. "Why Do White Evangelicals Staunchly Support Donald Trump?" *The Washington Post*, April 5, 2019. https://www.washingtonpost.com/outlook/2019/04/05/why-do-white-evangelicals-still-staunchly support-donald-trump/?utm_term=.1c3ddddf7c3e.
Felitti, Vincent J., et al. "Relationship of Childhood Abuse and Household Dysfunction to Many of the Leading Causes of Death in Adults: The Adverse Childhood Experiences (ACE) Study." *American Journal of Preventive Medicine* 14 (1998) 245–58.
Harari, Yuval N. *Sapiens: A Brief History of Humankind*. New York: HarperCollins, 2015.
Herman, Judith. *Trauma and Recovery*. New York: Basic, 1992.
Hunter, James D. *To Change the World: The Irony, Tragedy, and Possibility of Christianity in America*. New York: Oxford University Press, 2010.
Hurley, Dan. "Grandma's Experiences Leave a Mark on Your Genes." *Discover* (May 2013). http://discovermagazine.com/2013/may/13-grandmas-experiences-leave-epigenetic-mark-on-your-genes.
Karen, Robert. "Becoming Attached." http://www.psychology.sunysb.edu/attachment/online/karen.pdf.
Kinniburgh, Kristine J., et al. "Attachment, Self-Regulation, and Competency." *Psychiatric Annals* 35 (2005) 424–30.
Kippenberg, Hans G. "The Social Matrix of the Attack." In *The 9/11 Handbook: Annotated Translation and Interpretation of the Attackers' Spiritual Manual.*, edited by Hans. G. Kippenberg & Tilman Seidensticker, 59–70. London: Equinox, 2006.
Levers, Lisa L., and Debra Hyatt-Burkhart. "Immigration Reform and the Potential for Psychosocial Trauma: The Missing Link of Lived Human Experience." *Analyses of Social Issues and Public Policy* 12 (2012) 68–77.
Levine, Amir, and Rachel Heller. *Attached*. New York: Penguin Random House, 2010.
Longman, Timothy. *Christianity and Genocide in Rwanda*. New York: Cambridge University Press, 2010.
Massachusetts Advocates for Children. *Helping Traumatized Children Learn: Supportive School Environments for Children Traumatized by Family Violence*, 2005.
Massey, Brandon. "James Dobson's Anti-Immigrant Rhetoric is Dangerous." *Sojourners* (July 2019). https://sojo.net/articles/james-dobsons-anti-immigrant-rhetoric-dangerous.
McCall Garcia, Guadalupe. *All the Stars Denied*. New York: Lee & Low, 2018.
McCleary, Jennifer, and Charles R. Figley. "Special Issue on Resilience and Trauma: An Introduction." *Traumatology* 23 (2017) 1–3.

McCubbin, Hamilton I., and Joan M. Patterson. "The Family Stress Process: The Double ABCX Model of Adjustment and Adaptation." In *Social Stress and the Family: Advances in Family Stress Theory and Research*, edited by Hamilton I. McCubbin et al., 7–38. New York: Haworth, 1983.

McDurmon, Joel. *The Problem of Slavery in Christian America: An Ethical-Judicial History of American Slavery and Racism*. Braselton, GA: Devoted, 2019.

Morton, Barbara. M. "Barriers to Academic Achievement for Foster Youth: The Story Behind the Statistics." *Journal of Research in Childhood Education* 29 (2015) 476–91.

———. "The Grip of Trauma: How Trauma Disrupts the Academic Aspirations of Foster Youth." *Child Abuse & Neglect* 74 (2018) 73–81. doi.org/10.1016/j.chiabu.2017.04.021.

Morton, Barbara M., and Anna A. Berardi. "Creating a Trauma-Informed Rural Community: A University-School District Model." In *Making a Positive Impact in Rural Places: Change Agency in the Context of School-University-Community Collaboration in Education*, edited by R. Martin Reardon and Jack Leonard, 193–213. Charlotte: Information Age, 2018.

———. "Trauma-Informed School Programming: Applications for Mental Health Professionals and Educator Partnerships." *Journal of Child & Adolescent Trauma* 11 (2017) 487–93. doi.org/10.1007/s40653-017-0160-1.

Muniz de la Pena, Christina, et al. "Working with Parents and Children Separated at the Border: Examining the Impact of the Zero Tolerance Policy and Beyond." *Journal of Child & Adolescent Trauma* 12 (2019) 153–64.

Noddings, Nel. "An Ethic of Caring and Its Implications for Instructional Arrangements." *American Journal of Education* 96 (1988) 215–30.

Palmer, Parker J. *To Know as We are Known: Education as a Spiritual Journey*. San Francisco: Harper, 1993.

Perry, Bruce D. "Examining Child Maltreatment Through a Neurodevelopmental Lens: Clinical Applications of the Neurosequential Model of Therapeutics." *Journal of Loss and Trauma* 14 (2009) 240–55.

———. "Fear and Learning: Trauma-Related Factors in the Adult Education Process." *New Directions for Adult and Continuing Education* 110 (2006) 21–27.

Porges, Stephen W. *The Polyvagal Theory: Neurophysiological Foundations of Emotions, Attachment, Communication, and Self-Regulation*. New York: W. W. Norton, 2011.

Porges, Stephen W., and Senta A. Furman. "The Early Development of the Autonomic Nervous System Provides a Neural Platform for Social Behavior: A Polyvagal Perspective." *Infant and Child Development* 20 (2011) 106–18.

Ptak, Carolyn, and Arturus Petronis. "Epigenetic Approaches to Psychiatric Disorders." *Dialogues* 12 (2010) 25–35. https://www.ncbi.nlm.nih.gov/pmc/articles/PMC3181944/

Rosino, Michael. "The ABC-X Model of Family, Stress, and Coping." In *The Wiley Blackwell Encyclopedia of Family Studies*, edited by Constance L. Shehan, 1–6. Hoboken, NJ: John Wiley & Sons, 2016. doi:10.1002/9781119085621.wbefs313.

Samuels, Alex. "People Want to Donate Diapers and Toys to Children at Border Patrol Facilities in Texas." *The Texas Tribune* (June 2019). https://www.texastribune.org/2019/06/24/texas-border-facility-donations-turned-away/.

Scaer, Robert C. *The Trauma Spectrum: Hidden Wounds and Human Resiliency*. New York: W. W. Norton, 2005.

Schore, Allan N. *Affect Dysregulation and Disorders of the Self.* New York: W. W. Norton, 2003.

———. "The Right-Brain Implicit Self: A Central Mechanism of the Psychotherapy Change Process." In *Unrepressed, Unconscious, Implicit Memory, and Clinical Work,* edited by Giuseppe Craparo and Clara Mucci, 73–98. New York: Routledge, 2017.

Shapiro, Francine. *Eye Movement Desensitization and Reprocessing (EMDR) Therapy.* 3rd ed. New York: Guilford, 2018.

Shire, Warsan. "Home," https://www.facinghistory.org/standing-up-hatred-intolerance/warsan-shirehome.

Siegel, Daniel J. *The Developing Mind: How Relationship and the Brain Interact to Shape Who We are.* 2nd ed. New York: Guilford, 2012.

Souers, Kristin, and Pete Hall. *Fostering Resilient Learners: Strategies for Creating a Trauma-Sensitive Classroom.* Alexandria, VA: Association of Supervision and Curriculum Development, 2016.

Van Der Hart, Onno, et al. "Pierre Janet's Treatment of Post-Traumatic Stress." *Journal of Traumatic Stress* 2 (1989) 1–11. http://www.onnovdhart.nl/wp-content/uploads/2008/09/treatmentptsd.pdf.

van der Kolk, Bessel. *The body Keeps the Score: Brain, Mind, and Body in the Healing of Trauma.* New York: Penguin, 2014.

Vermetten, Eric, and J. Douglas Bremner. "Circuits and Systems in Stress. I. Preclinical Studies."

Depression and Anxiety 15 (2002) 126–47.

———. "Circuits and Systems in Stress. II. Applications to Neurobiology and Treatment in Posttraumatic Stress Disorder." *Depression and Anxiety* 16 (2002) 14–38.

Woodley, Randy. "The Fullness Thereof: How Indigenous Worldviews Offer Hope to a Besieged Planet." *Sojourners* (May 2019). https://sojo.net/magazine/may-2019/fullness-thereof.

World Health Organization. "Adverse Childhood Experiences International Questionnaire (ACE-IQ)." https://www.who.int/violence_injury_prevention/violence/activities/adverse_childhood_experiences/en/.

Chapter 4

GAME-BASED TEACHING METHODOLOGY AND EMPATHY

Angel Krause, Scot Headley, Danielle Bryant, Alicia Watkin, Charity-Mika Woodard, & Sherri Sinicki

While ethics instruction in initial teacher education and advanced preparation in education fields is fairly common,[1] less common is the particular curriculum and teaching methodology described herein. Professional educators make many daily decisions regarding curriculum, instruction, and assessment.[2] A number of those decisions reflect a need for and commitment to ethical frameworks that inform professional decision-making. Indeed, as Shapiro and Gross point out, "The most difficult decisions to solve are ethical ones that require dealing with paradoxes and complexities."[3] Often, educators find themselves at decision points in which ethical systems seem to clash.

A number of approaches to ethics education involve exposing the participants to ethical systems and then asking them to apply those systems to challenging dilemmas and decision situations. Among these systems are the

---

1. Shapiro and Gross, *Ethical Educational Leadership*; Strike and Soltis, *Ethics of Teaching*.

2. Griffith, "Preservice Teachers' In-the-Moment Teaching"; Parker and Gehrke, "Learning Activities."

3. Shapiro and Gross, *Ethical Educational Leadership*, 3.

ethic of the profession, the ethic of justice, and the ethic of care. While professional ethics and the ethic of justice seek to establish a legal and correct-action approach to decision-making, the ethic of care:

> ... asks that individuals consider the consequences of their decisions and actions. It asks them to take into account questions, such as: Who will benefit from what I decide? Who will be hurt by my actions? What are the long-term effects of a decision I make today?[4]

Recent work by Christian scholars has examined the value of the ethic of care as a paradigm for adoption by Christian professional educators, though the ethic of care has its roots in postmodern feminist thought, as reviewed by Freytag.[5] Indeed, in studying the work of Noddings, a noted authority of the ethic of care, Freytag concluded that, "There is clearly a need for Christian scholars to take a more active role in the dialogue on care in order that misconceptions or partial understandings surrounding Christian views of care might be elucidated."[6]

Earlier work by Palmer investigated how the Christian commitment to a life of love influenced an educator's view of curriculum and instruction.[7] Palmer presents the idea that love is the source of knowledge and also the means by which a community of trust is established between a teacher and students, thereby permitting a fuller and deeper learning experience. Wolterstorff, in discussing how to educate for human flourishing, addresses a particular aspect of love that reveals the depth of commitment needed to establish a meaningful and truthful view of the world, with all its brokenness. The author states:

> How can we teach our students to see the wounds of God behind the world's injustice? I do not know. Maybe teaching cannot do it. Maybe only through one's own tears can one see God's tears. Maybe we as teachers must humbly acknowledge our limitations before the mysterious and troubling fact that suffering illuminates.[8]

Reflecting on Christian conceptions of care, love, and suffering provides fertile ground for examining ethical education. The purpose of this chapter is to describe the experience of a professor and a group of students

---

4. Shapiro and Gross, *Ethical Educational Leadership*, 6.
5. Freytag, "Exploring Perceptions of Care."
6. Freytag, "Exploring Perceptions of Care," 3.
7. Palmer, *To Know as We are Known*.
8. Wolterstorff, *Educating for Life*, 154.

who participated in a doctoral level course on ethics, equity and justice in the summer semester of 2017. This experience is worth examining in order to gain insight as to how classroom climate and teaching methodology influence ethics education, and in particular the ethic of care.

Ethics, Equity, and Justice is a required course in a Doctor of Education (Ed.D.) program at a Council for Christian Colleges and Universities (CCCU) institution on the west coast of the United States. The course approaches the study of ethics through an examination of ethical models, applying them to the dilemmas of leadership. A particular emphasis in the course is an investigation of equity and justice for marginalized students. The primary text for the course presented four ethical models. These models are the ethic of the profession, the ethic of care, the ethic of justice, and the ethic of critique.[9]

Students in the Ed.D. program are educational practitioners, teachers, and leaders in PK-12 and higher education organizations. Five of the students who participated in the course joined with the course instructor to form a collaborative writing group to continue the learning process that occurred in the course. The authors of this chapter include assistant professors of education at two west coast CCCU schools, an art professor at a regional state university in the Midwest, a high school teacher and instructional coach at a rural Oregon high school, and an elementary educator in Hawaii. A professor of education at the university, who had recently returned to a faculty role after a four-and-a-half-year tenure as a full-time academic administrator, taught the course described herein and co-authored this article.

COURSE DEVELOPMENT PROCESS

With the retirement of a longtime faculty member, the professor accepted the assignment of teaching the course in a four-week summer term. In preparation for teaching, he initiated a process to learn about the culture and expectations of the program and the abbreviated summer term. As a result of interviews with faculty members and students, and a review of course-related documents, he concluded that an active learning environment was appropriate, which would provide an opportunity for students to fully engage with ethical dilemmas and inequities. For continuity in the curriculum of the program, the course objectives were retained. The course objectives were:

---

9. Shapiro and Gross, *Ethical Educational Leadership*.

1. Examine and articulate issues of ethics, equity, and social justice through a Christian and various additional ethical theories and worldviews.
2. Critically evaluate one's ethical framework and its implications for the application of social justice within educational contexts.
3. Reflect critically and ethically on matters of equity and social justice in educational settings, while explaining and defending the role of educational institutions in promoting social justice within contemporary contexts.
4. Collaborate on the analysis of educational problems and implement strategic actions that reflect justice for all students and stakeholders.

As the professor reflected on the unique opportunity he had in returning to teaching after a number of years in full-time administration, and regarding his own concerns about what he hoped to accomplish with the course, he developed an informal set of personal wonderings about the course. These wonderings included:

- What teaching methods could be used in a compressed summer schedule to get students fully engaged in the learning process?
- Would students seek to apply game-based methods in their teaching?
- How would the teaching methods employed influence the students?
- What could be done to foster doctoral students' empathy for the marginalized students and families in their schools and classrooms?
- What impact would the course experience have in challenging and affirming students' faith and worldview?

Due to his course preparation and in reflecting on how he might explore his personal wonderings for the course, the instructor chose to alter the primary learning activities in the course from a lecture/discussion and case-study approach to methods that featured a game-based learning environment, including a predesigned game and student game-design teams. This choice reflected his belief, based on his understanding of adult learning theory,[10] that an active learning approach would foster student engagement, provide an opportunity for reflection, and foster empathy for marginalized student populations amongst students in his course.

---

10. Vella, *On Teaching and Learning*; Wlodkowski, "Fostering Motivation in Professional Development."

The professor had not met any of the students prior to them arriving on the first day of the face-to-face phase of the course and had only course-related communication with them prior to that day. Course-related communication included instructions on the opening of the course in the learning management system, supplying detailed information about the course, and addressing a few questions for students about expectations they had for the course.

During the course preparation, the instructor read an article by Squire in which that author reviewed the lessons that video games held for educators. Squire asserted, "I argue that educators (especially curriculum designers) ought to pay closer attention to video games because they offer designed experiences, in which participants learn through a grammar of doing and being."[11] At that point, the professor realized that learning about video games, and other types of games, including role-playing games, would be advantageous in his preparation for the course and in meeting his personal objectives for the course. From that time forward, his course preparation included a commitment to developing a game as the focal point of the course. Key concepts from the texts and other resource materials on ethics and on gaming became the broader content for course preparation and game design.

The following definitions aid in an understanding of the nature of games and gamification of learning. A game is defined as an activity "in which one or more players make decisions through the control of game objects and resources, in pursuit of a goal."[12] Role-playing games in particular are ones in which players assume a role within a particular milieu, use resources as a character, and work both with and against other players to accomplish a task or tasks in order to achieve an objective.[13] The gamification of learning is the selection of elements, such as character, theme, goals, competition, and immediate feedback, and then applying those elements to a learning activity for the purpose of enhancing participant engagement and enjoyment.[14]

---

11. Squire, "From Content to Context," 19.

12. Overmars, *Game Maker Tutorial*, 3.

13. Arjoranta, "Defining Role-Playing Games"; Daniau, "Transformative Potential of Role-Playing Games."

14. Squire, "From Content to Context"; Bell, *Gamification, Gameful Design*,.

CONTRIBUTING COURSE TEXTS

The texts used in the ethics course included *Ethical Educational Leadership in Turbulent Times,* written by Shapiro and Gross, and *Confident Pluralism,* written by Inazu. In their text, Shapiro and Gross examine multiple ethical paradigms including the ethic of justice, ethic of critique, ethic of care, and the ethic of the profession, in conjunction with turbulence theory.[15] The four ethical models are presented to help educational leaders develop an ethical framework for approaching challenges. Inazu explores how through embracing confident pluralism in the American culture, people can and should live together in peace, accepting and appreciating our differences rather than allowing them to divide us.[16] Through these texts, the ethic of care is alluded to and described as an essential element in schools and society.

The ethic of care is described as an approach to be taken in moral decision-making, in contrast with the ethic of justice. The ethic of justice focuses on law and fairness in particular, while the ethic of care approaches dilemmas with consideration to how decisions will affect people.[17] The ethic of care considers a variety of voices, which comes as a result of listening. Inazu speaks to this in his discussion of humility as a component to confident pluralism.[18] He maintains that listening to others can pave the way for people to understand each other while accepting that everyone does not have to agree on everything. People are able to truly listen when they release their agenda and simply listen to understand.

In educational settings, serving students is critical to the purpose of the profession and educators must listen to their students if they are to live out the ethic of care. The emphasis of relationship with others is essential to the ethic of care and allows people to grow in empathy toward others.[19] Attention to the larger society also allows social justice issues to be associated with the ethic of care, for there is consideration of more than just the specific parties involved in a dilemma.

The ethic of care can include caring through discipline, caring through attention, and caring through prompting action. For example, caring through discipline may be viewed as a more logical approach, while giving

---

15. Shapiro and Gross, *Ethical Educational Leadership.*
16. Inazu, *Confident Pluralism.*
17. Shapiro and Gross, *Ethical Educational Leadership.*
18. Inazu, *Confident Pluralism.*
19. Shapiro and Gross, *Ethical Educational Leadership.*

attention through compassion is more emotion based.[20] Both responses should be valued and viewed as necessary aspects to a caring response to others. What is important to consider is that there is an intention by the educator to view individuals and situations through more than a rules-based approach, but also by including a commitment to care. While Shapiro and Gross do not write from an overtly Christian point of view, their stance is similar to Shotsberger's assertion that a Christian ethic of care can inform an organization, such as a school or college, and that is accomplished through ". . . intentionally thinking through the implications of a caring model and consciously implementing them . . . ."[21]

Teachers daily interact with students who are in need, and when the needs of the student do not fit neatly into the structure of the system, ethical dilemmas abound. Approaching these needs through the lens of an ethic of care is imperative for educators to learn in order to grow in empathy and respond with consideration of the broader effects in decision-making.

THE FUNCTION OF ROLE-PLAYING GAMES IN EDUCATION

Teachers understand that their work includes daily interpersonal communication with learners, and during these interactions emotions are occurring within teachers, students, and between teacher and student. Thus, it is understandable that the study of emotions in education has become a valid subject matter as seen by the increase of research within the last few decades.[22] Yet, even with all the information available in current research, understanding how to emotionally connect and even empathize with students can still be a challenge. Add to this the fact that classrooms in America are becoming more and more diverse each year,[23] and the task of connecting with all students can seem impossible. While personal experience can lend itself to the concept of understanding students, it is not possible for every teacher to have experienced the variety of races, social status, and cultural backgrounds found in one's classroom. However, there is a way for teachers to develop a deeper sense of emotional connection with their students through the concept of perspective-taking.

20. Shapiro and Gross, *Ethical Educational Leadership*.
21. Shotsberger, "How a Christian Ethic," 8.
22. Zembylas, "Theory and Methodology."
23. Lichter, "Integration or Fragmentation?"

The ability to take on students' perspectives greatly improves a teacher's ability both to respond to and interpret student behavior.[24] Lam, Kolomitro, and Alamparambil, in a review of empathy training in the human services field, characterized empathy as a form of perspective-taking, where a person reacts to the observable behaviors of others.[25] Research in education has begun to explore the concept of using role-playing games (RPGs), to equip educators in understanding and utilizing perspective-taking with students. Squire argues that games offer a new way in which to package learning so that experience is at the forefront. He writes:

> Game-based learning can be understood as a particular kind of designed experience, where players participate in ideological worlds, worlds designed to support a particular kind of reaction, feelings, emotions, and at times thoughts and identities, which game-based learning designers are leveraging for education and training.[26]

While RPGs are not a new phenomenon, their use as a way of exploring marginalized or misunderstood students is a recent development. Through the use of the RPG, teachers can mindfully incorporate personality traits and information about their students into gameplay, which leads to higher levels of empathy and understanding for their students.[27] The RPG enables teachers to bridge the gap between their own background and their students' backgrounds. Research has also shown that the learning benefits of RPGs are not limited to educators; students can benefit from the RPG experience through the development of empathy[28] and by exploring concepts such as social-class inequality,[29] morality,[30] and other societal issues.[31]

---

24. Barr, "Relationship Between Teachers' Empathy and Perceptions"; Davis, "Measuring Individual Difference in Empathy."

25. Lam et al., "Empathy Training."

26. Squire, "From Content to Context," 103.

27. Kaufman and Libby, "Changing Beliefs and Behavior"; Belman and Flanagan, "Designing Games to Foster Empathy."

28. Carnes, *Minds on Fire*.

29. Sandoz, "Game Design Assignment."

30. Sicart, "Game, Player, Ethics."

31. Kaufman and Flanagan. "Psychologically 'Embedded' Approach to Designing Games."

THE COURSE EXPERIENCE

Given the positive response in the research literature around RPGs and preparatory interviews with professional gamers, the professor of the ethics class planned a transformation of the course that would lead his students and educators in settings ranging from elementary school to college, through an RPG experience. An initial draft of the course featured a two-week role-playing game. Upon further refinement, the final plan for the class featured a one-day gameplay followed by a debriefing session. In addition, students worked in two teams in which two additional games were designed, played and debriefed during the course.

The course was delivered in three phases. Phase one (online) was the preparatory phase in which students read the syllabus, much of the text and resource material, and completed several assignments. Phase two (face to face) was two weeks long and consisted of eight three-hour sessions, plus related out-of-class work. Phase three (online) was one week long and consisted of a student's choice assignment, completion of course journaling, and two post-course assessments.

A primary aim of the reformatted four-week summer course was to have students assume the role of a marginalized student. To help prepare students for the new experience of participating in a RPG, the professor provided several research articles[32] focused on the usefulness of role-playing games in education, especially in ethics education. During the first phase of the course, students read related articles and contemplated questions about role-playing games. In addition, sections of the two course texts were assigned in the first phase of the course, introducing key ethical models. Key reading content for students included an introduction to turbulence theory and an examination of practices to successfully live and work within a pluralistic society.

Understanding the research around role-playing games, and building knowledge on ethical models and pluralistic society were not the only objectives for the first week of class. Students were also asked to look at a list of possible characters that would be played during an instructor-created RPG and choose a character they would become during the game. Students created a backstory for their character given the limitations or special needs that the professor previously assigned to each character before the start of the course. The characters represented a wide range of students that can be found in many American classrooms today. These students included:

---

32. Belman and Flanagan, "Designing Games to Foster Empathy"; Daniau, "Transformative Potential of Role-Playing Games"; Overmars, *Game Maker Tutorial*; Simkins and Steinkuehler, "Critical Ethical Reasoning"; Squire, "From Content to Context."

English as Second Language students, students from poverty, students coping with substance abuse issues, students with special needs, undocumented students or deferred action for childhood arrival (DACA) students, recently immigrated students, and homeless students. Students in the class were free to choose whatever student they wished to embody for the RPG experience. Many of the doctoral students had decided to develop characters that they had previously interacted with through their own personal or professional lives. As such, many of the backstories or additional information provided about the characters were based on real individuals.

Another key assignment during phase one was for each student to listen to the song "Rockin' in the Free World," by Neil Young. The song was written by Young in 1989 and was intended to be a critique of American society. In addition to listening to several versions of this song, reading the lyrics, and viewing an original work of art representing the themes of the song, students read commentary on the song from a number of sources. After carrying out these activities, students then reflected on the song and its meaning. The professor selected this song as a metaphor for the RPG he developed, entitled *Rockville: Life on the Margins*, and a number of the themes in the song (e.g. homelessness, poverty, consumerism, and drug abuse) were alluded to in the game.

Phase two, the face-to-face portion of the course, featured a review of content, and engagement in ethical decision-making and the constructs of equity and justice. The primary learning activities in this phase were game-based play and related experiences. Rockville, the teacher-developed game, became the defining activity and focus of the course. Players assumed the role of their character and journeyed through challenging times and chance misfortunes as they attempted to win. The setting for the game was a small town in which two students would be awarded a scholarship for life at the end of the game. Course participants referred to the entire course as Rockville well after the conclusion of the course, yet it was only the focus of the first few days of the face-to-face meetings. In the remaining time allocated to the course, some significant activities and interactions occurred. With Rockville as a model, two student teams created role-playing games that were used to apply course content, create ethical dilemmas, and provide experiences for meaning-making with regard to ethics, equity, and justice. Phase three of the course provided time for each student to complete a choice assignment, reflect on the course experience, and complete several course-related assessments.

RESEARCH METHODS

The professor recognized the possibility for carrying out research related to the course during the course development stage. He submitted paperwork to the Institutional Review Board and obtained approval to conduct a study related to the course experience. During the first face-to-face session of the course, he discussed the possibilities with students. All ten agreed to participate in the study and completed informed consent forms. The primary means of data collection were game debriefing notes, course assessments, an online journal with entries made during the course, and post-course interviews. For the purposes of this chapter, only data from participant interviews were analyzed.

The general aim of the study was to examine the experience of the course participants and what their reactions were to their experience in the course. In particular, the personal wonderings of the professor were used as the lens by which the data were examined. The essential question to be investigated was: What was the evidence from the experience of the course participants regarding the professor's personal wonderings about engagement, application, empathy, impact on faith/worldview, and reaction to the professor's teaching methods?

FINDINGS

Structured interviews were completed over the course of a three-week period, two to three months after the course's conclusion. Appendix A contains the interview questions. The five contributing student co-authors served as interviewers in two to three structured interviews each, using the predetermined interview questions. Nine interviews with student participants were conducted and recorded using video conferencing tools (Zoom and Adobe Connect). Responses to the interview questions were collected from a tenth student via email communication due to circumstances which would not allow a virtual interview to occur. The structured interview with the professor was conducted by two student researchers in a face-to-face format using an audio recording device. Ten of the eleven interviews were transcribed using the same transcription service (GoTranscript), with the eleventh interview not requiring transcription due to the email format in which it was received.

Transcripts were reviewed for accuracy and coded using preset codes. These initial codes were derived from the personal wonderings of the professor, which became the conceptual framework for analysis. The preset codes for student interviews included: a) student engagement, b) applications of participants, c) empathy developed, d) faith impact, and e) reaction to professor modeling. Three additional categories emerged during the coding process of student interviews. These themes included: a) contributing factors to success of RPG, b) barriers to implementation, and c) initial student perception of pedagogical approach. See Table 1 for an overview of the preset and emergent themes with associated concepts.

Table 1
Student Interview Themes

Major thematic categories*	Associated concepts
Student Engagement	curious, meaningful, ownership, involved, really matters, immersed, connection to learning
Applications of Participants General	heightened awareness of equity & ethics, how to treat or respond to others, self-reflection, concept of right versus right
Professional Setting	getting to know students better, simulations or RPG development, debriefing after a lesson, focus on building empathy in students
Empathy Developed General	"my" person/character, connected to students/others they knew, saw classmates as characters, put myself in their shoes, labeling as an empathetic person
Feelings during "The Day After" (fictional accounts of what happened later in the lives of student-created characters)	upset, sad, aches, concerns, regrets, invested, anger
Reaction to Professor Modeling	promoted understanding, made it work, gave deeper understanding, exaggerated approach
RPG Success Attributed to Cohort Cohesion	preexisting cohort, honest, trust, felt safe, empathetic as a group, length of time together
Identified Barriers to Implementation	required standards/curriculum, large class sizes, short time to build cohesion, student readiness, need for trust, online setting, K-12 setting, frequency of courses
Initial Student Perception of Pedagogical Approach	a unique way to learn, uncertainty, unknown, unsure, unexpected, intimidated, irritated, nervous, concerned

> *The bold categories were preset codes used in analyzing student interviews. A fifth preset code, Faith Development/Impact, was not present in student interviews to substantiate inclusion. The three additional themes which emerged are bold italicized.

Student Engagement

Throughout the interviews, student participants used terms to describe how they were engaged in the course experience and how they were engaged with the learning. Students described their experiences as meaningful and said that it really mattered. Additionally, curiosity in the approach to learning and an immersion in the learning were experienced. Six of the student interviewees used derivatives of the term *invested* in their description of how they viewed the course and learning experience. The preset code of student engagement was affirmed in the analysis process. The concept of engagement with the course experience, others in the course, and the content of the course was prominent in all student interviews. Several students stated in their interviews that they had taken an ethics class before this one, but the game design aspect was a new concept. Interviews pointed to the character design as an early connection because the characters were based off students or friends that participants had known in the past.

Applications of Student Participants

Student applications of the course experience and learning emerged in two areas: general applications and application in a professional setting. Two interviewees noted a general heightened awareness and more self-reflective practices (post-course) around the concepts of equity and ethics. "I think it [the experience] just gives me a heightened awareness, that no matter what group you're in, you don't know their backstory. You don't know where they have come from. You don't know their history. Our language is so powerful, even when we don't know that it's powerful" (student interview B, 2017). One participant reflected that how they treat and respond to others was impacted by the course experience; "I think it makes you think twice about how you treat people" (student interview D, 2017). Additionally, the phrase "right vs. right" was used by three participants as they described their self-reflection and how they have applied the course learnings. The phrase indicates that there is not always a right and a wrong decision which can be made, that in fact there are many times where we are choosing between two right decisions.

In addition to general applications from their learning, students indicated there were applications in their professional settings. Professional applications included: a desire to get to know their students better, adding simulations in their teaching repertoire, RPG development, the importance of debriefing after a lesson, and focus on building empathy in students. Participants described the ability to create empathy and a similar experience. "Creating empathy through role-playing, I began to see that this could be something that we could do, and it could work" (student interview G, 2017). "I want the students to have this, I want them to walk away with the ability to experience something that I've just experienced that they would be able to really take away personally from, this is not just an intellectual experience" (student interview G, 2017). While learning how to implement RPGs was not a direct course objective it was evident as a learning result as one student stated, "Implementing this [pedagogy of RPG] into a professional practice is, it was very concrete for me. That was the secondary learning objective in the class" (student interview E, 2017).

Empathy Development

True ownership of the game characters was developed and fostered within the class as participants shared their empathy toward and for characters, which then transferred to real-life situations as the course learning stretched beyond the course. Interviewees used the term "my person" or "my character" throughout, speaking for them and sometimes as if the characters were real people. One response included "I was much relieved when I made the right decision for them" (student interview H, 2017) as they spoke about awarding the scholarship. Concepts of right treatment and justice were applied to fictional characters in the game. Additionally, students noted how they began to see their classmates as the characters they were playing.

Three of the ten students who participated labeled themselves as empathetic during the interview process. While this may have contributed to the amount of empathy-related items evidenced in the interviews, three additional interviewees included the concept of putting themselves in someone else's shoes during the experience. One student noted, "I didn't really start internalizing it, and processing it, until I was feeling something about it" (student interview A, 2017). Another student evidenced a new understanding or empathy as they noted, "It [the experience]...reminded me that when we're dealing with people, we're dealing with living people with free will and the ability to mess and up and the ability to just have life happen to them" (student interview I, 2017).

While the concept of empathy was found throughout the course experiences, the emotions used to describe student experiences were most poignant during The Day After experience, which was the closure of the Rockville game. Words used to describe how students felt during The Day After included: upset, sad, aches, concerns, regrets, invested, and anger. One student noted, "I had an actual physical response to [the professor] reading it [The Day After script]" (student interview G, 2017).

Reaction to Professor Modeling

The final preset theme evidenced in the interview data was how students reacted to professor modeling during the RPG experience. Student responses focused on the professor RPG implementation and also generally to how the instructor approached the course material and students. In relation to the RPG implementation, students noted the professor had an "exaggerated approach," that he was "Zen-like" in how he implemented the game, and "he made it work." Some questioned if his approach and personality were contributing factors to what they saw as a successful pedagogical approach. The overall impact of the professor's modeling was captured in a student's response as they stated, "[He] has influenced and given me a deeper understanding of people" (student interview C, 2017).

Additional Emerging Themes

Through the coding process three additional themes were found: attributing the success of the RPG experience to cohort cohesion and established community, significant barriers preventing the implementation of RPG in participants' settings, and initial student responses to the course's pedagogical approach.

RPG Success Attributed to Cohort Cohesion

There was an overwhelming amount of discussion around the success of the RPG experience being attributed to the specific group members who participated. The cohort had completed a two-week summer residency the year prior and they entered into the course as a preexisting group who had spent time in both face-to-face settings and online courses throughout the previous year. Participants described the group as honest, trusting, and the group provided a place where they felt safe. One student stated, "We were such a cohesive group—I don't want to use the word cohort because it seemed more" (student interview C, 2017). Additionally, others described the cohort as a whole as empathetic. "I think we were right for this type of experience" (student interview D, 2017).

Identified Barriers to Implementation of RPG

While professional applications were discussed in the interview data collected, as participants did note that the experience had direct pedagogical applications, there was a continued identification of barriers to actual RPG implementation in their own professional settings. Constraints of implementing a RPG as a pedagogical approach included structural challenges like large class sizes, frequency of face-to-face class sessions, and online course delivery. "How do we teach that [RPG] given the constraints of curriculum and testing and all of that" (student interview I, 2017)? In addition to these structural barriers, participants questioned the ability for their students to experience a RPG as they had experienced, questioning student dynamic barriers. Limited time to build group cohesion, questioning of student readiness for the experience, and the challenge of building trust all came to the surface as they reflected on their ability to use RPGs in their own professional settings.

Initial Student Perceptions of Pedagogical Approach

The first interview question asked students to reflect on their expectations beginning the ethics course after reading the syllabus and realizing that the major focus was a game. These initial thoughts and feelings toward a course using RPG as a core learning element show a sense of student anticipation and uneasiness. "When I first read it [syllabus], I thought it was kind of out there" (student interview I, 2017). Another student noted, "I was feeling apprehension; I didn't understand how a game could be done at a doctoral level" (student interview G, 2017). Students described it as a "unique way to learn," but more prominent were the concepts of being uncertain, unsure, or nervous. Other terms used regarding the precourse reading and preparation included "intimidated," "irritated," and "concerned." Concern prompted one student to action: "I still remember, I was very nervous about the [course] design. I even wrote to [the professor] and told him my concern" (student interview H, 2017).

Connections Between Student Interviews and the Professor's Interview

A theme comparison was completed using the ten student interviews and the single professor interview. Connections were found within two distinct areas: course design for empathy development and discussion of barriers to RPG implementation. The professor's interview demonstrated a core desire behind course development. "It was like I wanted you to feel what those kids were going through and you did it. That was the main goal" (professor interview, 2017). Student "feeling" was present throughout student interviews as they shared their empathy and connection to the characters and their lives, even though they were fictional. Debriefing and reflection at multiple points during the RPG experience was purposefully planned by the professor. "I happen to think that the debriefing times that happened after the game were very valuable. I think there was a lot of learning there for me and for you, I wouldn't sacrifice that" (professor interview, 2017). Student interviews confirmed the value of the debriefing process as they transferred this concept into their own professional practices.

Structural barriers of class size and curricular freedom were noted by both student participants and the professor. While student interviews focused on the challenge of implementing this approach in their own curriculum, the freedom within a doctoral program was noted by the professor in addition to how others might view the approach to the course. The professor indicated that there may be restraints to this approach in some settings (i.e., programs with external requirements, licensure programs). The ideal student dynamics were also a common thread between both student and professor responses, noting trust as a critical element required for successful use of RPGs.

The professor noted, "Part of my desire was to have a meaningful experience for us and not just a typical experience" (professor interview, 2017). The course was atypical for students, but it was a meaningful experience, and powerful. The pedagogical approach was noted during one interview, "We could have easily done the typical course of action [read articles], but I was able to see that games can be used to transcend these and other ways of how we do things . . . not just discuss things in theory or in a vacuum but actually to get them to truly experience things at a deeper level" (student interview G, 2017). Noting the impact of the course, one student commented, "I really felt this is one of the most powerful courses I've ever taken" (student interview F, 2017).

CONCLUSIONS

The revised version of the course "Ethics, Equity, and Justice" was a deliberate decision on the professor's part to implement a teaching methodology that he hoped would be engaging and allow for application of course content. Further, the intent was to put course participants in difficult decision-making situations and to foster within them empathy for marginalized students. A limitation of the analysis of the data in this study is that participant interviews were the only data pool examined, and what was found is not the complete picture of the experience and the meaning made by the participants. However, three conclusions can be drawn along with considerations for future game-based methodology use.

First, the course experience was meaningful for the participants and it felt to them that the course really mattered. Repeatedly, interviewees used the word *invested* in their responses. They were invested emotionally, and they were invested in learning the course content. They also invested their time in the course; indeed, some invested an inordinate amount of time.

Second, it is apparent that the participants found professional applications in the course methodologies. The applications that students intended to use included instructional techniques such as simulations and role-playing games, and the use of debriefing sessions after lessons. In addition, they desired to get to know their students better, wanting to develop focus in their teaching on building empathy in their students.

A third conclusion arose in regard to fostering empathy amongst this group of students. They described their experience and how they felt about their characters in particular from an empathetic perspective. The character development aspect of the course, and assuming the role of the character during gameplay, created the means by which participants experienced empathy. The two instructor-written follow-ups, fictional accounts of what happened later in the lives of student-created characters, also fostered strong feelings and empathy in the participants.

FUTURE CONSIDERATIONS

An important consideration regarding the students' reactions to the professor and the potential for game-based methodology, if it is to be used in other courses and by other teachers, is the fact that participants recognized the unique aspects of this experience. The cohort nature of the program in which the course is situated fostered a close learning community with strong trust amongst students and several pointed to that as a possible contributing factor in the success of the course. Participants also pointed to the particular personality and teaching style of the professor as an enhancement, while wondering if other instructors had the inclination or wherewithal to successfully carry out a similar course experience. While participants expressed appreciation for the instructor and the course, they cited structural constraints in other learning environments that might make the implementation of game-based methods difficult.

The professor had a personal wondering about how the course would affect the participants' faith and worldview. However, the interview data yielded scant information about this aspect, perhaps due to the fact that no interview questions directly addressed this element. It is possible that once the data from other sources are analyzed a more adequate picture of that theme will be seen. A question that remains unanswered is: What is the possibility for challenging people of faith regarding their view of care and the price to be paid for caring for students and others in need in their community? It is quite possible that RPGs can be effective tools in this regard. For Christian educators, those who are at their core concerned for the well-being of their students, the ethic of the profession is insufficient in providing guidance in addressing the difficult dilemmas of practice. Brueggemann stated,

> The vision of shalom is so great that it would be nice to manage and control it—to know the formula that puts it at our disposal—either by religion or piety or morality or by a technology that puts it on call . . . But shalom is not subject to our best knowledge or cleverest gimmick. It comes only through the costly way of caring.[33]

The experience of the course participants related that the process itself—that is, how the course transpired, the methodologies chosen, and professor's areas of emphases—had a meaningful and positive influence. If the intent of an educational experience is to convey the significance of human flourishing (shalom), the commitment must go beyond knowing what it looks like or building a system to bring it forth, that it is represented by empathy for the other, care for individuals, and the intentional creation of culture. That commitment is costly in time, attention, and emotional investment. And that commitment made it all worthwhile.

---

33. Brueggemann, *Living Toward a Vision*, 22.

THE YEAR AFTER

After a learning experience, a teacher often wonders to what extent the learning will transfer to new settings and situations. And further, was there a community of trust established, rooted in love, which permitted a fuller and deeper learning experience?[34] The interviews conducted with Rockville participants occurred two to three months after the ethics course. At that time, participants noted a desire to transfer what they learned through the RPG experience into their professional setting. The potential professional applications included getting to know and care for their students better, facilitating simulations and RPGs, RPG development, and a focus on building empathy in students. The following stories, of both students in the course and the professor, paint a picture of what occurred in the years following the original Rockville learning experience.

The Graduate Teacher Educator's Story—Building Empathy Through Perspective Writing

I remember the first days of our ethics class vividly. A question was posed asking if we liked to play board games. I was truthful, sharing that I like to win, but beyond that, games were not my thing. Knowing this about myself, I wanted to approach the Rockville RPG experience with an open mind. I took a few words from the directions very seriously: "from here forward you will play the game in character." Since my character, DeAnna, was based on a best friend from high school, and I had spent years teaching high schoolers, becoming her was easy, but I did not realize how being "in character" would open my emotions and my heart. Fully immersing myself in character, I felt angst towards those around me and disdain for decisions that were made. I made it to the final stage of the game, giving a speech to win the scholarship. Unexpectedly I broke down in tears during my speech, barely finishing, as I knew I was not going to win. I was attempting to give a voice to DeAnna, and to so many students who have been labeled as not worthy, and that voice was not being heard. A week after the Rockville experience I wrote in my class journal, "Can I use games to encourage empathy and understanding in my courses?"

I began the next semester working with in-service teachers unsure of how RPGs could be used. I was teaching new courses, learning new program requirements, and trying to prepare for a large state licensure visit. I was overwhelmed with the idea of creating a full RPG experience. Then I

---

34. Palmer, *To Know as We are Known*.

was gently reminded of my powerful "in character" experience. I worked with teacher candidates who were interacting with students daily; they were beginning to hear stories like DeAnna's. I started to regularly use "in character" student perspective writing to see if it could build cognitive empathy, how well we can perceive and understand the emotions of others.

During the first class of a secondary curriculum course, I ask teacher candidates to think critically about a question that their students will repeatedly ask: "Why should we learn this?" They take on the role, the persona, of a student in their classroom to write the internal dialogue (what you think but do not say) when a teacher responds to the valid question with "because it is in the standards," "because we have to," or "because you need to learn this." The responses have immediately brought forward student perspectives of anger, frustration, apathy, and distaste for the subject matter, for the teacher, and school in general. As volunteers read the internal dialogues of students, some censor out the expletives, but no one sugarcoats their students' internal thoughts and feelings. For a moment, they gave a voice to students who have felt marginalized in the learning process. Each time internal dialogues are read out loud, it brings tears to my eyes. Then through those tears, we begin our journey together looking at how intentional curriculum design can be revolutionary for the student who feels they are often not heard, or that they are not worthy.

I also use student perspective writing in an online health education course. After reviewing health priorities for K-12 students, candidates were asked to take on the role of a student who is faced with one of the eight health issues (vision, asthma, teen pregnancy, aggression and violence, physical activity, breakfast, inattention, and hyperactivity). In character, they were asked to share: How do you feel? What are your daily obstacles? Describe your interaction with your teacher(s).

As I read their responses each semester, my eyes swell. Their writings are often based on students they have observed. One teacher candidate wrote from the perspective of a teenage father, a voice which is often silenced. Using student perspective writing at the beginning of a course can help set the tone, the focus, for our learning experiences, but can it do more? Perspective-taking has demonstrated the ability to reduce stereotypes.[35] Using perspective-taking as a pedagogical approach with teacher candidates may prove to be a powerful way to develop care dispositions in our teacher candidates and, in turn, for them to develop in their future students.

---

35. Moskowitz and Galinsky, "Perspective-Taking"; Wang et al., "Cultural Boundaries of Perspective-Taking."

The High School Educator's Story—Personal Impact and Potential Future Impact

As I sat teary-eyed at the end of summer term listening to our professor regale us with the postscript of our characters, I thought how this experience was unique and beautiful and a once-in-a-lifetime thing. While I still hold fast to the emotional ties I have with my cohort and my experience of Rockville, I will again tell you my experience is a once-in-a-lifetime deal. I will also say that the idea itself, the idea that an RPG can teach empathy, is definitely not a once-in-a-lifetime experience.

I have the privilege of being a veteran RPG player as I have been playing since my early twenties; I am familiar with the ins and outs of gaming. However, I worried about how difficult it is to release the anxiety of role-playing . . . in front of people. I worried about people committing to their characters. I worried that this type of gaming is out of people's comfort zone, and the whole concept may be a failure. I was wrong, oh so wrong.

The fact that the professor helped us to achieve agency in the process by asking us to create our characters was one of the critical factors in the buy-in process. We loved and still love our characters; they are our people. The parameters put in place (poverty, sexual orientation, etc.) were extraordinarily helpful, but we were also encouraged to be creative and to create real, meaningful, genuine people. The attachment to our characters paired with the trust we had in the professor and the trust we had within our cohort made this role-playing within the game even more powerful.

As we played the game in class, we became more and more comfortable, truly being our characters. The entire cohort interacted with each other in character during the game, even when their character would react to a situation/player utterly different than the player. When the time came in the game to pick winners of the scholarship, we were all torn, who did deserve it? Who needed it more? Was the person with the most need even a finalist to win? How do we choose? It was a transformative experience for all involved. We left class wondering if we were doing the right thing and if we had chosen the correct person. The game made us question our values in the best way: it made us open up to discussions, and to confessions, we may not have ever had.

I currently teach high school, and the characters in this game are my students. I often know their daily struggles as well as those of their siblings; I also know that is not the case for all teachers. It certainly is not the case for people who are far removed from the classroom. This RPG allowed all people who are involved with education to remind themselves of what it is like to be a young adult (or a child) who is struggling, who has some intrinsic factor in their lives that makes it more challenging to succeed.

With the daily grind of classroom teaching, it is easy to forget the grind your students are going through. Most teachers are not aware that they have distanced themselves from their students, that they have lost the connection to their student's daily lives and daily struggles. That is why I am working with our administration to bring this RPG to our high school staff as a way to build empathy that teachers may have unintentionally let fall to the wayside. The game is a safe way to remind educators that our students have things in their lives that they don't know about. It also is an excellent reminder of the privilege that some of us live in.

While my initial statement holds true, our experience in the first class to teach empathy with an RPG isn't too replicable; it was the perfect collision of professor and cohort, and I do believe we won't see the experience again. However, I do think Rockville is an accessible, amazing teaching tool. Empathy sometimes feels like an amorphous concept. Yet becoming another person, a marginalized person, even for a little while, can change everything.

The Undergraduate Teacher Educator's Story—The Use of Role-Play to Promote Empathy

After the original Rockville experience, I was personally impacted. While I had entered the course skeptical about the idea of role-playing, I had no idea how powerful this type of experience would be on me. Overall, the experience left me with a new appreciation for the struggles many students have to go through, a new understanding of empathy, and an interest in the benefits of role-playing.

Like many teachers, whenever I come across a great idea or have an amazing experience, one of my first desires is to share this experience with my students. Noddings notes that "schools can contribute [to students] by helping [them] learn how to care and be cared for."[36] Walking away from the profound experience with Rockville, I wanted to bring something similar to my students. In the following fall semester, I had the flexibility to adjust the curriculum in my Educational Psychology class by adding role-playing experiences. The course consisted primarily of sophomore undergraduate students, and it serves as one of the courses that determines entry into the teacher preparation program at the university.

36. Noddings, *Educating Moral People*, 38.

Before I was ready to bring this concept to my students, I knew that building relationships and trust was necessary to the process. As such, I spent the first five weeks of class in preparation for implementing the role-playing scenarios by building a culture of honesty and transparency by building a judgment-free zone. The first scenario explored what happens in a family when one parent has decided to leave the family. Students were placed into groups of four, given background cards, and walked through a family dinner playing one of the family member roles (mother leaving, father staying, older child, and a younger child). After a set amount of time, students switched groups and switched roles to experience being both a parent and a child.

The second role-playing scenario explored trying to learn a new concept as a child with special needs. For this scenario, one student role-played being a teacher, while the three other students role-played being a student with special needs (a student who is deaf, a student who is blind, and a student who is deaf and blind). During the role-play, an eye mask and noise-canceling headphones were used to simulate the students with special needs. Similar to the first role-playing scenario, I had students switch roles after a set amount of time, so students would have the opportunity to play multiple roles. Before and after each role-playing experience, students would journal their thoughts, impressions, and takeaways about the topic at hand, as well as the role-playing experience. Across the board, students responded at first that they thought the role-playing activity "was weird," but afterward were glad they had participated in the activities. One student wrote in their journal:

> My perspective is that I am now more aware of how my words directly affect the children I speak to. I have the power to use my words for good or for bad. My words can either tear the children down and cause their lights to go out or have the opposite effect and give life to their eyes.

At the beginning of the process, I felt apprehension from the unknowns. Having completed Rockville with working professionals who had at least five years of teaching experience, would eighteen-to-twenty-year-old students be able to engage in the process? My experience has shown that students could engage in this process, and I have incorporated at least one role-playing scenario into every course I have taught. Students still seem hesitant and even doubtful at the beginning of the role-play, yet the majority of students have walked away expressing gratitude in getting to explore student perspectives in such a hands-on method.

The Art Educator's Story—Rockville: The Next Generation

The experience of the ethics class and game design pedagogy was a natural tie into my love of board games and the project-based nature of my art classes. I felt mimicking the experience would be a natural fit. As an art education professor working with future teachers in their sophomore and junior years, I folded game design pedagogy into preservice teacher training through a class on theory and practice in the classroom. I have been able to expose my traditional preservice art educators to the same game design literature readings as well as the project-based collaborative work to design and prototype their games in the classroom. The experience followed the three-phase format of the summer ethics course, including a preparatory phase, Rockville gameplay and collaborative student-created games, and post-experience journaling.

As a part of the initial curricular unit, the students read assigned articles and had several class discussions to flesh out the necessary parts of game design theory. Next, the class followed the example of the original Rockville experience by listening to Neil Young's "Rockin' in the Free World" and analyzing the many themes that come from that song. As many students were not familiar with the references within the song, such as the Thousand Points of Light Foundation, additional time was spent examining and researching that song's symbolism. Student journal writing and online discussion boards were used to take the class interaction to a virtual space where students could take time for thoughtful exchanges.

Next, the students were allowed to select their character from a list that included different attributes and social and economic statuses. The students used the listed information to create a game card and game token for their chosen character. The students spent time diving into the character lists and asking questions regarding the socioeconomic status of their game character. The original doctoral students who played Rockville developed their characters based on former students, while the art education students also selected characters that they felt they knew in real life. Clarification was given to undergraduate students on specific character traits that were not familiar (i.e., DACA status). When the class played Rockville, the ethical dilemmas of moving ahead or holding another player back based on what each character would do were still in place. The students wrestled with their group decision on which character should receive the lifetime education grant and what characters should not get the money. Different dynamics based on the characters that made it to the finals, how the game was played, and the students behind the characters led to varied conversations and different conclusions. The next class session was used as a debriefing tool, which was an eye-opening revelation into the ethical dilemma and the individual student's thought processes. In one instance, a student refused to give the money to a character that she felt was not a natural-born citizen. This comment was a shock for some participating students, but I praised this student for her openness to share her opinion even if it is not a popular opinion in the diverse classroom setting. Due to the classroom dynamics and relationship building that had occurred, the student felt comfortable sharing a contrary opinion.

Following the model of the game Rockville, students next divided into small groups and created their board games. Being preservice art teachers, the games needed to be something they could use in their future classrooms, so they were based on the elements of art and the principles of design. Like the game Rockville, the student-created games included an ethical dilemma that the characters would face while playing the game. The student game design could fit into any category of gaming, including collaborative games, party games, deck building, or roll-and-move games. The RPG games developed by first-year students were trivia question or roll-and-move games. To counter this, the instructor adapted the unit to allow second-year students to play board games before starting their game design to show game possibilities and modern adaptions of classic board games. Because of this extra time and attention to the structure and format of game design, the games designed by the second-year students were more complex and collaborative.

The first year I implemented game design in my classroom, the students in my class were gamers and more familiar than I with role-playing games. By the second year, the class was made up of individuals who had not played a board game in the last ten or more years and did not know any current role play games, including *Dungeons and Dragons*. This confirmed the importance of knowing and understanding that the learning context is critical to implement the concept of RPG in a learning environment.

The Professor's Story

Since the summer of 2017, when we played Rockville for the first time, much has changed in my thinking and practice about teaching and learning. My decision to implement a game-based approach in teaching and learning was based on my belief that this method would enhance student engagement, and I hoped that it would foster empathy for marginalized students. In this follow-up, I am going to present some ideas about what I have taken away from that initial experience and what I am currently working on. I'll present a brief update on the game itself and how I continue to use it, and how I plan on using it in the future. I will also share some insights I gained from the game and how I apply those insights.

I constructed the first version of the board game Rockville from a large piece of cardboard, cardstock, color markers, and tape. In the winter of 2017/18, I sought out an art student who would accept a commission to reconceptualize the game as an actual manufactured game that had a real board and game elements. Design students at my institution played the game with me, interviewed me several times, and then produced an elegantly designed board, character cards, and the related game elements, all contained within a beautifully designed box. In anticipation of working with larger groups, I purchased two sets of game elements. This well-designed and produced version of Rockville was ready for use in the spring of 2018. At that time, I was curious about whether the game had utility for courses other than my graduate course in ethics. I sought out a colleague in teacher education and asked for a venue to use the game in his senior seminar, for fourth-year teacher candidates who were in their final semester prior to graduation. Those twenty-five students played the game in two groups simultaneously. I served as the game master for one group, and an original Rockville participant served as the game master with the second group. I worked with teacher education faculty to develop content questions that were related to their coursework, replacing the content questions I originally developed for my course. Debriefing afterward with the students, I learned that the undergraduates were also moved by the experience and did a good job of developing their characters and playing the roles during gameplay. Students suggested that the game would be better played in a sophomore- or junior-level course as a good prelude to student teaching. These students were similarly impacted by the game as my graduate students in that they experienced empathy for their characters. I noted, though, that this group found it a little more difficult to play a role than my graduate students. I also noticed that it was harder for me to play the role of the game master, possibly because I had never worked with this group of students before. From this experience with the preservice students, I reflected on the following:

a) The context for the game matters and the nature of the group who plays the game needs to be taken into consideration when preparing for gameplay.

b) Debriefing after gameplay is a valuable tool and leads to powerful learning, regardless of the type of group that is playing.

c) The game has broader utility than I first thought and caused me to reflect on what other populations might benefit from its use.

During the summer of 2018, I used Rockville again in my doctoral-level ethics course. While I was pleased with the reaction of this group of students to the experience, I noted that their level of enthusiasm for the game was not as high as the previous group. This reinforced my emerging belief that the nature of the group playing the game and the context for the game are vital for its success, and are important elements to consider for the facilitator who is doing the game mastering. I reflected back to a conversation I had in the spring of 2017 with a *Dungeons and Dragons* game master, who told me that he spent at least eight to ten hours of preparation time prior to leading a game session that might take two to four hours. He told me that this preparation was necessary to facilitate the type of engaging experience he wanted his players to have.

As I move forward, I am making amendments to the game to improve it for my purpose: to help foster empathy for marginalized students. I am also taking ideas from the game experience and exporting them into other teaching and scholarly work. The following are the elements I'm working on:

a) Story: One element I had not anticipated but realized was invaluable was the use of fiction, introduced as "The Day After" in the first playing of Rockville. The words of Parker Palmer are relevant here, as he stated, "Why does a literary scholar study the world of 'fiction'? To show us that the facts can never be understood except in communion with the imagination."[37] I'll continue to explore the use of fiction in my courses, to stimulate imagination and foster student engagement.

b) Character development: Asking students to develop a character and then become a character is one of the highlights of the game. Participants developed empathy for others as a result of this activity. I want to export this aspect to other courses and for other purposes. Empathy for others who are similar to oneself is common, as supported by recent research in cognitive science.[38] However, I desire to help my students develop empathy for those who are different, and therefore intentional efforts to help my students gain the perspective of the other are needed.

---

37. Palmer, *Courage to Teach*, 55.
38. Han, "Neurocognitive Basis of Racial Ingroup Bias."

c) Gameplay: Enhancing game flow by making the game more challenging and engaging. My initial research into games and what they offer to educators revealed that games could be quite engaging to players, and I desired that high level of engagement for my learners. Continued modifications of Rockville, with attention to the player experience will enhance engagement.

d) Tie to academic objectives: I am wondering how important it is to overtly include academic content in the game. While an original purpose of the game was to reinforce learning of academic content in a particular course, I am currently working with the idea that removing academic content allows the game to be used in multiple courses or not tied to a course at all.

Where to Go From Here?

Since most of my teaching is done online, I am interested in discovering how I can move the game of Rockville, or similar games and activities, to the online environment. I shared the concept with colleagues at two conferences and with others within my network. I implemented the Rockville game in Second Life, a Mult-user Virtual Environment, and alpha-tested it with a group of participants who had previously played the game as a board game. I received feedback from those alpha-testers, and I am at the point of recruiting participants to try the game out in the online environment. Through the alpha-testing online and through additional rounds of the board game, I made some additional modifications to the game, including tokens in the game for defining financial levels for characters, and introducing a nonplayer character (NPC) who is a privileged character to act as a foil to the other players.

Other educators who have played Rockville have made the following observations:

a) The character development component has broad utility in providing perspective-taking and empathy-building for students in various courses and outside of a game environment.

b) The scholarship competition has good application in reviewing ethical decision-making and in setting up discussions of family and community context, privilege, and marginalization.

I now have confidence that game-based learning, in particular role-playing games for the purpose of fostering empathy and providing the environment for ethical decision-making, are worthwhile instructional tools for use with preservice and in-service educators. I will continue to use Rockville and look for opportunities to develop additional games for similar purposes.

CLOSING THOUGHTS

In reflecting on the meaning of the Rockville experience for those of us who lived it, we conclude that our desire and commitment is to engage our students in authentic relationships and to make the process of teaching and learning far more than the dispensing of information. We seek to provide an experience that will influence the thinking of our students, shape their attitude toward others, and create the grounds by which care is given and received, and given again. In working toward the development of empathy for those students on the margins, we seek to follow the example of Christ who taught us that the neighbor whom we are directed to love is the one who is in need. The ethic of care is evident in the life of Jesus where need was more prominent than rights. The story of the good Samaritan in Luke 10:25–37 is a good reminder:

> On one occasion an expert in the law stood up to test Jesus. "Teacher," he asked, "what must I do to inherit eternal life?"
>
> "What is written in the Law?" he replied. "How do you read it?"
>
> He answered, "'Love the Lord your God with all your heart and with all your soul and with all your strength and with all your mind,' and, 'Love your neighbor as yourself.'"
>
> "You have answered correctly," Jesus replied. "Do this and you will live."
>
> But he wanted to justify himself, so he asked Jesus, "And who is my neighbor?"
>
> In reply Jesus said: "A man was going down from Jerusalem to Jericho, when he was attacked by robbers. They stripped him of his clothes, beat him and went away, leaving him half dead. A priest happened to be going down the same road, and when he saw the man, he passed by on the other side. So too, a Levite, when he came to the place and saw him, passed by on the other side. But a Samaritan, as he traveled, came where the man was; and when he saw him, he took pity on him. He went to him and bandaged his wounds, pouring on oil and wine. Then he put the man on his own donkey, brought him to an inn and took care of him. The next day he took out two denarii and gave them to

the innkeeper. 'Look after him,' he said, 'and when I return, I will reimburse you for any extra expense you may have.'

"Which of these three do you think was a neighbor to the man who fell into the hands of robbers?"

The expert in the law replied, "The one who had mercy on him."

Jesus told him, "Go and do likewise."

This story sums up for us the essence of care and the importance of developing empathy for those on the margins. Jesus points out that the neighbor to be loved and cared for is the person who is in need. And it is the Samaritan, the person on the margin, who is the hero of the story. Seeking to understand another's context and need is a vital step in building a relationship that leads to care in the classroom, the school, and the community. To care does come with a cost and yet, if we choose to follow the model and direction of Jesus, there is no other way.

APPENDIX A: INTERVIEW QUESTIONS

1. What were your expectations going into an ethics class when you read the syllabus and saw the major project would focus around game design?
2. Did you become invested in the characters of the Rockville game, and if so, what factors led to your investment?
3. When you worked as a team creating your game what factors were most important for your team to include and why?
4. What have you learned from your experience playing, designing, and debriefing the games?
    - How has the experience influenced your current setting and/or role?
5. How do you see the role of RPGs (role-playing games) as a teaching tool?
6. Did you experience empathy and the desire to care during your participation in the course? Explain a bit about . . .
    - When you felt empathy? For whom?
    - How you felt when [the professor] read the "day after" presentation?

7. As you reflect back now on the EDDL 700 "Ethics, Equity, & Justice" experience, how do you feel today about the course topics/experiences? Has there been a change in your point of view, or professional practice?

BIBLIOGRAPHY

Arjoranta, Jonne. "Defining Role-Playing Games as Language-Games." *International Journal of Role-Playing* 1 (2011) 3–17.

Barr, Jason J. "The Relationship Between Teachers' Empathy and Perceptions of School Culture. *Educational Studies* 37 (2011) 365–69. doi:10.1080/03055698.2010.506342.

Bell, Kevin. *Gamification, Gameful Design, and the Rise of the Gamer Educator.* Baltimore: John Hopkins University Press, 2018.

Belman, Jonathan, and Mary Flanagan. "Designing Games to Foster Empathy." *International Journal of Cognitive Technology* 14 (2010) 5–15.

Brueggemann, Walter. *Living Toward a Vision: biblical Reflections on Shalom.* 2nd ed. New York: United Church, 1982.

Carnes, Mark. *Minds on Fire: How Role-Immersion Games Transform College.* Cambridge, MA: Harvard University Press, 2014.

Daniau, Stephanie. "The Transformative Potential of Role-Playing Games: From Play Skills to Human Skills." *Simulation and Gaming* 47 (2016) 423–44.

Davis, Mark H. "Measuring Individual Difference in Empathy: Evidence for a Multidimensional Approach." *Journal of Personality and Social Psychology* 44 (1983) 113–26.

Freytag, Cathy. "Exploring Perceptions of Care in Christian Teacher Education Communities: Toward a Faith-Informed Framework of Care." *International Christian Community of Teacher Educators Journal* 10 (2015). https://digitalcommons.georgefox.edu/cgi/viewcontent.cgi?article=1129&context=icctej.

Griffith, Robin. "Preservice Teachers' In-the-Moment Teaching Decisions in Reading." *Literacy* 51 (2017) 3–10.

Han, Shihui. "Neurocognitive Basis of Racial Ingroup Bias in Empathy." *Trends in Cognitive Sciences* 22 (2018) 400–21.

Inazu, John. *Confident Pluralism: Surviving and Thriving Through Deep Difference.* Chicago: The University of Chicago Press, 2016.

Kaufman, Geoff F., and Mary A. Flanagan. "Psychologically 'Embedded' Approach to Designing Games for Prosocial Causes." *Cyberpsychology* 9 (2015) 20–37. doi:10.5817/CP2015-3-5.

Kaufman, Geoff F., and Lisa K. Libby. "Changing Beliefs and Behavior Through Experience-Taking." *Journal of Personality and Social Psychology* 103 (2012) 1–19. doi:10.1037/a0027525.

Lam, Tony C., et al. "Empathy Training: Methods, Evaluation, Practices, and Validity." *Journal of MultiDisciplinary Evaluation* 7 (2011) 162–200.

Lichter, Daniel T. "Integration or Fragmentation? Racial Diversity and the American Future." *Demography* 50 (2013) 359–91. doi.org/10.1007/s13524-013-0197-1.

Moskowitz, Gordon B., and Adam D. Galinsky. "Perspective-Taking: Decreasing Stereotype Expression, Stereotype Accessibility, and In-Group Favoritism." *Journal of Personality and Social Psychology* 78 (2000) 708–24.

Noddings, Nel. *Educating Moral People: A Caring Alternative to Character Education.* New York: Teachers College Press, 2002.

Overmars, Mark. *Game Maker Tutorial: Designing Good Games.* Dundee, UK: YoYo Games, 2007.

Palmer, Parker. *The Courage to Teach: Exploring the Inner Landscape of a Teacher's Life.* San Francisco: Wiley, 2012.

———. *To Know as We are Known: Education as a Spiritual Journey.* San Francisco: Harper and Row, 1993.

Parker, Walter C., and Nathalie J. Gehrke. "Learning Activities and Teachers' Decision-making: Some Grounded Hypotheses." *American Educational Research Journal* 23 (1986) 227–42.

Sandoz, Joli. "A Game Design Assignment: Learning About Social Class Inequality." *On The Horizon* 24 (2016) 121–25.

Shapiro, Joan P., and Steven J. Gross. *Ethical Educational Leadership in Turbulent Times: Solving Moral Dilemmas.* 2nd ed. New York: Routledge, 2013.

Shotsberger, Paul. "How a Christian Ethic of Care Can Inform the Organization and Structure of Schools of Education." *International Christian Community of Teacher Educators Journal* 7 (2012). http://digitalcommons.georgefox.edu/icctej/vol7/iss2/4.

Sicart, Miguel. "Game, Player, Ethics: A Virtue Ethics Approach to Computer Games." *International Review of Information Ethics* 4 (2005) 14–17.

Simkins, David W., and Constance Steinkuehler. "Critical Ethical Reasoning and Role Play." *Games and Culture* 3 (2008) 333–55.

Squire, Kurt. "From Content to Context: Videogames as Designed Experience." *Educational Researcher* 35 (2006) 19–29.

———. "Video Game-Based Learning: An Emerging Paradigm for Instruction." *Performance Improvement Quarterly* 26 (2013) 101–30.

Strike, Kenneth, and Jonas F. Soltis. *The Ethics of Teaching.* 5th ed. New York: Teachers College Press, 2009.

Vella, Jane. *On Teaching and Learning: Putting the Principles and Practices of Dialogue Education Into Action.* 1st ed. San Francisco: Jossey-Bass, 2008.

Wang, Cynthia S., et al. "The Cultural Boundaries of Perspective-Taking: When and Why Perspective-Taking Reduces Stereotyping." *Personality and Social Psychology Bulletin* 44 (2018) 928–43.

Wlodkowski, Raymond J. "Fostering Motivation in Professional Development Programs." *New Directions for Adult and Continuing Education* 98 (2003) 39–47.

Wolterstorff, Nicholas. *Educating for Life: Reflections on Christian Teaching and Learning.* Grand Rapids: Baker Academic, 2002.

Zembylas, Michalinos. "Theory and Methodology in Researching Emotions in Education." *International Journal of Research & Method in Education* 30 (2007) 57–72.

Chapter 5

EMPATHY AS A CHRISTIAN CALLING

Danielle Bryant

After his miraculous resurrection, Jesus breakfasted and conversed with his disciples on the shore of the Sea of Galilee. In one of his last earthly conversations, Jesus turned to Peter and said to him, "Take care of my sheep" (John 21:16). Jesus often referred to the people he ministered to as his sheep and even described those who were not walking with God as "lost sheep" (Matt 10:6). Thus, Peter would have understood that to take care of Jesus' sheep meant he was to step into the role of being a teacher, healer, confidant, and friend to those in his care, much like Jesus had been to him and others.

Jesus' words to Peter are also a call to me, one that is both personal in my role as a wife and mother, and professional in my work teaching children and adults. This calling means that there are certain people God has entrusted me to watch over and care for during my brief time here on earth. I felt the importance of this calling in a deeper way after some serious medical challenges and scares a few years ago. In this time of uncertainty and sickness, I was overwhelmed and humbled by the care I received from others. This experience left me wanting not only to understand care in a deeper way but to fulfill the calling to care for others. As a result, I have spent the past few years studying how to care for others, in particular those directly under my care, including my students. This in-depth study has revealed the importance of empathy as part of caring for others, which has convinced me that it is an essential element of my teaching practice. At that same time, the understanding I have gained about showing care through empathy applies not only to myself as a teacher, but also to my students. This chapter will explore the impact that empathy can have for both teachers and students.

Cooper's definition of empathy resonates with my experiences. She defines empathy as the ability to "... accept others for who they are, to feel and perceive from their perspective and to take a constructive and long-term attitude towards the advancement of their situation by searching for solutions to meet their needs."[1] Empathy has also been described by Lam, Kolomitro, and Alamparambil as "... an individual's capacity to understand the behavior of others, to experience their feelings, and to express that understanding to them."[2] Along with these definitions, Slote offers two classifications for empathy, projective empathy, and emotional or associative empathy.[3] While projective empathy allows an individual to imagine what another is experiencing consciously, associative empathy entails feeling emotions alongside another. Considering the key pieces of these definitions and Slote's classifications, as well as my own views of empathy within an educational setting, it seems Peck, Maude, and Brotherson's description best captures an understanding of empathy for the purposes of this article: Empathy is the ability to "... feel what the child or family member is feeling, understand what the child or family member is feeling, communicate that understanding to them, and then respond in ways that meet their needs."[4]

In addition to educational settings, the idea of empathy is gaining traction in other aspects of society, but I question whether it is truly lived out. Brené Brown's books and short films have begun to bring empathy to a mainstream audience, and yet current political and digital climates seem to have shifted away from empathy in speech and treatment of others with differing views.[5] An increase in the charged and often anonymous rhetoric found in Internet interactions is a primary example of this shift. Fulfilling the call of Jesus in these current times can be challenging, but ultimately essential. I also recognize that if I can better understand and implement empathy in my classroom through my interactions and classroom set-up, perhaps I will model tools for my students to use in practicing care in an often harsh world.

1. Cooper, "Empathy, Interaction, and Caring," 14.
2. Lam et al., "Empathy Training," 163.
3. Slote, "Empathy as Instinct."
4. Peck et al., "Understanding Preschool Teachers' Perspectives," 170.
5. Brown, *Daring Greatly;* Brown, "Brené Brown On Empathy."

MY SHEEP

My professional life has been split between two educational worlds the last couple of years. I have spent several days a week substitute teaching in elementary classrooms and balanced the rest of each week working as a teacher educator at a Christian university. Both of these worlds have brought me fulfillment, but a highlight was the opportunity to offer real-life examples to my undergraduate students about what it is like to be an elementary school teacher. Diversity in student ability abounded in both of these environments. Some students could easily focus and do their work without assistance, while others faced daily physical and mental challenges, something that I have experienced personally since the birth of my son.

A couple of months before his birth, I closed my second grade classroom doors and became the vice principal of my school. I was excited to start a new adventure of being a mom and an administrator at the same time. However, about four months after the birth of my son I was diagnosed with Stage III colon cancer. As a newer mom, I had no idea how I was going to take care of my son while also starting my treatments. During the next eight months of treatment, my husband, my son, and I were cared for by those around us, people who felt our pain, understood, and graciously responded in practical and helpful ways. As a recipient of this thoughtful care, I gained a new understanding for students with health struggles and their need for care, recognizing empathy as a powerful tool for meeting the needs of struggling students. Yet even with my own experience of care, the busyness and demands of the classroom can cause me to forget to engage with empathy toward my students. I believe this is also true for others. A recent collegial conversation highlighted that empathy is not always our first response. As a result, I began to think about ways to make empathy more prevalent in my teaching and interactions with others, while also creating a model that could be used by myself and my students.

FINDING EMPATHY

A few years ago, one of my undergraduate students had been struggling with various medical issues, including chronic migraines resulting from computer usage. When his migraines would hit, he would often be bedridden for up to three days. At one point, this student had two migraines in a row, causing him to miss a full week of classes. During lunch one day, my colleagues raised concerns about how often this student had asked for extensions in each of our classes, which led to questions about the validity of his medical struggles. Knowing that each of us cared profoundly for our students and that we had chosen to work at a college where we could be teacher educators, I wondered how we might express empathy to this student through our actions. I attempted to turn the conversation toward an empathetic response by bringing up my own experiences with migraines and how they affected me. I proposed that this student probably needed our empathy first, rather than our criticism. My colleagues admitted that they were probably not thinking with empathy or compassion towards this student, but were instead focusing on the extra work they had to take on because of his absences. That conversation proved a turning point for me in my considerations of empathy as it caused me to reflect on how easy it is to become focused on the class or course objectives, to the point that I can become numb to the personal needs of my students. I wondered how to help myself move from a theoretical understanding of empathy to incorporating it into my teaching practice, modeling it for others, and encouraging students to engage in this type of interaction with their peers.

My journey into the study of empathy has led me to many researchers; however, these are not the only voices of authority to whom I listen and learn. As a Christian, I also seek wisdom and knowledge through God's Spirit and his word. I found the Bible offered insight into empathy as it states, "Rejoice with those who rejoice; mourn with those who mourn" (Rom 12:15). This verse is a direct call to feel alongside others, reaffirming a key component of Slote's associative empathy.[6] Considering the idea of feeling alongside another and responding in the context of both Cooper's and Peck, et al.'s definitions of empathy, it appears that there is a component of response or action to engaging in empathy.[7] In fact, I would state that action is the crux of empathy. Warren supports this belief by stating, "The application of empathy ends when the target—the individual on the receiving end of an empathetic response—confirms that the observer's actions effectively alleviate their personal distress."[8] My own research into empathy has shown that empathy only occurred for students when they felt some relief after interacting with their teachers.[9] Ultimately, we are called not only to recognize emotions and feel alongside others, but also to respond in a way that alleviates another's physical, emotional, or mental discomfort. Noddings adds, "I

---

6. Slote, "Empathy as Instinct."

7. Cooper, "Empathy, Interaction, and Caring"; Peck et al., "Understanding Preschool Teachers' Perspectives."

8. Warren, "Empathy, Teacher Dispositions, and Preparation," 171.

9. Bryant, "Exploring High School Seniors' Lived Experience."

must take into account the feelings and desires that are actually there and respond as positively as my values and capacities allow."[10]

STARTING WITH SELF-REFLECTION

I started this journey of studying care and empathy by setting time aside for self-reflection, to better understand the places where I find myself resisting empathy and the places I recognize my own need for it. Part of my self-reflection process was to understand how care and empathy would impact my students in future situations. The other part of the process was to engage in Schön's type of self-reflection, known as reflection-in-action, to see how care and empathy would benefit both my current student population and future students.[11] Although the self-reflection process can be difficult during busy times, I have seen the benefit of how self-reflection helps adjust and change plans based on needs and interactions from the day. I also knew that one's beliefs about empathy would impact how it is expressed to others,[12] and I wanted to delve into my own beliefs about empathy.

In addition to self-reflection about care and empathy, I found it important to reflect on my teaching style. With overcrowded classrooms and current testing pressures, it is easy to fall into thinking about students as a group versus seeing each student as an individual. Cooper offers the term "functional empathy"[13] as a way to describe empathy used with students in large groups. However, she stresses that "profound empathy,"[14] which occurs in one-on-one or small-group situations, is the most impactful and transformative. During my self-reflection I realized that previous assumptions that everyone must be doing well when a class was moving along could have led to specific students feeling overlooked or ignored.

During this time of self-reflection, I also sought the advice of some trusted mentors; I have found that others can help me clearly identify positive or negative aspects of my teaching. This time of reflection made it possible for me to begin to build empathy into my day-to-day practice with my students.

---

10. Noddings, "Caring in Education," para. 5.
11. Schön, *Reflective Practitioner*.
12. Warren, "Conflicts and Contradiction."
13. Cooper, "Empathy, Interaction, and Caring," 17.
14. Cooper, "Empathy, Interaction, and Caring," 16.

THE ACTS MODEL

While contemplating empathy, I used personal journal writing to explore my interactions with students, as well as my own thoughts about what I was learning in the research and feedback from mentors. I began to recognize the need to slow down the busy moments of my teaching in order to contemplate the spaces for empathy.

From the concepts and definitions of empathy in research and my reflective process, I was able to develop a model to help me engage with empathy and care towards my students in day-to-day interactions. The model is known by the acronym ACTS, which stands for Actively Listen, Communicate Back, Think with Empathy, and Speak a Response. Practicing the ACTS model has enabled me to do a better job of approaching each student with the empathy required to care for their needs. A recent interaction with one of my first-grade students indicates how this model works.

The ACTS Model for the Elementary Classroom

The class was already late for lunch when I felt a tug on my sleeve and a little voice saying, "Teacher! Teacher! He cut in front of me!"

I looked down to find a slightly red-faced girl, Susan, tugging on my sleeve. I followed her pointing finger to find Peter in line, waiting to go to lunch. As I glanced around the room, I noticed that a handful of students were still hanging out by their desks, and a pile of papers had been knocked to the floor. I will admit that my first thought was to tell Susan that we were all going to make it to the cafeteria, so one's place in line doesn't really matter that much. Yet I also could tell by Susan's exasperated tone of voice and angry facial expressions that she was unhappy. So instead of dismissing her obvious emotion, I decided to practice the ACTS model.

I asked her to tell me what happened and chose to actively listen to her (rather than thinking about the students still standing by their desks instead of lining up for lunch, or the upcoming meeting I had scheduled with the principal during my lunch break). After Susan finished telling me what had happened, I communicated back to her what she said while validating her feelings. I asked, "You are feeling frustrated because you were in line and he cut in front of you?" I have found the step of calmly communicating back to be especially vital in ensuring that I have heard the student. I also want to make sure I have accurately identified the emotions the student is experiencing. My experience in using the ACTS model has shown that this step not only validates my students' feelings but begins to calm the situation immediately.

Once Susan confirmed that she was frustrated by Peter cutting in front of her, I moved into the critical stage of ACTS, which is to think with empathy. I took a moment to reflect on what it means to be a first-grader and to have someone cut in front of you while you are in line. Although this scenario does not seem like a big deal to adults, I do know that young children think in black-and-white terms with regard to fairness and justice. Susan knew that an injustice had been done to her: She had followed the rules, while someone else had broken the rules in a way that impacted her.

Even though we were now five minutes late to lunch, I knew from empathy research that my student required me to speak a response to her first.[15] I affirmed it was not kind to cut in front of others and walked with her over to Peter. I gently prompted Susan on how to talk with Peter and express to him how she was feeling. Peter apologized for cutting in front of her and went to the end of the line. Susan returned to her spot in the line, content with the resolution. I gathered up my remaining students, and we headed to the cafeteria.

The ACTS Model for the University Classroom

This relatively simple scenario in first grade was well-served with the ACTS model, but I need to state that this model is not just for young children. The ACTS model can be applied at any level. Recently, a sophomore in my undergraduate education class came to me, visibly upset. He shared that his girlfriend had just broken up with him at breakfast, an hour before class. He was expected to give a presentation in my class that morning, and I could see he had all of his materials ready. The ACTS model helped me to recognize this student needed a caring and considerate response to his emotional distress. After listening and communicating back, I then thought with empathy about his situation and responded with a resolution that worked for both of us: I informed him that he could do the presentation at our next class session. At the following class, he came up to me and said, "Professor, thank you for really listening to me on Tuesday. I appreciate that you gave me an extra day, even though you didn't have to."

The ACTS model has helped me to communicate empathy in new ways. My experiences have shown that all four principles of the model are

---

15. Cooper, "Empathy, Interaction, and Caring"; Peck et al., "Understanding Preschool Teachers' Perspectives"; Warren, "Empathy, Teacher Dispositions, and Preparation."

necessary to create effective and relational interactions with others. Skipping steps results in frustration. Choosing not to engage in active listening or communicating back can result in inaccurate assumptions about what a student is saying or experiencing. These faulty assumptions can lead to a lack of empathy. Beyond that, if one chooses to listen actively and communicate back, but forgets to engage with empathy, the response could lead to a failed sense of resolution or connection.

The ACTS Model for Students

The previous two sections explored personal experiences of using the ACTS model as a teacher. In the past year I have begun to dig deeper into care and empathy. One of the fundamental aspects of care that I have pondered is the continuation of empathy. At my church it would not be unusual to hear the phrase, "I have been blessed to be a blessing." The core of this phrase is the concept that as Christians we are called to pass along goodness we experience. This idea has challenged me in how I look at and respond to students with empathy. I have come to realize that there is a fundamental need not only to respond to my students with empathy, but to help them develop this crucial life skill, so that in turn they may respond to others with empathy.

The idea of helping students develop and practice empathy with others is not a new idea. Noddings has challenged educators to begin to look at the need to help children in the area of care.[16] Noddings wrote, "Children today need desperately to know how to care for themselves and for intimate others."[17] Answering Noddings's call to help students learn how to care for others, I began to incorporate the ACTS model, not just as a teaching strategy, but as a classroom model for encouraging positive peer relationships between students. While it is important that teachers demonstrate the ACTS model when interacting with their students, I believe this model can also be used by students in scaffolding their care for others through empathy. This next section discusses how I moved the ACTS model from a teacher strategy to a classroom strategy.

This last year I had the opportunity to work a longer sub assignment in a second-grade classroom. During this time I noticed that a group of students struggled in talking to each other while exhibiting frustration or anger. It was during this time that I began to wonder if it would be possible to teach the ACTS model to the students, and possibly have them practice the four components when talking with their peers.

16. Noddings, *Educating Moral People*.
17. Noddings, *Educating Moral People*, 33.

During a weekend, I went into the classroom and cleared out a small corner to put up two chairs. I created a bulletin board to hang on the wall between the two chairs that had the ACTS model spelled out: A= Actively Listen, C= Communicate Back, T=Think with Empathy, and S=Speak a Response. On Monday, I had the students gather in a community circle and I introduced that we were going to try something new. I talked about what I had been seeing in the interactions between students, and how the words many had been using toward others were not showing care or kindness. I then explained that I had added a special place in our room that was called the ACTS Corner. This corner would be available for students to go to anytime during the day to talk with another student. As a group we went through each of the letters of ACTS and talked about what each component meant. A large part of our time was spent talking about empathy, and what it means to think about what a person would be feeling and thinking, while also trying to feel alongside them as outlined in the empathy literature.[18] After discussing these components, the class as a whole did a couple of role-playing scenarios where students acted out being upset, frustrated, or hurt about something. During the role-playing practice I led the students through the ACTS steps, starting with Actively Listening, to practice how to work through a problem or concern with another in the classroom.

For the first day, I encouraged students to have me come with them when they wanted to meet with a peer in the ACTS corner. This way I could help explain anything or step in if the students were struggling to go through the steps. As might be expected, a lot of students wanted to "try out" the ACTS corner that day, so it was a very busy day with me going back and forth between the ACTS corner and the rest of the classroom. On Tuesday, I encouraged students to continue to use the ACTS corner to discuss issues or concerns with their peers, but told them to try and use the model without me present. However, I made it clear that I could come over at anytime if students felt like they were having trouble engaging with the process. For Tuesday and Wednesday, I was still called over to the ACTS corner at least half of the time to help students communicate, listen, and respond. However, Thursday I saw a clear change, as I wasn't called over to assist any of the groups that day. Students self-managed in choosing when to go to the corner, what happened in the corner, and what resolution came about as a result of their time in the corner. From discussions about not sharing a ball at recess, to feeling left out of a game, to wanting to do something different for a group project, students were able to express their

---

18. Davis, "Measuring Individual Differences in Empathy"; Cooper, "Empathy, Interaction, and Caring."

thoughts and feelings to others, while also receiving a response from their peers. Overall, my experience was that the ACTS model could be adapted for student interactions with great success.

THE ACTS MODEL AND BRAIN RESEARCH

With the increased awareness and study of brain research in education, new information is continually being made available that is helping to shape and develop new teaching practices. One of the more recent discoveries in brain research is Rizzolatti, et al.'s discovery of mirror neurons,[19] a concept that was further clarified by Iacoboni's practice of mirroring—the imitation of gesture, speech pattern, or attitude of another.[20] This research has highlighted that mirroring has been shown to influence one's ability to connect empathetically. Gallese, et al. note that the concept of mirroring enables individuals to understand "the meaning of other's behavior from within."[21] New information has also revealed that mirroring has more value than just confirming and validating another's feelings. Mirroring also produces a calming effect on the individual expressing their emotions.[22] Although the terminology of mirroring is not used in the ACTS model, the concept is seen in the step "Communicate Back." Through the process of communicating back what was said, the teacher or student can start the process of calming the other individual before moving onto the next step of the ACTS model. In the case of younger children, this mirroring step can also help provide language for an emotion the teacher recognizes, but the student may not have yet been able to articulate.

Another area of brain research is the study of the empathy gap occurring between individuals when one person has gone through the same experience that another is currently experiencing.[23] People who have had similar experiences may assume that empathy comes more naturally because of the shared experience, but hindsight for the individual who has overcome the experience can bias their view of the other person's situation and emotions.[24] This is why the third step in the ACTS model, "Think with Empathy," is especially vital. This stage compels the one caring to consider what specific background knowledge they may have about another and how this may be

---

19. Rizzolatti et al., "Mirrors in the Mind."
20. Iacoboni, "Imitation, Empathy, and Mirror Neurons."
21. Gallese et al., "Mirror Neuron Forum," 370.
22. Reid, *Hypnosis for Behavioral Health*.
23. Ruttan et al., "Having 'Been There' Doesn't Mean I Care."
24. Nordgren et al., "Visceral Drives in Retrospect."

impacting the carer's emotions. The "Think with Empathy" step may not be a complex or in-depth procedure for students, as it is for the teacher, but students can still engage in a more simplified version of thinking with empathy about their peer. It is important to note that even if we ourselves have had a similar experience, we must not assume we know how the other person is feeling. I know I have engaged, unintentionally, in the concept of empathy gap when interacting with others. When colleagues have expressed their level of stress from busyness, I may discount their stress compared to the stress I have experienced as a wife, mom, student, and teacher. Instead of choosing to think with empathy and considering the other teacher's feelings, I found myself assuming that the teacher was feeling the same kind of stress as myself. It is only through a conscious effort that I am able to overcome my own empathy gap and truly empathize. Awareness of an empathy gap is a beginning step in the process of connecting with others.

EMPATHY AND EXPECTATIONS

It is important to note that even when I consciously use empathy with my students, I do not always resolve a situation the way the student wants. This section explores looking at empathy and the expectations of others when offering a response, especially in the case of a teacher responding to students.

A colleague asked me about showing empathy and continuing to maintain expectations. Specifically, she wondered how I balanced showing empathy to my students while continuing to maintain high standards and expectations. Learning this balance is where the practice of empathy can become murky. There is no easy answer to this question because each student and situation is unique. Responding to a sick student using the ACTS model, I feel the student's stress of not being able to do their work with looming deadlines, and I express empathy to the student about their dilemma. However, at times I must maintain the established deadline, telling them that their late work will face the appropriate consequences. I have both felt and expressed empathy for my student, but the academic standards remain the same. For these situations, I have learned to rely on my knowledge of the student, the immediate situation, and reasonable expectations, trusting that care is often more important for the student to experience than adjusted expectations.

THE ACTS MODEL AND JESUS' CALL

Empathy is not always the easiest course of action, particularly in the bustle of busy classrooms. During the last year of self-reflection, I have noted that there have been times that I did not engage in the ACTS model towards my students because I was overwhelmed or tired. In those moments, I found myself responding quickly and thoughtlessly. One particular day I saw an elementary student sitting at her desk with her head hanging low after a recent conversation with me. Seeing the student upset, I went to her and tried to engage her in conversation. After a few minutes of talking to the student, I was able to get her to share that she had felt unheard when I brushed off her concerns. Despite my desire to be empathetic, I had not been so. With sincere apologies to my student, I asked her to share again what she had tried to tell me before. This time while she was speaking, I consciously employed the ACTS model. A hug and smile at the end of our conversation let me know that I had not only resolved the situation for my student but had also reconciled with her. Although I may still miss opportunities for empathy, my hope is that ongoing practice of the ACTS model in my day-to-day teaching will cause these incidents to lessen over time. The ACTS model has allowed me to connect with others in more meaningful ways, and I believe that this type of connection is a vital element of a Christian ethic of care. I have also seen that the ACTS model can be utilized by students, as young as elementary school, in helping to create meaningful and positive peer-relationships. I move forward, grateful for the example of Christ and others, striving to learn, seeking feedback, and practicing empathy in all aspects of my personal and professional life, growing in Jesus' calling to care for his sheep.

BIBLIOGRAPHY

Brown, Brené. "Brené Brown on Empathy." https://www.youtube.com/watch?v=1Evwgu369Jw.

———. *Daring Greatly: How the Courage to be Vulnerable Transforms the Way We Live, Love, Parent, and Lead.* 1st ed. New York: Gotham, 2012.

Bryant, Danielle. "Exploring High School Seniors' Lived Experience of Teacher Empathy: A Phenomenological Study." PhD diss., George Fox University, 2019.

Cooper, Bridget. "Empathy, Interaction, and Caring: Teachers' Role in a Constrained Environment." *Pastoral Care in Education* 22 (2004) 12–21.

Davis, Mark H. "Measuring Individual Differences in Empathy: Evidence for a Multidimensional Approach." *Journal of Personality and Social Psychology* 44 (1983) 113–26.

Gallese, Vittorio, et al. "Mirror Neuron Forum." *Perspectives on Psychological Science* 6 (2011) 369–407.

Iacoboni, Marco. "Imitation, Empathy, and Mirror Neurons." *Annual Review of Psychology* 60 (2009) 653–70.

Lam, Tony C. M., et al. "Empathy Training: Methods, Evaluation Practices, and Validity." *Journal of Multidisciplinary Evaluation* 7 (2011) 162–200.

Noddings, Nel. "Caring in Education." http://infed.org./mobi/caring-in-education.

———. *Educating Moral People: A Caring Alternative to Character Education*. New York: Teachers College Press, 2002.

Nordgren, Loran F., et al. "Visceral Drives in Retrospect." *Psychological Science* 17 (2006) 635–40.

Peck, Nancy F., et al. "Understanding Preschool Teachers' Perspectives on Empathy: A Qualitative Inquiry." *Early Childhood Education* 43 (2015) 169–79.

Reid, D. B. *Hypnosis for Behavioral Health: A Guide to Expanding your Professional Practice*. New York: Springer, 2012.

Rizzolatti, Giacomo, et al. "Mirrors in the Mind." *Scientific American* 295 (2006) 54–61.

Ruttan, Rachel L., et al. "Having 'Been There' Doesn't Mean I Care: When Prior Experience Reduces Compassion for Emotional Distress. *Journal of Personality and Social Psychology* 108 (2015) 610–22.

Schön, Donald. *The Reflective Practitioner: How Professionals Think in Action*. London: Temple Smith, 1983.

Slote, Michael. "Empathy as Instinct." In *Forms of Fellow Feeling*, edited by Neil Roughley and Thomas Schramme, 133–41. Cambridge: Cambridge University Press, 2018.

Warren, Chezare A. "Conflicts and Contradiction: Conceptions of Empathy and the Work of Good-Intentioned Early Career White Female Teachers." *Urban Education* 50 (2015) 572–600.

———. "Empathy, Teacher Dispositions, and Preparation for Culturally Responsive Pedagogy." *Journal of Teacher Education* 69 (2018) 169–83.

Chapter 6

THE ETHIC OF CARE AND INCLUSIVE EDUCATION

David W. Anderson

INTRODUCTION

THE ETHIC OF CARE espoused in this article should be evident in every classroom, preschool through university. This ethic is especially significant to classrooms in which students with disabilities are included. I begin by briefly reviewing historical and legal issues which led to the movement toward inclusive education, and continue by considering issues of moral development important to understanding the ethic of care. Finally, I discuss biblical principles which are foundational aspects to an ethic of care in the classroom.

LEGAL AND HISTORICAL BACKGROUND LEADING TO INCLUSION

Arguments regarding inclusion are generally founded on ideas of social justice and equal rights, following the same logic as that which prevailed in the movement toward desegregation.¹ The Individuals with Disabilities Education Act² required that students with disabilities be included in regular classrooms to the extent possible. This position was argued largely from an ethic of justice in response to the history of injustices inflicted on students with disabilities, which ranged from denial of access to public schools, to being warehoused in institutional settings, to advocating elimination of some disabled persons. These unjust practices were thought necessary to build a strong society by eliminating or isolating certain people groups. The eugenics movement of the early 1900s even received judicial support through the infamous ruling of Oliver Wendell Holmes, which concluded:

> Still, it is better for all the world if, instead of waiting to execute degenerate offspring for crime or to let them starve for their imbecility, society can prevent those who are manifestly unfit from continuing their kind. The principle that sustains compulsory vaccination is broad enough to cover cutting the Fallopian tubes ... Three generations of imbeciles are enough.³

This ruling shows a distinctly negative view of people who had disabilities. It is reasonable to argue that the eugenics movement is still alive in the U.S. and other countries in the form of prenatal assessment and the recommendation to terminate pregnancy rather than give birth to a child who may have a disability.

Over time the approach to serving children with special needs changed from having them in the regular classroom to the extent possible (which, arguably, still cast a negative pall over those with disabilities) to the language of inclusion. The definition of inclusion preferred for the purpose of this discussion is one that recognizes that inclusion refers not simply to placing individuals with disabilities in the regular classroom, but to a change in school culture such that all teachers accept responsibility for the learning of all children, including those who have typically been excluded.⁴

WHAT IS NEEDED FOR INCLUSIVE EDUCATION?

A change in school culture such as Mittler envisioned has direct implications for the ethic of care in the classroom. Pudlas wrote of "Head and Heart

---

1. Anderson, "Teacher as Servant-Leader"; Schaffner and Buswell, "Ten Critical Elements."
2. Individuals with Disabilities Education Act, PL 114–95.
3. Buck v Bell, Opinion Section, para. 6.
4. Mittler, *Working Toward Inclusive Education*.

and Hands" as necessary elements of inclusive education.[5] I have used this model in helping teachers in Christian schools in Kenya transition into inclusive programming, but added a fourth "H" to emphasize that when the head, heart, and hands work together, they result in *habits* of teaching and interaction that benefit both students with a disability and students with conventional minds and bodies. Simply stated:

Head focuses on the teacher's knowledge of curricular content, teaching methodology, and disabling conditions and their impact on various areas of functioning;

Heart refers to the teacher's convictions, such as worldview and beliefs, their attitudes and values in regard to students (with and without disabilities), and the teacher's inclination to do things in a certain manner;

Hands relates to the customary practice and conduct of the teacher in implementing various teaching methodologies;

Habits refers to effective educational practice that follows when the head, heart, and hands consistently work together.

Teacher preparation programs typically emphasize the head and the hands. Students preparing to serve as teachers commonly take many general and/or special education courses and conclude their educational preparation with one semester of student teaching. Assessment of their teaching ability is primarily through course exams and observation of their performance in a student teaching or practicum setting to evaluate the adequacy with which the head and hands function. Assessment of the heart may be limited or absent, since it is difficult to measure this aspect objectively. Many who have been involved in preparing teachers over a period of years can recall students for whom the head and hands were firmly established, but whose heart seemed cold to the *persons* with whom they worked. The heart, however, is the most important and should guide the head and the hands toward developing the habits desired of Christian teachers. True inclusion begins not with what we know (head) and are able to do (hands), but with *who we are,* i.e., the heart. The heart is the fount out of which the ethic of care flows.

ETHIC OF JUSTICE VS. ETHIC OF CARE

Owens and Ennis defined caring as "a set of relational patterns that foster mutual recognition and realization, growth, development, protection, empowerment, and human community, culture, and possibility."[6] They

---

5. Pudlas, "Head and Heart and Hands."
6. Owens and Ennis, "Ethic of Care in Teaching," 393.

maintained that teachers should be expected to establish an ethic of care in the classroom, but noted that the ability to care is "assumed rather than nurtured or taught."[7] They proposed that teaching on the ethic of care should be included in the teacher-training curriculum. Their point is valid, but needs clarification: teaching them *to care* is not directly a part of the teacher-training curriculum, but teaching the *how* and *why* to be caring is important and should be modeled in preparing our students to become teachers.

In presenting their position, Owens and Ennis contrasted the work of Kohlberg[8] and Gilligan[9] on moral development. Kohlberg focused on the concept of fairness and suggested a developmental process moving from an egocentric attitude of fairness based on individual needs, to a more principled understanding of fairness resting on the ideals of equality and reciprocity. Kohlberg essentially equated morality with a broadly though not necessarily biblically understood concept of justice.[10] Gilligan, on the other hand, was unsatisfied with Kohlberg's conclusions. Based on his study of primarily male subjects, Kohlberg's system tended to show females as morally less developed. From her study of female subjects, Gilligan attributed the observed difference in moral development between males and females to dissimilarities in how boys and girls are socialized. She suggested an ethic of care is more central for females than the cold justice Kohlberg described. The voice of care, as Gilligan described it, understands moral judgment to be context-specific and based on sensitivity to a person's needs and on interpersonal relationships.

Both Kohlberg's and Gilligan's ideas are pregnant with implications, but Gilligan provides more direction for an ethic of care in the classroom. Morris, whose life experience includes becoming disabled, claimed that recognition of interdependence, relationships, and responsibilities is central to a feminist ethic of care (as per Gilligan), and spoke critically about the masculine view (as per Kohlberg) that separates individuals from one another because of its emphasis on autonomy, independence, and individual rights.[11] With regard to inclusion, Morris argued that an ethic of care acknowledges the common humanity of able-bodied and disabled persons and pointed to negative consequences for both groups resulting from denying equal human rights.

7. Owens and Ennis, "Ethic of Care in Teaching," 392.
8. Kohlberg, *Philosophy of Moral Development*.
9. Gilligan, *In a Different Voice*.
10. Anderson, *Toward a Theology of Special Education*.
11. Morris, "Impairment and Disability."

Noddings argued that ethics should be based on *natural caring* and grounded her approach in a longing for goodness rather than simple moral reasoning (as did Kohlberg and Gilligan).[12] She argued that schools should encourage the growth of competent, caring, and loving (and lovable) persons.[13] Noddings identified four major components of moral education from a care perspective:

Modeling: demonstrating for students what a caring relationship looks like through the teacher's behavior

Dialogue: calling attention to actions or words (the teacher's or other students') that reflect caring for others, or asking students to evaluate their own behavior as to its caring nature

Practice: giving students opportunity to display caring behavior to their peers; e.g., peer-to-peer tutoring and group activities to help shape caring behaviors and relationships

Confirmation: affirming and encouraging students as they engage in caring behaviors.[14]

A BIBLICAL BASIS FOR AN ETHIC OF CARE

Noddings, as noted previously, spoke generally about establishing an ethic of care in the classroom. Seeking to establish a biblical basis for an ethic of care is consistent with her suggestions, but has deeper implications (and importance) since it is based on the word of God.

What Gilligan[15] and Morris[16] described as a feminist ethic of care is more consistent with biblical teaching than Kohlberg's theory. Caring is eminently biblical, not something we have invented. God reveals himself as a carer throughout Scripture, most prominently in and through the ministry of Jesus, but God's caring nature is evident from the beginning of time. After creating the garden of Eden, God provided a watering system (Gen 2:10–14) for the plants and animals. God then "placed the man in the garden of Eden to tend and watch over it" (Gen 2:15), to *"keep it in order."*[17] Adam's appointment as manager or steward of God's creation made mankind responsible to care for God's creation. Adam's naming the animals (Gen 2:20) also suggests a responsibility of care, while simultaneously helping Adam realize he was

12. Noddings, *Caring: A Feminine Approach*
13. Noddings, *Challenge to Care in Schools.*
14. Noddings, *Caring: A Feminine Approach*
15. Gilligan, *In a Different Voice.*
16. Morris, "Impairment and Disability."
17. Peterson, *Message* (emphasis added).

without a suitable co-worker or companion. Creating Eve and presenting her to Adam evidences God's care for Adam, and Adam's recognition of their unity ("one flesh," Gen 2:24), implies a caring relationship between the couple. Even expelling Adam and Eve from the garden was an act of care and grace on the part of God, preventing them from eating of the Tree of Life (Gen 3:22–24). Though Adam and Eve had fallen, their responsibility to care for God's creation—and for one another and their progeny—remained.

Some people see God portrayed in the Old Testament as an angry God who brings judgment on the nations. However, the history of Israel bears further witness to God's ongoing care for his chosen people, even though that often meant disciplinary action on God's part.

Jesus' incarnation, crucifixion, and resurrection most clearly demonstrate God to be a caring God. Jesus' announcement of his mission in Luke 4:18–19 reveals the scope of his care:

> "The Spirit of the Lord is on me,
>   because he has anointed me
>   to proclaim good news to the poor.
> He has sent me to proclaim freedom for the prisoners
>   and recovery of sight for the blind,
> to set the oppressed free,
> to proclaim the year of the Lord's favor."

The Gospels make evident Christ's care for all: diseased, disabled, outcasts, widows, Jews, gentiles, tax-collectors, adulterers—all who are kept in any form of bondage or oppression. Christ provided a model that all Christians are called to emulate, a call to love and to care for others.

HOW DOES THIS APPLY TO TEACHERS?

"What God is determines what we ought to be."[18] Since God is characterized by love and caring, these qualities must be evident in our interactions with our students and others. Teaching is a way of expressing God's love to others and demonstrating our love for God. Caring love leads us to seek the best interests of those with whom we work. In this sense, teaching *is* caring. Shurley spoke of caring as a Christian's calling:

> God wants all of God's children to take good care of each other. God's desire is not simply a gentle invitation: it is a directive, a summons, a call . . . all Christians are called to give care to and

---

18. Wiersbe, *Bible Exposition Commentary*. 1 John 4:17.

receive care from one another as a reflection of who they are as the body of Christ.[19]

This call to be caring is not restricted to how we interact with other believers, just as God's love and care is not only for those who respond to the gospel message. Caring should be a prominent characteristic of our lives, in and out of school. The role of the Christian teacher is not limited to teaching facts and concepts, but includes (demands?) establishing a caring classroom and school community. Such a community can lead to the transformation of unjust societies in which historically marginalized people, such as those who are disabled, "have an equal place at the table."[20] The actual methods of teaching used by a Christian teacher will not necessarily be different from those of other teachers, but being a Christian should flavor our demeanor such that a mood of caring pervades the classroom, influencing the manner of teacher-student, student-student, and teacher-peer interactions in the educational community.

Establishing a Christian ethic of care in the classroom is "good news" in action. It is an aspect of spiritual care for others: *spiritual* because it impacts both our students' spirits and our own; and *Spiritual*, because we act in the power of and in response to the Holy Spirit who seeks to conform us to the image of Christ. All people, including our students, have the same basic spiritual needs: to love and be loved, to forgive and be forgiven, and to find meaning and purpose in life.[21] Being a spiritual care provider is the job of every Christian; our faith uniquely equips us to relate to the needs of others.[22]

God's love is an all-encompassing characteristic of God by which he continually gives of himself to others, seeking their benefit. An educator's love and care for students must involve self-giving as well. God has poured his love into our hearts (Rom 5:5), and that love should spill over into our relationships with others, especially those we teach. Love and care should infuse our thoughts, attitudes, and actions (Gal 5:22) such that we ". . . walk in the way of love . . ." (Eph 5:2). As agents of the kingdom of God, our work as teachers should attest to the characteristics and values of God's kingdom,[23] displaying unconditional love and creating an environment where students feel welcomed and accepted by teachers and by one another. The ethic of care and love means seeing our students, including those with a

19. Shurley, *Pastoral Care and Intellectual Disability*, 1.
20. Cohall, "Developing an Ethic of Care," 15
21. Shelly, *Spiritual Care*.
22. Haugk, *Christian Caregiving*.
23. Snyder, *Community of the King*.

significant disability, as having value in themselves and helping others in the school community to see this as well. Our interactions must communicate respect for all students as individuals made in the image of God. We allow for their weaknesses, imperfections, or difficulties, accepting our students where they are (developmentally, academically, and behaviorally), though not being content to leave them at that level, but seeking their betterment.[24]

Ethics and morality are not merely derived from human or social thought, but are dependent on God.[25] The author of Hebrews tells us that Jesus ". . . is the radiance of God's glory and the exact representation of his being . . ." (Heb 1:3). Christ is our model for ethical, caring behavior. To display the ethic of care in our lives and classrooms requires patterning our love of others after God's love and care as we see it embodied in Christ. Christian teachers should be a visible representation of Jesus—his grace at work, his love outreaching, his desire for people to be free from oppression, and to be reconciled with and to serve one another.

WHAT ARE CHARACTERISTICS OF A CLASSROOM FOUNDED ON AN ETHIC OF CARE?

Teachers must actively seek to promote in the classroom a community of acceptance, respect, and caring. Ethics is more than making right decisions; its scope includes affect and behavior.[26] Anderson's discussion of a theology of special education relates to all classrooms and teachers, especially given the emphasis on including children with disabilities in general education classes.[27] The ethic of care should be evident at all levels of education, and felt by everyone involved: teachers, administrators, school board members, students, and families. In classrooms established on an ethic of care several qualities will be evident.

Compassion

Inclusive programming requires the display of unconditional love. Teachers must create an environment where all students feel welcomed and accepted by the teacher and by their peers. Interaction with the students must

---

24. Anderson, *Toward a Theology of Special Education*.
25. Estep, "Moral Development. and Christian Formation"
26. Estep, "Moral Development and Christian Formation."
27. Anderson, *Toward a Theology of Special Education*.

communicate respect for them as individuals made in the image of God.[28] Benevolence will have a prominent role as teachers seek to give each student what he or she requires in order to learn effectively. Using various teaching methods and approaches, or creatively developing a new approach may be necessary, along with providing constructive and compassionate affirmation of the students.

Long, whose primary focus was children with behavioral problems, wrote of the importance of kindness, which he described as ". . . the source of energy that maintains and gives meaning to humanity."[29] Kindness is the outworking of compassion and is linked to forgiveness. Both are crucial to maintaining a classroom informed by an ethic of care. Acts of kindness help students who struggle academically or behaviorally because of disability to establish trusting relationships with others.

Presence

An ethic of care requires teachers to be physically and emotionally available to their students. The teacher must actively listen to the student and reflect on teaching-learning activities by attending to the teaching-learning activity that does not go as planned. Care for the student's development should lead to questioning whether something was overlooked in the lesson planning or missed in assessing the student's strengths and weaknesses.

Teachers who manifest an ethic of care understand that fairness does not mean all students are treated (or taught) equally, as if all are alike or have the same needs. They recognize that to be fair requires that the needs of each student be considered and that they seek to furnish what is needed for the student to learn effectively. Above all, caring teachers will, through their attitudes, actions, and words, communicate hospitality and acceptance of all students.

Interdependence and Hospitality

An ethic of care highlights the interdependence of all people. The ethic of love, as expressed in reconciliation, acceptance, and interdependence promotes inclusive education through community building. Interdependence recognizes the mutuality of responsibility and interconnectedness of each member of the classroom community.

---

28. Anderson, *Toward a Theology of Special Education*.
29. Long, "Therapeutic Power of Kindness," 242.

The biblical concept of hospitality expresses the desired classroom environment, one in which students with disabilities and other marginalized students are effectively incorporated into the body of the class. Hospitality is a necessary quality for classrooms to be truly inclusive by creating a milieu that conveys a sense of welcome, acceptance, and belonging for each student. A hospitable classroom will present a welcoming environment in which all students, with or without a disability, feel valued and safe within a "... shelter of relationships."[30] Critical to hospitality is "... maintaining an open and ready heart."[31]

Relationship

The relationships teachers establish with students are paramount in the ethic of care, and begin with recognizing the worth and dignity of every student, including those with a severe or profound impairment. A classroom infused with an ethic of care recognizes and promotes the human rights of persons with impairments. A caring attitude must also be maintained when offering assistance to students whose disability may interfere with their success, so that such students are not seen simply as a need or as a drain on limited resources. Pairing a nondisabled student with one who has a disability shows care for both, but the pairing should be bidirectional, recognizing that sometimes students with a disability may be able to assist their nondisabled peers. This counteracts the mistaken idea that disability always means dependence. An ethic of care encourages students who have a disability to do as much as possible for themselves, thereby gaining a sense of self-achievement and self-control while at the same time fostering interdependence, relationships, and mutual responsibility.[32] A caring teacher-student relationship requires that teachers believe in the potential of their students and cultivate mutual trust and confidence between the students and themselves.

Authenticity

For teachers to be real requires knowing their personal strengths while also acknowledging their weaknesses. Authenticity includes a willingness to admit and take responsibility for mistakes or misjudgments, and a readiness

---

30. Pohl, "Hospitality, a Practice," 39.
31. Reynolds, "Welcome Without Reserve?," 201.
32. Morris, "Impairment and Disability."

to try something new. Modeling this authenticity affirms that both teacher and students are unique human beings, individually designed and loved by the God who created them both, whether disabled or able-bodied. Teachers who show themselves to be authentic persons become a ". . . source of life . . .,"[33] a motivating force for students with disabilities, by displaying an encouraging attitude, confidence that the students can be successful, an unwillingness to give up on the students, and a preparedness to search for or create new ways of teaching that may enable students to demonstrate their learning and growth. Authentic teachers will keep their expectations of the students high but realistic, accommodating to each student's needs but not settling for minimal gains. The authentic lifestyle of the teacher becomes a powerful tool in working with students, with or without disabilities, as well as with students' parents and other professionals. Authenticity promotes the establishment of relationships and puts teachers in a better position to advocate for others.

Service

The Bible is unambiguous in its emphasis that Christians are called to serve others. As servant-leaders, Christian teachers are servants first, and in serving, they lead out of concern for the needs and welfare of the students.[34] Teaching is a ministry to which God has called and equipped us. As we exercise our teaching gifts we demonstrate obedience to God's call to be a part of his grand mission. In the ministry of teaching we directly serve our students, and indirectly serve God as we exercise the gifts he has bestowed on us. Serving our students involves caring for them, seeking to promote their growth and development, academically, socially, and emotionally, and championing their inclusion in the educational community and beyond. We also serve society at large in helping to develop an educated and responsible citizenry.

CONCLUSION

An ethic of care can also be called an ethic of love, or even an ethic of life— a commitment to upholding the dignity of each person as someone created in the image of God (see, for example, Gathje[35]). Christian teachers,

---

33. Steensma, *To Those Who Teach*, 90.
34. Anderson, "Teacher as Servant-Leader."
35. Gathje, "Shalom and a Consistent Ethic."

as caregivers, become mediators of God's presence as they create a healing community in the classroom by extending grace in practical ways to their students. Caring as Jesus cared involves reaching out to people at their level, coming alongside, being present with them and entering into their experience as best we are able.

Shortt wrote metaphorically to describe the Bible as an environment that shapes each Christian, but especially emphasized how the Bible shapes us as teachers in the classroom. Paul's exhortations in Colossians explain the desired effect of this shaping: "And whatever you do, whether in word or deed, do it all in the name of the Lord Jesus . . ." (3:17); and "Whatever you do, work at it with all your heart, as working for the Lord, not for human masters" (3:23).

In Colossians 3:17 and 23, Paul uses a form of the Greek word *ergon* to describe our work or labor—what we do. But in 1 Corinthians 9:1, Paul uses *ergon* in a different way, to refer to the *result* or *product* of work: ". . . Are you not the result of my work in the Lord?" Paul is using the word to describe the Corinthian believers themselves; literally in the Greek he calls them "the work of me." What difference would it make to think of our students as "the work of us?" Establishing a Christian ethic of care in the classroom would seem essential if this was how we thought of our students and our work.

BIBLIOGRAPHY

Anderson, David W. "Inclusion and Interdependence: Students with Special Needs in the Regular Classroom." *Journal of Education & Christian Belief* 10 (2006) 43–59.
———. "The Teacher as Servant-Leader." In *Nurturing Christians as Reflective Educators. Proceedings of the Second Biennial Symposium for Christian Professional Education Faculty*, edited by H. Van Brummelen and D. Elliot, 23–38. San Dimas, CA: Learning Light Educational, 1997.
———. *Toward a Theology of Special Education: Integrating Faith and Practice*. Bloomington, IN: WestBow, 2012.
Buck v. Bell, 274 US 200 (1927). https://supreme.justia.com/cases/federal/us/274/200/.
Cohall, Kirkpatrick G. "Developing an Ethic of Care: An Educational Response." *The Living Pulpit* 21 (2012) 15–19.
Estep, James R. "Moral Development and Christian Formation." In *Christian Formation: Integrating Theology and Human Development*, edited by James R. Estep and Jonathan H. Kim, 123–59. Nashville: B & H Academic, 2010.
Gathje, Peter R. "Shalom and a Consistent Ethic of Life." *The Living Pulpit* 15 (2006) 10–12.
Gilligan, Carol. *In a Different Voice*. Cambridge, MA: Harvard University Press, 1982.
Haugk, Kenneth C. *Christian Caregiving: A Way of Life*. Minneapolis: Augsburg, 1984.
Individuals with Disabilities Education Act. PL 101–476. Reauthorized in 2004 as PL 114–95, 1990. https://sites.ed.gov/idea/

Kohlberg, Lawrence. *The Philosophy of Moral Development: Moral Stages and the Idea of Justice.* San Francisco: Harper & Row, 1981.

Long, Nicholas J. "The Therapeutic Power of Kindness." *Reclaiming Children and Youth* 5 (1997) 242–46.

Mittler, Peter. *Working Toward Inclusive Education: Social Contexts.* London: David Fulton, 2000.

Morris, Jenny. "Impairment and Disability: Constructing an Ethic of Care that Promotes Human Rights." *Hypatia* 16 (2001) 1–16.

Noddings, Nel. *Caring: A Feminine Approach to Ethics and Moral Education.* 2nd ed. Berkeley: University of California Press, 2003.

———. *The Challenge to Care in Schools: An Alternative Approach to Education.* New York: Teachers College Press, 1992.

Owens, Lynn M., and Catherine D. Ennis. "The Ethic of Care in Teaching: An Overview of Supportive Literature." *Quest* 57 (2005) 392–425.

Peterson, Eugene H., ed. *The Message: The Bible in Contemporary Language.* Colorado Springs, CO: NavPress, 2002.

Pohl, Christine D. "Hospitality, a Practice and a Way of Life." *Vision* 3.1 (2002) 34–43.

Pudlas, Ken. "Head and Heart and Hands: Necessary Elements of Inclusive Praxis." *Journal of the International Community of Christians in Teacher Education* 3 (2009). https://digitalcommons.georgefox.edu/icctej/vol3/iss1/.

Reynolds, Thomas E. "Welcome Without Reserve? A Case in Christian Hospitality." *Theology Today* 6 (2006) 191–202.

Schaffner, C. Beth, and Barbara E. Buswell. "Ten Critical Elements for Creating Inclusive and Effective Communities." In *Inclusion: A Guide for Educators*, edited by William Stainback and Susan Stainback, 49–65. Baltimore: Paul H. Brookes, 1996.

Shelly, Judith A. *Spiritual Care: A Guide for Caregivers.* Downers Grove, IL: InterVarsity, 2000.

Shortt, John. *Bible-Shaped Teaching.* Eugene, OR: Wipf & Stock, 2014.

Shurley, Anna K. *Pastoral Care and Intellectual Disability: A Person-Centered Approach.* Waco, TX: Baylor University Press, 2017.

Snyder, Howard A. *The Community of the King.* Downers Grove, IL: InterVarsity, 2004.

Steensma, Geraldine. *To Those Who Teach: Keys for Decision-making.* Signal Mountain, TN: Signal, 1971.

Wiersbe, Warren W. *The Bible Exposition Commentary—New Testament, Volume 2.* Colorado Springs, CO: Victor, 2001.

Womack, Morris M. *The College Press NIV Commentary: 1, 2 & 3 John.* Collegedale, TN: College Press, 1998.

Chapter 7

INCLUSION AND THE ETHIC OF CARE
Our Responsibility as Christian Special Educators

Alicia Watkin

I REMEMBER BEING A student teacher, sitting with my teacher education advisor and making the decision to add a credential in special education to my program coursework. "It's only three additional classes and one more student teaching experience. You might as well get it now, while you're still in school," I remember her convincing me. I can say with complete confidence that was the best decision I could have made. My credential in special education is the reason I was hired in a district that had too many elementary teachers. It is the reason I received a pink slip only once and then promptly had it taken back when they checked my credentials to find out they included special education. Yes, special education has benefited me. However, beyond these somewhat surface advantages, my teaching experience in special education has allowed me to gain a depth of understanding in my personal calling as a Christian educator.

My teaching career began with being hired as a Resource Specialist in a large district. I was assigned to an elementary school, then quickly reassigned to another school due to shifting numbers in caseloads. I ended up at a middle school in which I was expected to "push in" to support the students on my caseload. Though a somewhat dated term, "push in" refers to supporting students in their general education classes, in order to provide more inclusive delivery of service for students with Individualized Education Plans (IEPs). In a classroom, the special education teacher works with students to provide specific scaffolds in supporting students' access to the curriculum. One example is helping students to work on an assignment in a small group rather than independently. The Resource Specialist is in the classroom to focus specifically on those students who require additional supports. This was my first experience with inclusive education and one I am grateful for, as it has brought such depth of purpose to my career as an educator.

Entering those general education classrooms, with the eagerness of a first-year teacher, I quickly became frustrated with the barriers I encountered as I worked to support the students on my caseload. I was surprised to find that one teacher did not want me in his class at all. This was difficult to understand because I felt we were both there to help students learn. I was left wondering why a classroom teacher with an overflowing roster would not want another teacher to support student learning. As we worked together during the school year, he became more welcoming of my support. I learned that he had enormous pressure put upon him by the district to cover specific curriculum in a specific time frame. It became clear that the system was not structured to accommodate these well-meaning mandates of inclusion, which left teachers and any other stakeholders frustrated with unrealistic expectations.

INCLUSION

Inclusion of students with IEPs is not a new practice. Federal policies have been in place for more than forty years to set the parameters for supporting students with disabilities. The Individuals with Disabilities Education Act of 2004 (IDEA) included the consideration of Least Restrictive Environment (LRE). This means a student with disabilities should receive educational support in the environment that is least exclusive from the general population of students.[1] Additionally, with the enactment of the No Child Left Behind Act (NCLBA), which specified almost all students attain grade-level proficiency, inclusion of students with disabilities has grown. This growth is in response to meeting not only student learning needs, but now meeting federal education achievement goals.[2] Inclusion may look differently depending on the student being supported. Some students may be fully included, meaning they have an IEP, but are taught and supported in the

---

1. DeMatthews and Mawhinney, "Addressing the Inclusion Imperative."
2. Friend, "Co-teaching."

general education classroom with no exclusion. Some students may be included a certain percentage of the school day because the IEP team has agreed they require some support outside of the general population, perhaps in a setting where curriculum can be modified more extensively. The degree of inclusion for students varies according to their learning needs and what the IEP team has agreed upon.

Though federal mandates have been in place for students with disabilities, there are disconnects in how these policies are applied in public school classroom structures. The prevailing approach in public education is knowledge-centered, with goals focused on meeting learning standards and grade-level proficiency for all learners.[3] There is great pressure put upon classroom teachers to increase test scores, and to have students with disabilities included in that expectation can seem overwhelming.

The more experience I gained in working with students and teachers, the more I understood the benefits of including students with disabilities. Winter explains that inclusion is more than the simple location of classes.[4] The Department for Education and Skills expands on location and notes that inclusion is about being able to fully participate in the "life of the school."[5] I began to realize that placing students in separate classes, away from their peers, was not an accurate representation of life. Surely, some students need individualized instruction in a separate setting, so I am not claiming full inclusion for all, but inclusion as it is appropriate for each student to be a part of the school community.

When I consider the purpose of education, I sense deeply that school must be a place where teachers help students prepare for life through experience and relationship with others. I believe teachers cannot claim to have imparted a quality education to a student if the student has not been given experience in working with peers and being part of a community.

I remember being on the blacktop one morning before school as students were playing handball, and I watched a group of students including a boy who had Down Syndrome. As I watched them, I never heard a student tease the boy or act as if they did not want him there. In fact, they cheered loudest when he got a point or made a good hit. For me, this illustrates Romans 12:5, when Paul writes, ". . . in Christ we, though many, form one body, and each member belongs to all the others." The students I observed that day were living in community. There was no pity for the boy with Down Syndrome, just full acceptance and evidence of support for each other.

3. Ellis, *Exemplars of Curriculum Theory*.
4. Winter, "Preparing New Teachers."
5. Department for Education and Skills, *Removing the Barriers to Achievement*, 12.

THE GREATEST COMMANDMENT AND THE ETHIC OF CARE

Recently, I moved out of the K-12 classroom and into higher education at a Christian university. This has caused me to reflect deeply upon the role of Christian educators in public schools, specifically in special education.

Mark 12:30–31 tells us that the greatest commandment is to love God with all we have and to love our neighbor as we would love ourselves. This passage is an obvious call that if we profess to love God we will love our neighbor; the two "cannot be divorced."[6] If I love God, I must love my neighbor. As special educators, neighbors include students, parents, colleagues, and administrators. Additionally, Noddings acknowledges that life is lived in relation with others and that this forms us as individuals.[7] Building relationships with my students and their parents is how I love God and bring God's kingdom to Earth. There is a great opportunity for reconciliation in the relationships teachers have with parents and students, especially those who have had negative experiences in special education. In my view, the IEP process is set up for relationship, so I take full advantage to make that relationship meaningful.

In speaking of the ethic of care, Noddings writes that it is "other-oriented."[8] There is a denial of self. It is apparent that the ethic of care, and in particular a Christian ethic of care, aligns with God's commandment. God-followers must care for others. Noddings explains that teachers have asked how they are to create a caring climate in the classroom when there are so many other pressing needs. Her response is that creating a climate of care is "... *underneath* all we do as teachers."[9] I would add to Noddings's idea that, as a Christian, my motivation to care for my students is in response to my love for God. God is what is underneath all the other duties of teaching.

It follows that if I am to truly care for my students with God's love, then I must be working to bring them into community with others. Looking at the life of Jesus, he consistently loved the marginalized and those that did not quite *fit*, such as children (Matt 19:14), people who are blind (John 9:1–6), Samaritans (John 4:1–26), and tax collectors (Luke 19:1–10). Within special education, the term "SPED" itself expresses exceptionality and labels students. This common label is simply an abbreviation of the term "special education." The label serves practical purposes, certainly, but works against

---

6. Brower, *Mark*, 318.
7. Noddings, "Caring Relation in Teaching."
8. Noddings, "Caring Relation in Teaching," 777.
9. Noddings, "Caring Relation in Teaching," 777 (emphasis added).

the very mandates of inclusion that are promoted through it. Jesus modeled an inclusive love and care for people, and as a Christ-follower, I am called to do the same.

TEACHER EDUCATION FOR SPECIAL EDUCATORS

In teacher education, I have found it easy to focus on pedagogy and promoting academic rigor, without a consideration of the relationship of a teacher with his or her students. Nouwen writes that, ". . . perhaps we have paid too much attention to the content of teaching without realizing the teaching relationship is the most important factor in the ministry of teaching."[10] In my credential coursework in special education, the role of the parent was repeatedly used in negative, combative examples to show the importance of communication and following laws, which certainly must be addressed in order to prepare special education teachers. However, this taught me to view the parents of my students in a negative way. It took me longer than I would like to admit to understand that the parent can be an incredible support and partner in teaching students with disabilities. I was frustrated that my teacher preparation did not instruct me about the impact of good relationships with parents.

I argue that teacher education programs at Christian universities need to spend time addressing the importance of relationships with colleagues, beyond mere collaboration, which is primarily centered in curriculum. There is interdependence in our humanity and that is significant in the lives of educators. Anderson asserts that, from the beginning, God designed humanity to need others in his creation; he did not want Adam to be alone, so he created Eve. Throughout Scripture, followers of Jesus are referred to as the body of Christ, showing that ". . . our dependence on one another is part of God's design."[11] This is a difficult concept in education where the classroom can be quite lonely and even become personal turf for some. I use the term "turf," meaning ownership, in the sense that some teachers believe the space within their walls belongs to them. Any other adult entering is treated as an outsider. This mentality promotes the opposite of loving one's neighbor and living in relationship. Knowing this, special educators have work to do in order to build bridges with colleagues and help gain trust so that the practice of inclusion of students with disabilities is welcomed into general classroom settings.

---

10. Nouwen, *Creative Ministry*, 11.
11. Anderson, *Toward a Theology of Special Education*, 149.

Special education requires a collaborative mentality, centrally expressed in the IEP. It is meant to be a team effort and decision. So often personal agendas get in the way of what is best for the student. But if teachers are working from a motivation of love, then they must be working to reconcile these issues. To reconcile these issues, teacher education programs should give more attention to preparing student teachers for building relationships.

COMMUNICATING CARE

I would like to offer a look at how loving one's neighbor might be practically applied, but first want to stop and frame the perspective of those applications. In his chapter in this book, Sean Schat reported on a study looking at how care was communicated between teachers and students.[12] As many of us can assume, most teachers desire to care for their students. Schat studied why intentions of care failed to be experienced by students. It is important not only to consider the actions that show care on the part of the teacher, but to also consider how care is received by the student. Noddings emphasizes that, in the classroom, the ethic of care can only be fulfilled within the relationship of the teacher and student; both are participants.[13]

This is important to recognize because well-meaning intentions can easily be miscommunicated if the one being cared for is not considered. As educators, we know that each student is unique and I believe this applies to parents, colleagues, and administrators as well. For those in special education, each IEP meeting holds a distinctive dynamic because each team member brings an individual perspective. Each member has ideas about what is best to support the student. I have to admit here that in my early days leading IEP meetings I felt my opinion was in some way more knowledgeable than others' because I saw the student in the classroom; I knew the reality of what the learning goals and accommodations looked like in practice. As I wrote earlier, I'm ashamed of how long it took me to see the value in the parents I worked with, and even the service providers at times, when their opinion did not match my own.

In considering the format of an IEP team and my experience in IEP meetings, I cannot help but think of Parker Palmer's discussion of what he calls the "community of truth."[14] Palmer explains that, in education, there cannot be a single master in command. There are multiple voices and perspectives that come together, even across time, to consider a specific focus.

12. Schat, "Successful Communication of Educational Care."
13. Noddings, *Caring*.
14. Palmer, *Courage to Teach*, 90.

To me, this aligns well to the purpose of an IEP team, with the student as the focus.

In writing about academic culture, Palmer discusses the dilemma of being confronted with new ideas and perspectives. He writes, "Startled by otherness, reacting out of fear, we destroy the possibility of learning anything new by allowing the ancient fight or flight syndrome to have its way."[15] I think this applies to our relationships, not only with other educators, but with the parents and other stakeholders with whom we interact. As a teacher, whether I am in an IEP meeting or a staff meeting, I need to work to understand the perspectives of others. Their stories and knowledge can enrich my own practice, and thus inform my way of caring.

In Schat's study, he identifies three dimensions of educational care. He names the personal, pedagogical, and interpersonal dimensions, according to what students shared with him relating to care from teachers.[16] I want to draw attention to the interpersonal dimension because it aligns with the idea of the community of truth that Palmer writes of.[17] Interpersonal care refers to the care for a person as a member of the classroom community, and Schat's research identified that this role in the community must be communicated and received in order for a student to feel truly cared for.[18] Though Schat's research focused on the role of the student as the one receiving care, I think it can be applied to each member of the learning community as well. I believe it is critical for any teacher, not just those in special education, to understand their place within the community of those they work with and the parents and students they support. Each participant is valuable. Remember Palmer's claim that there is not one holder of truth, but together there is a clearer truth.[19]

The following section speaks to practical ways to build relationships and care for those we interact with as educators. Some references are specific to special education; however, all three action steps can be implemented in any educational community.

NOW WHAT?

As I consider my role in helping to prepare future teachers, and my deep belief that advocating for inclusive practices is a responsibility of Christian

15. Palmer, *Courage to Teach*, 113.
16. Schat, "Successful Communication of Care."
17. Palmer, *Courage to Teach*.
18. Schat, "Successful Communication of Care."
19. Palmer, *Courage to Teach*.

special educators, I have landed on three essential action steps that future special educators must put into practice: *listen, show up,* and *advocate*. I believe putting these actions into place helps build relationships amongst everyone involved and leads to more positive experiences for all.

Listen

In special education, there can be myriad voices speaking in support of a single student. Every student has an IEP team, which includes those adults supporting the student in working toward their specified goals. For some students, I have had IEP teams consist of fifteen people. While there are many voices grabbing for our attention as special educators, I believe the student, parents, and classroom teacher must take priority in these conversations. They are the *neighbors* who must be loved and cared for, and listening is an outward expression of care. Listening sounds like a simple act, but it requires time and intentional effort. As most educators would agree, time is something teachers get very little of in meeting the demands of teaching. However, through listening, teachers can build trust and relationships are strengthened. Through strong relationships, teachers can work together in a more positive way to help students reach their goals.

One year, I worked with a parent who demanded more time than what I would have expected according to their child's IEP. While I acknowledge that boundaries must be set with parents, which I had to do in this case, I did schedule time to meet with her because I felt she wanted me to hear her concerns. The more I listened, the more I learned of her story with her son and his learning disability. I learned that her previous special education experiences had been negative and that she felt the last school told her what was best for her son and never listened to her. I learned that she was desperately grasping to find a reason her son had a learning disability and wanted to discover the remedy, as most parents would. My experience with this parent, though frustrating at times, allowed me to build a relationship with her and she grew to trust me. This trust allowed us to have difficult conversations. While we did not always agree, there was shared respect and she knew I was listening. I could not meet all of her demands, but listening is how I cared for her. As Noddings says, "Time spent on building a relation of care and trust is not time wasted."[20]

---

20. Noddings, "Caring Relation in Teaching," 774.

Show Up

Additionally, special education teachers need to know that they must show up for their students, making time for them. This is especially important in the public school system, which historically can tend to be more structured with the goal of having all students achieve the same learning outcomes, with little consideration of the whole person.[21] However, it should be noted that some public school districts are taking steps to change this. Special educators must do the hard work of showing up to support students, even in a misaligned system. The rigid structure of public school requires special educators to be attentive to the students with whom they work.

For example, I worked with a student who had emotional and behavioral challenges. He had a difficult time self-regulating his feelings. One morning, as students packed up to get ready for the bell to ring, I noticed he was still in the corner of the class where I had a reading area set up. His head was down and covered with his hands, clearly showing something had upset him, even though there had been no outburst or incident reported to me. I watched him as the bell rang and students left. My own schedule required me to teach a computer elective class in another part of the building, but I knew this student needed time before moving on to his next class. I felt the pressure of time and quickly went across the hall to ask if the English learner support teacher could start my elective class while I helped the student. She agreed and I returned to find the boy crying. When he did not want to talk, I simply sat there on the floor with him. After several minutes, he wiped his face and lifted his head. I asked if there was anything he needed, he said no and that he was going to go to class.

I learned that day that I cannot always be a problem-solver for my students, but I can sit with them in their struggles and frustrations. I can show up. Showing up for this student meant I had to make him a priority over an inflexible bell schedule. The rigid requirements of my schedule had to take second place in order to care for this student and show him the love that God has called me to in teaching. This is important for teacher candidates to be aware of, especially when they feel the pressure to prove themselves as new teachers.

Special educators also need to show up for their colleagues. To promote inclusive practices, relationships with general education teachers must be built if students are to be accepted into the classroom community. One powerful approach to inclusion is co-teaching. Co-teaching is two credentialed teachers, usually a general education teacher and a special educator,

---

21. Freytag, "Reimagining Excellence in Inclusive Education."

teaching a diverse group of learners in the same classroom.[22] Respect is also a critical component in showing up for colleagues.[23] Consideration of schedules and planning time are examples of opportunities to respect another teacher's time. While passing in the hallway, unplanned conversations may occur, but intentionality should be given to scheduling specific times to meet about student needs. To be an effective teacher, Friend explains that educators must invest in their relationship with each other, and as a result student outcomes are more positive.[24]

Advocate

In responding to loving and caring for students, special education teachers must also be advocates. As a new teacher, in a district focused on inclusion, I expected everyone I worked with would be supportive of inclusive practices for students. When I experienced otherwise, I was unsure of what to do. In one instance, I had a classroom teacher who gave me the assigned packet of reading and questions and directed me to work with "my" students, referring to those students with IEPs, in the library. With another student, I was told by a lead special education teacher that I could not ask for assistive technology for a student to take home because the district would not allow it, even though I knew IDEA supported this. I had not been taught how to advocate for my students within the system of the school district. Though my students were my priority, I was an employee of the district, so I felt torn. The program for my special education credential taught me the law of special education, as well as best practices and how to teach diverse learners. However, it had not prepared me to stand up as a voice for my students and parents. Freytag notes that many teacher education programs lack preparation in this area. She states that teacher education programs must help special educators ". . . develop their voice in a system that too often fails to listen from the bottom up."[25] I did not have a voice then, but over the years I have learned how to advocate for students. I have learned to pay attention to that feeling when I know the system is not supporting students the way it should. Preparing future teachers for this reality must be addressed or a great disservice is done in preparing teachers to serve and care for students.

22. Cook and Friend, "Co-teaching."
23. Friend, "Co-teaching."
24. Friend, "Co-teaching."
25. Freytag, "Reimagining Excellence in Inclusive Education," 139.

CONCLUSION

Loving God and loving neighbor is the greatest commandment. In educating future teachers at Christian universities, the motivation should be different from that of secular programs. Teaching an ethic of care should be integral to teacher education programs, preparing genuine educators who consider the whole person. The motivation to care is in love for God. In special education, teachers are specifically called to care for students who have been labeled and often marginalized, as well as their parents and caregivers. It cannot be forgotten that teacher peers are neighbors as well. As I have taught and supervised student teachers, I intentionally bring attention to students who have IEPs. I want to help teachers notice their *neighbors* and care for them as they teach.

When I think back to sitting with my advisor and our discussion about me pursuing special education, I wish there had been more meaningful discourse, aside from it being an easy time to add the credential. Though my current role in higher education has not yet required me to act as an advisor, when I think of myself in that chair advising a teacher candidate, I will answer differently.

BIBLIOGRAPHY

Anderson, David W. *Toward a Theology of Special Education: Integrating Faith and Practice*. Bloomington, IN: WestBow, 2012.

Brower, Kent. *Mark: A Commentary on the Wesleyan Tradition*. Kansas City: Beacon Hill, 2012.

Cook, Lynne, and Marilyn Friend. "Co-teaching: Guidelines for Creating Effective Practices." *Focus on Exceptional Children* 28 (1995) 1–16. doi.org/10.1007/s13398-014-0173-7.2.

DeMatthews, D E., and Hahn Mawhinney. "Addressing the Inclusion Imperative: An Urban School District's Responses." *Education Policy Analysis Archives* 21 (2013) 1–27.

Department for Education and Skills. *Removing the Barriers to Achievement: Executive Summary*. Nottingham, UK: DfES, 2004.

Ellis, Arthur K. *Exemplars of Curriculum Theory*. New York: Routledge, 2004.

Freytag, Cathy E. "Reimagining Excellence in Inclusive Education: Transforming Edict to Ethic." *Journal of Education & Christian Belief* 12 (2008) 129–43.

Friend, Marilyn. "Co-teaching: A Simple Solution That Isn't Simple After All." *Journal of Curriculum and Instruction* 2 (2008) 9–19. doi.org/10.3776/joci.2008.v2n2p9-19.

Noddings, Nel. *Caring: A Relational Approach to Ethics and Moral Education*. Berkeley: University of California Press, 2013.

———. "The Caring Relation in Teaching." *Oxford Review of Education* 38 (2012), 771–81. doi.org/10.1080/03054985.2012.745047.

Nouwen, Henri. *Creative Ministry*. New York: Image, 2003.

Palmer, Parker. *The Courage to Teach: Exploring the Inner Landscape of a Teacher's Life.* San Francisco: Jossey-Bass, 1998.

Schat, Sean. "The Successful Communication of Educational Care." In *How Shall We Then Care?: A Christian Educator's Guide to Caring for Self, Learners, Colleagues and Community,* edited by Paul Shotsberger and Cathy Freytag, [x-ref].. Eugene, OR: Wipf & Stock, 2019.

Winter, Eileen. "Preparing New Teachers for Inclusive Schools and Classrooms." *Support for Learning* 21 (2006) 85–91. doi.org/10.1111/j.1467-9604.2006.00409.

Chapter 8

DISPOSITIONS
Real-Time Active Practice

MICHELLE C. HUGHES

INTRODUCTION

IN THE LAST SEVERAL decades, educational initiatives such as No Child Left Behind, Race to the Top, and the Every Student Succeeds Act altered the educational landscape. Linking the ever-changing demands of these initiatives with the reality that teaching is a complex and constructive process, preservice programs must develop and prepare candidates with content, skills, and pedagogy. Additionally, because of the increasing social-emotional demands placed on teachers, preservice programs like the one I teach in must equip teacher candidates with dispositions and a level of care that transfers to K-12 students.

In 2011, in an effort to care for and nurture preservice candidates' dispositions, a formal focus on dispositions was introduced in the program of study at my university. My faculty team and I initiated efforts to infuse three dispositions through instruction, collaboration, and assignments: *Lifelong Learner, Reflective Practitioner, and Compassionate Professional.* With each new cohort, faculty and candidates made a commitment to seek and nurture dispositions throughout the preservice program. In order to identify the program's dispositional expressions and build a profile for dispositional development, I collected data from multiple sources, including personal interviews of graduates in their first year of teaching, faculty interviews, and archived course artifacts. The initial case study in 2014 revealed four program expressions for dispositional development: an early focus on dispositions, modeling by faculty, embedded coursework, and multiple practice contexts. This study validated that dispositions were embedded throughout the preservice program and graduates carried dispositional awareness into their first year of teaching. Future research was recommended to investigate the impact of the program's dispositional focus after the first year of teaching.[1]

For this subsequent longitudinal study, I sought to widen my program's dispositional lens and add to the initial findings. My team has since added the fourth disposition of *Grateful Servant*.[2] Although this new study does not provide a specific roadmap for dispositional development during or after completion of a preservice program it does provide a snapshot into new teacher dispositional awareness and practices. Results will be used to inform my preservice program, as well as advance similar-sized preservice programs, and promote dispositional development with school districts that prioritize dispositions with new hires.

DISPOSITIONS ARE SIGNIFICANT FOR TEACHER PREPARATION

Dispositions are most often defined as the professional attitudes, values, and beliefs that influence the decisions and actions of educators.[3] Over the last several decades, researchers agreed that fostering dispositions in teacher candidates contributed to the academic, social, and emotional well-being of new teachers.[4] Today's educational climate, linked with the complexities of teaching, requires preservice programs to prepare candidates with professional teaching dispositions alongside content knowledge, skills, and pedagogy.[5] This responsibility validates the approach to educate, care for,

---

1 Hughes, "One PreService Program's Dispositional Development."

2. Program of Study, *Dispositions Statement*.

3. National Council for Accreditation of Teacher Education, "Standards for Professional Development Schools."

4. Day, *Passion for Teaching*; Giovannelli, "Relationship between Reflective Disposition"; Wake and Bunn, "Teacher Candidate Dispositions."

5. Conderman and Walker, "Assessing Dispositions"; Shively and Misco, "But How Do I Know?"

and develop the whole person.[6] Recently, the President of the Association of Independent Liberal Arts Colleges for Teacher Education affirmed that teachers need to operate with pedagogical and content knowledge, and with professional ethics and dispositions.[7]

For the purpose of this study, dispositions are defined as, "the habits of professional action and moral commitments that underlie an educator's performance."[8] Two additional terms highlighted in this study are: 1) *dispositional awareness,* or the conscious perception or self-awareness to name, define, and understand professional teaching dispositions, and, 2) *dispositional development,* or the ongoing process of cultivating and applying professional teaching dispositions in practice.

Dispositions remain a priority in teacher education.[9] Over the years, researchers agreed that dispositions are essential to teaching and teacher preparation; empirical research affirms that dispositions impact learning outcomes.[10] Educators repeatedly reference philosopher John Dewey's call for dispositions in practice; Dewey first highlighted reflection and open-mindedness to develop individuals as strong, contributing citizens.[11] Dewey claimed that reflection led to active thinking and then practice. Farrell revisited Dewey's recommendation and encouraged teachers to listen to the many sides of an issue, consider the impact of instructional decisions, and commit to review teaching practices.[12] Farrell concluded that teachers, often resistant to change, should demonstrate increased open-mindedness. In 2002, one set of researchers recommended providing opportunities for reflection for teacher development.[13] The team encouraged a focus on contexts for reflection to empower new teachers to make informed instructional decisions.

Reviewed literature affirmed increased efforts to infuse dispositions throughout preservice programs. DaRos-Voseles and Moss specifically promoted dispositions to foster student achievement, naming dispositions as

---

6. Cronon, "Only Connect"; Holmes, *Idea of a Christian College;* Noddings, *Caring: A Relational Approach.*

7. Email from David Denton, January 17, 2017.

8. Council for the Accreditation of Educator Preparation Standards, "D."

9. Costa and Kallick, *Dispositions;* Evans-Palmer, "Building Dispositions and Self-Efficacy."

10. Schussler, "Defining Dispositions"; Schussler and Knarr, "Building Awareness of Dispositions"; Hill-Jackson et al., *What Makes a Star Teacher.*

11. Dewey, *Democracy and Education;* Dewey, *Experience and Education.*

12. Farrell, "Teacher You are Stupid!"

13. Risko et al. "Preparing Teachers for Reflective Practice."

fundamental to elevate the teaching profession.[14] Additionally, preservice teachers need opportunities to develop dispositions in a variety of classroom contexts.[15] These softer skills are more than just warm, fuzzy feelings since they play a significant role in teacher preparation.

In 2016, *Phi Delta Kappan*'s Educators Rising Standards for prospective teachers encouraged reflective practice as a habit of mind that is fundamental for teacher development.[16] This focus was a shift in direction from an educational system previously centered on data-driven assessment.[17] Researchers then recommended making dispositions explicit in practice for further development in teachers and to create meaningful experiences for students.[18] As priorities and standards continue to shift, new expectations require preservice programs to demonstrate professional dispositions throughout coursework and clinical experiences, adding strength to the notion that dispositions are habits that can be learned with practice.[19]

In the last decade, associations emerged between dispositions and growth mindset theory.[20] The development of a growth mindset encourages habits for student motivation and learning. Similarly, fostering academic mindsets to develop learning habits lends support to thinking about education as a mindset journey for meaningful work and improvement for both students and teachers.[21]

Specific to my program, California's revised Teacher Performance Expectations for preservice programs now require preservice teachers to demonstrate dispositions such as caring, support, and acceptance.[22] At the same time, researchers have linked dispositions for the classroom to attributes such as resilience and flexibility.[23] Additional research recommends that school leaders create capacity for academic success by looking beyond the individual to prioritize values such as empathy, care, and listening in and

14. DaRos-Voseles and Moss, "Role of Dispositions."
15. Claxton et al., "Hard Thinking about Soft Skills."
16. Educators Rising, "Educators Rising Standards."
17. Ravitch, *Death and Life*.
18. Claxton et al., "Hard Thinking about Soft Skills."
19. Council for the Accreditation of Educator Preparation Standards, "Vision, Mission and Goals"; Costa and Kallick, *Dispositions*; Noddings, *Caring: A Relational Approach*; Thornton, "Case Analysis."
20. Dweck, *Mindset*; Dweck, "Recognizing and Overcoming."
21. Schwartz, "What's Your Learning Disposition?"
22. California Commission on Teacher Credentialing, "Teacher Performance Expectations."
23. Evans-Palmer, "Building Dispositions and Self-Efficacy"; Farrell, "Teacher You are Stupid!"

outside of school.[24] This focus advances best practices to build emotionally healthy schools and develop thoughtful teachers.

WHERE IS THE BLUEPRINT?

Although national teaching organizations affirm the role of dispositions and set expectations that many teacher preparation programs in the United States follow, programs continue to approach dispositions differently; there isn't a single prescribed approach to infusing and assessing dispositions.[25] Over the years, a variety of models, such as the Disposition Assessment Aligned with Teacher Standards, were created to help programs measure dispositions. Models like this suggested that teacher preparation fails if new teachers do not use the dispositions they have been taught in preservice.[26] Yet, even with sample structures, preservice programs continue to approach dispositions in unique ways without a universal framework for dispositional development.[27] Some programs use preassessments or surveys to gauge dispositional development; others, like the program of study, use an embedded approach to connect curriculum, clinical contexts, and modeling for dispositional development.[28] One collection of case studies recognized a variety of approaches in teacher preparation to develop, implement, and assess dispositions with intentional practice contexts to grow dispositional awareness.[29]

Conderman and Walker affirmed that dispositions in teacher preparation lead to exemplary professional practice.[30] An earlier study examined two teacher preparation programs with different models. One of the programs emphasized dispositions in coursework, the other focused on dispositions in field experience. Recommendations included connecting theory and practice.[31] Another research team recommended activities like community service to develop dispositions in candidates.[32] Additionally, to prepare individuals as effective character educators, preservice

---

24. Smylie and Murphy, "Call for Caring School Leaders."
25. Choi et al., "Assessment of Teacher Candidate Dispositions."
26. Wilkerson and Lang, *Assessing Teacher Dispositions*.
27. Shively and Misco, "But How Do I Know?"
28. Hughes, "One PreService Program's Dispositional Development."
29. Schussler et al., "Swimming in Deep Waters."
30. Conderman and Walker, "Assessing Dispositions."
31. Bercaw et al., "Mirror Images."
32. Meidl and Baumann, "Extreme Make Over."

programs can identify expectations for dispositions.[33] Similarly, one study suggested a preservice emphasis on dispositions to develop reflection and decision-making.[34] Likewise, Cummins and Asempapa affirmed that dispositions embedded in preservice experiences fostered dispositional awareness; the scholars validated that action-oriented opportunities in preservice foster dispositional awareness and growth.[35]

NEW TEACHER ISOLATION

When preservice programs make dispositions a priority, teachers begin their careers with some dispositional footing.[36] Yet, even when a new teacher is introduced to dispositions in preservice there are a variety of factors, such as school climate, school leadership, and district support, that can impact dispositional growth. One team of researchers suggested that meaningful professional development and mentoring strengthens the developing teacher's dispositional response.[37] Bialka noted that for preservice programs to focus on dispositions, preservice teachers must have the opportunity to reflect on their decisions or they will not do so once they are in their first teaching positions.[38] Of particular interest, Wormeli cautioned that teachers who ignore the emotional elements of teaching and learning can become isolated.[39] Wormeli invited teachers to cultivate a sense of curiosity, infuse joy, and develop emotional wellness for the classroom; the author encouraged dedicated time to foster emotional habits needed in teaching, highlighting the idea that dispositions are often overlooked in schools since they are not easily measured.[40] Others affirmed that, like preservice teachers, teachers in permanent positions need experiences to develop dispositions.[41]

Additional literature exposed new momentum in teacher preparation to acclimate a teacher's thinking to care for and meet student needs, as well as to cultivate personal and professional growth. One educator highlighted that teaching remains a difficult and humbling challenge.[42] Soon after, Tosh-

33. Sanger and Osguthorpe, *Moral Work of Teaching*.
34. Johnson et al., "Let the Theory be Your Guide."
35. Cummins and Asempapa, "Fostering Teacher Candidate Dispositions."
36. Hughes, "One PreService Program's Dispositional Development."
37. Thornton, "Case Analysis."
38. Bialka, "Beyond Knowledge and Skills."
39. Wormeli, "Seven Habits."
40. Wormeli, "Seven Habits"; Smith and Skarbeck, *Professional Teacher Dispositions*.
41. Titone et al., "Cultivating Student Teachers' Disposition."
42. Tomlinson, "Caring Teacher's Manifesto."

alis cautioned about inequities found in the educational system, suggesting that teacher isolation and apathy can be overcome with give-and-take in the classroom and action-oriented practices that demonstrate care and trust for and with students.[43] Similarly, Aguilar endorsed prioritizing and cultivating emotional resilience for professional growth.[44]

Hayward reinforced building self-awareness in teachers; for teachers to nurture attributes such as grit in their students, teachers need self-awareness.[45] Hayward recommended modeling risk-taking and telling personal stories to build trust with students. This recommendation supported Day's earlier suggestion to nurture a reflective disposition in teaching.[46] Day highlighted professional qualities such as reflection, hope, curiosity, and commitment. Likewise, after analyzing teacher dispositions over five years, one study concluded that if a new teacher developed a dispositional foundation in preservice, the teacher was then more responsive to student needs.[47]

WHAT'S NEXT?

Although much has been written about how preservice programs integrate dispositions throughout preparation, the direction of dispositional development appears to narrow after the preservice experience. I found that there is a traditionally heavy focus on content, pedagogy, and skills following preservice programs, and as a result less attention is directed toward long-term dispositional development. Dispositions appear to take a backseat to knowledge, skills, lesson planning, and assessment.[48]

Because the current literature promotes exploring dispositional development to strengthen teacher self-efficacy and teacher performance,[49] as well as recognizes the need to develop dispositions beyond traditional preservice programs,[50] I decided to explore the following questions:

1. Do new teachers carry dispositions and dispositional awareness from the preservice program into the first years of teaching?

---

43. Toshalis, "Correcting Our Connecting."
44. Aguilar, *Art of Coaching Teams*.
45. Hayward, *"Got Grit?"*
46. Day, *Passion for Teaching*.
47. Thornton, "Case Analysis."
48. Wake and Bunn, "Teacher Candidate Dispositions."
49. Conderman and Walker, "Assessing Dispositions"; Wake and Bunn, "Teacher Candidate Dispositions."
50. Meidl and Baumann, "Extreme Make Over."

2. If new teachers carry dispositions and dispositional awareness from the preservice program into the first years of teaching, what is the impact?
3. Are there specific practices that nurture and sustain dispositional awareness and dispositional development in the new teacher?

DIVING IN

I started the study by conducting personal interviews with four original participants (New Teacher A, B, C, D) from the program's initial study.[51] At the start of the study, two of these New Teacher participants were teaching in elementary classrooms, one in public school, and the other in private school. The other two New Teachers were teaching in public high school classrooms. All participants lived and worked in close proximity to the preservice program. Each New Teacher was interviewed privately in their own classrooms for convenience.

I also added a focus group meeting with New Teachers to enlarge the dispositional profile of the New Teacher and increase the number of participant voices. Ten recent graduates teaching in close proximity to the program were invited to attend; five committed to do so (Focus Group Teacher 1, 2, 3, 4, 5). These New Teachers gathered after school in a local elementary school classroom; one completed the program in 2015 and was in her second year of elementary teaching; the other four completed the program in 2016 and were in the first year of teaching. At the time of the focus group meeting, four New Teachers were working in public elementary schools and one taught in a public high school.

I attempted to tell the story of the New Teachers using case study framework,[52] asking all participants the same group of open-ended questions for consistency in order to examine growth over time (see Appendix A). Just like the 2014 study, I served as interviewer and facilitator, giving explicit acknowledgment to former roles with the New Teacher participants to reduce possible bias. I attempted to enlarge the dispositional profile of the New Teacher and increase understanding of the New Teacher experience.[53] Although the sample size was small and could limit broader generalizations, the pool of New Teachers represented the program's small cohort size, revealing specifics about the program and adding insights to the needs and progress of New Teachers.

51. Hughes, "One PreService Program's Dispositional Development."
52. Creswell, *Qualitative Inquiry and Research Design*.
53. Creswell, *Qualitative Inquiry and Research Design*.

Dispositions Build Self-Awareness

New Teacher perceptions revealed agreement that dispositions introduced in the preservice program build self-awareness. "I think they [dispositions] inform what I do. They're subconscious" (New Teacher D). When asked about the program's dispositions (see Appendix B), participants repeatedly commented that the program's dispositions were "engrained" throughout preservice preparation. Focus Group Teacher 4 shared, "I had really good practice with [dispositions] with the program . . . and lots of good habits that I've kind of just carried into teaching in a way that works for me." Focus Group Teacher 1 affirmed the program's focus on dispositions: "They [the dispositions] helped with dealing with just the practice of student teaching and then transitioning into full time."

Additionally, New Teachers highlighted links between dispositions and self, dispositions and students, and dispositions and colleagues. Participants appeared to grasp the big picture and the significance of their role with students. When asked to define professional teaching dispositions, New Teacher D noted, "They are like characteristics or tendencies or traits that professional teachers should be fostering throughout their career." This New Teacher continued, "They [dispositions] are guiding principles in the way I interact with my students." Likewise, New Teacher A shared, "Dispositions are the plumb-line for where I want to be. I keep the long-term goals in mind. Because I approach teaching with those dispositions . . . I feel like it's given me a long-term vision of doing something greater."

New Teachers recognized dispositions in themselves and in colleagues; they named a desire to practice dispositions in their classrooms and shared personal examples where they demonstrated dispositions in and outside the classroom. Examples included creating space for students to reflect about their work, sharing materials with colleagues, practicing humility and care with colleagues, and reflecting on lessons with colleagues. Notably, when asked about how New Teachers demonstrate dispositions, New Teacher A shared that modeling dispositions for students served as "relational clout that grows exponentially." New Teacher B noted, "Colleagues without dispositions are harder to work with and engage with collaboratively. I have seen a difference when colleagues have these dispositions and when they do not." New Teacher D affirmed this perception: "It is apparent when you go to meetings, which of your colleagues are compassionate, reflective, and seeking to grow and develop, and which ones aren't." New Teacher D stated in an essay, "To me, being a compassionate professional also means being a team player and working with fellow colleagues in a kind and professional manner."

Focus Group Teacher 5 revealed that dispositions are essential for positive school collaboration: "My team, they've both been grateful servants and they've generously given me what their class is doing, their lesson plans, the curriculum, they definitely display being grateful servants." New Teacher D explained, "I almost feel like it's something that will be helpful for teachers to have to sit through and say what are the dispositions that you think are most important and why." Focus Group Teacher 3 shared, "It's really helpful to have the mission or the dispositions as a school because it makes it easier to practice, I think, when everyone's more aware of them."

Real-Time Active Practice

New Teachers in the Focus Group repeatedly named developing dispositions as a professional choice. Focus Group Teacher 3 expressed that it is a decision to be grateful or compassionate. Focus Group Teacher 4 shared, "Dispositions are the practices or habits that I want to emulate as a professional." Focus Group Teacher 1 claimed, "They're [dispositions are] practices that can help strengthen your teaching." Focus Group Teacher 4 described, "[Dispositions are] things that are practices that you want to try and model and hopefully pass on to students."

Agreement emerged among New Teachers regarding developing dispositions with purpose. Focus Group Teacher 2 stated, "[Compassionate professional] reminds me to engage with the other teachers and have sympathy and empathy and really build relationships . . . instead of being isolated in my classroom and not helping others or hearing from them." New Teacher D coined her intentional daily reflective classroom practice as "real-time reflectiveness."

New Teachers in the Focus Group also noted that active practice occurs with one's self, with students, and with colleagues. This linked back to earlier findings that revealed when New Teachers develop a sense of dispositional awareness, there is a greater desire to practice and continue to increase awareness.[54] Furthermore, New Teachers expressed a desire for opportunities to experience dispositions in their work. New Teacher B explained:

> We [my students and I] have discussion, class discussions on different topics, learning how to dialogue with each other and then we'll step back and reflect on how our discussion went . . .

---

54. Hughes, "One PreService Program's Dispositional Development."

and that's been pretty special, like, they're [the students] starting to clue in to different things because of that space to reflect!

She continued, "It's [reflection is] definitely a constant, it doesn't turn off. You're constantly reflecting on how to make it [the lesson] better." New Teacher A stated, "Being able to reflect on your teaching practices constantly is what makes you become a better teacher." New Teacher B affirmed, "If there wasn't that reflective piece, I think there's a lot of days where you'd just throw in the towel."

Additionally, New Teachers expressed a desire to build dispositional capacity and provided support for real-time practice strategies and action. Citing the disposition of a lifelong learner, Focus Group Teacher 2 commented, "I need to bring in something that I am excited about learning. I think my students would really benefit from that, and it would be an easy way to implement [lifelong learner] into the classroom." Focus Group Teacher 4 stated, "I've learned a lot by getting into other people's classrooms and see[ing] how they interact with their students and [how they] treat their students." When asked about colleagues, New Teacher B responded, "We [colleagues] have lots of conversations before school, after school." She explained that she "talks and debriefs with colleagues each day." Another New Teacher A shared, "As I plan, I ask [myself] what do my students need from this lesson?" Her archived e-portfolio revealed, "Every situation and student is so different and I still have much to learn about what compassion looks like in the context of different [student] stories." These examples further highlight the expressed New Teacher desire for regular dispositional practice and engagement.

Agreement was noted around the idea that when dispositions are modeled, dispositions transfer to students. Examples included New Teacher perceptions linked to reflection and growth mindset theory: "By being able to reflect on what they [students] have accomplished they are more likely to go into upcoming projects with a growth mindset instead of a fixed mindset" (Focus Group Teacher 5 e-portfolio). The same New Teacher noted in an archived essay:

"Being a life-long learner instills in them [students] an unquenchable thirst for knowledge and curiosity (Philosophy of Education Essay). I will do this by modeling my own bottomless pit of inquiry, teaching them about the joy of learning and being interested in all things." When asked about the impact of dispositions, Focus Group Teacher 1 responded:

Remind them [students] that mistakes are part of learning and that it's okay to make mistakes. When they have that sort of mindset then when they get to challenges, they're able to be more resilient and sort of push through their challenges or ask for help if they don't understand something.

Focus Group Teacher 5 wrote in an e-portfolio: "By constantly reflecting I am able to learn things about myself and recognize patterns. From these reflections, I can then make changes to my instruction or management." Focus Group Teacher 3 explained, "I survey students and ask them to reflect on projects. I ask what do you like about this assignment? What are you proud of? What was important in the assignment?"

A Dispositional Toolbox?

New Teachers underscored and repeatedly articulated an understanding of the significance of dispositions for their professional big picture. They revealed self-awareness and the ability to focus on others. In particular, New Teacher A shared, "Building relational emotional skills and emotional intelligence I think is everything in this job. I have had to learn how to be in touch with my own skill set and be okay with what I'm strong at."

When asked about the role dispositions play in teaching, New Teacher A stated, "I think it is essential to have [these] dispositions if you are going to survive." Focus Group Teacher 2 reinforced this response: "I don't want to become a grouchy old teacher; I need to survive and I wonder about the habit of being compassionate." When asked about New Teacher support at school, New Teacher C concluded, "I'd say I think when I start to lose those dispositions is when I probably shouldn't be teaching anymore." Furthermore, Focus Group Teacher 4 stated, "And so I wonder if five years down the road if I'm not being intentional about it [dispositions] if I'll kind of lose that." New Teacher C shared, "[Do not] keep dispositions dusty or rusty, but sharp!" She continued, "Honestly, when I lose the dispositions I shouldn't be teaching." These perceptions exposed a concern from participants regarding their professional futures. New Teacher A reinforced the concern when she explained, "Sometimes I feel like [I'm] on an island . . . I would just love more time with colleagues for building those relationships." New Teacher C also shared:

> I think when I start to lose that love of learning or that compassionate heart towards students, I think that's a pretty good sign that maybe I would need, maybe it's time for a change for me because it's going [to] really impact students [if] they have a teacher that no longer, I think, values their profession and values the things that are important to being a teacher.

When New Teachers were asked about the role dispositions play in Induction, California's mentoring program,[55] responses varied. Focus Group Teacher 2 commented, "I am in the mentoring [Induction] program this year. I joined it so I could clear my credential. There is not an emphasis on dispositions. They do mention the inquiry cycle which I guess sounds like [being a] reflective practitioner but it's not really stated why we are doing the inquiry cycle." Focus Group Teacher 4 acknowledged, "There is not so much of an emphasis on dispositions, more on curriculum development and classroom management." In contrast, New Teacher A shared,

> I did finish my program two years ago. [Induction] definitely focused on the professional development and passion for your craft. They encouraged us to dig into areas where we wanted to grow, magnify aspects we were passionate about, and implement new things into our classroom.

Focus Group Teacher 3 shared: "I [also] have found it helpful to be with other first year teachers who are going through the same thing I am. That sense of support is especially helpful for a first-year teacher."

DISCOVERIES

This study should encourage greater dialogue in the field. Recommendations can be considered by similar-sized teacher education programs, school districts, principals, and new and veteran teachers. Of particular significance is the stated perception and concern by New Teacher participants regarding their professional futures; three of four interviewees and four of five focus group teachers named this concern. Responses suggested that it is an individual teacher's decision to develop dispositions in practice and any effort to nurture dispositional awareness among participants was essentially dependent on the individual teacher's actions, rather than a school district's or principal's leading. This implies that the responsibility for dispositional growth often falls to the New Teacher alone.

The study revealed strong agreement for creating space for dispositional development in collaboration with colleagues. It should be noted that New Teachers expressed a desire for space and time to grow dispositions in practice, exposing a need for dispositional strategies or a toolbox of practices to foster dispositional awareness and build capacity. Furthermore, New Teachers named strategies that they use as part of their dispositional practice;

---

55. California Commission on Teacher Credentialing, "General Education Induction Program Preconditions."

examples include being open to receiving criticism, discussing what a class can improve upon, naming what students and teachers are grateful for, and giving grace to students. A suggested toolbox of practices for New Teachers could include these and other strategies to nurture dispositional growth and practices in the developing teacher. Hence, my next steps are to explore and consider compiling a user-friendly manual with a collection of practices that promote ongoing dispositional growth in New Teachers.

The study's findings point preservice program faculty like me to connect with local mentoring programs; New Teacher concerns about professional survival should be shared. Preservice programs could also review transition plans that follow the preservice teacher into the first years of teaching. Suggested dialogue could highlight the inclusion of dispositional goals in the transition plan, adding support to new research that recognizes the need for dispositional development beyond traditional preparation.[56]

The study also reinforced reflection as a significant disposition for professional development. New Teachers engaged in reflection as part of their daily work and they expressed that they try to model, teach, and transfer reflective skills to students. Acknowledging the role of reflection in teacher practice demonstrates a leap of maturity in the study's New Teachers, revealing growth into the first years of teaching. This adds validation and affirms the need for a focus and framework for a New Teacher's dispositional development.[57]

The study provided a selection of perceptions specific to California's teacher mentoring program. New Teachers expressed a desire for increased focus on dispositions in their first positions. Preservice programs and school districts should revisit the Francis recommendation to explicitly link theory to practice and action.[58] Recently, Costa and Kallick suggested linking cognitive thinking with repetition and reflection to highlight and internalize dispositions; implementing intentional strategies invites a dispositional commitment and response from teachers and students.[59] Others in the field advocate for practices, such as core reflection, to cultivate a teacher's professionalism.[60] Regardless of the method or approach, these endorsements strengthen the need for ongoing dispositional training.

---

56. Meidl and Baumann, "Extreme Make Over."

57. Schussler et al., "Swimming in Deep Waters"; Schussler and Murrell, "Quality Teaching as Moral Practice."

58. Francis, "Reflective Journal."

59. Costa and Kallick, *Dispositions*.

60. Korthagen et al., *Teaching and Learning from Within*.

This study urges preservice programs, schools, and districts to consider how to collaborate on, support, and develop dispositions in New Teachers beyond preservice. Additional questions for future investigation include: How can preservice programs elevate their role in the transition from preservice to the first teaching position? How can preservice programs strengthen their efforts to care for candidates and increase dispositional awareness and practice? Lastly, can school and district leaders prioritize and create space for dispositional development as a way to demonstrate care for new teachers? These questions support the research that dispositions, knowledge, and skills can be learned as a form of best practice and for teacher leadership.[61]

NEXT STEPS?

In the first years of teaching, new teachers need both dedicated space to cultivate dispositions and time to nurture dispositional development. In addition to traditional expectations for content and pedagogy, developing teachers must collect and cultivate tools to build dispositional awareness. Concerns for professional longevity should serve as a significant red flag for preservice programs, especially since New Teachers exposed the need for an explicit focus on dispositions in schools. School leaders and districts should consider reframing professional development priorities to include time for dispositional reflection and dialogue. Some researchers recommend restructuring dispositions within the educational system and notably recognize that to internalize dispositions, individuals must choose to engage with them over and over.[62] More research opportunities are needed to care for and support developing teachers professionally and personally,[63] adding validation to the conclusion that education is an ongoing, continuous journey.[64]

This study affirms the need for increased dispositional practice and development in new teachers. Educators must consider and prioritize the individual and collective roles assumed in a teacher's dispositional development from preservice to new teacher to seasoned teacher. Collectively, educators should be encouraged to pause and ask, "Are we preparing new teachers for the short-term or the long-term?" Furthermore, if teaching

61. Levin and Schrum, *Every Teacher a Leader*.
62. Costa and Kallick, *Dispositions*.
63. Tomlinson, "Caring Teacher's Manifesto"; Wake and Bunn, "Teacher Candidate Dispositions."
64. Thiell, "Adapt and Evolve."

requires professionals to demonstrate love in practice,[65] then preservice programs, schools, and districts must make a courageous shift and presume a collective, ongoing responsibility to nurture, stretch, care for, and engage all teachers in real-time active dispositional practice. This intentional decision of time, space, and care to develop dispositions and the heart of a teacher can only increase the depth of care that K-12 students receive.

FOLLOW-UP AND UPDATES

Since completing this study, I have made concerted efforts to apply the recommendations. At the onset, my colleagues and I added a professional dispositions section to our program's transition plan. This plan, recently retitled the Individualized Development Plan (IDP), includes strengths and achievements observed during full-time clinical practice. The IDP also highlights professional goals for the first teaching position and becomes part of the goal-setting dialogue as each new teacher enters the state's mentoring program. This new emphasis serves to acknowledge and implement recommendations that strengthen dispositional focus and build new teacher self-awareness in the first teaching position.

Additionally, I continue to comb through my program's archived artifacts. I've discovered that the most recent artifacts continue to validate the pivotal role of dispositions and their significance in new teacher development. A recent graduate noted in an exit interview, "I still know that none of these dispositions will become personal habits of mine [without] personal discipline and starting each new morning with intentional recommitment." Another recent graduate shared, "If I don't work on myself first to adopt dispositions to strengthen and guide me, I am in danger of burning out and losing the joy I have already found in this profession. By internalizing spirits of gratefulness, compassion, reflection, and humility I will be able to continue growing into the best educator I can be." These anecdotes add validation to the significance and impact of dispositions within the program, which new teachers carry into their first teaching position.

I continue to ponder, write, and explore new dispositions such as empathy, resilience, and joy. As teacher burdens and pressures expand, the need to cultivate strengths of the heart remains.[66] Of particular significance, a colleague recently affirmed empathy as a valuable teaching tool and disposition; specifically, when a new teacher understands and practices empathy,

---

65. Paris, *Teach from the Heart*.
66. McKibben, "Grit and the Greater Good."

students see ways they can practice empathy when they encounter difficult circumstances.[67] Hence, there are more dispositions to explore.

Additional research continues to support my plans to write a textbook or workbook for teachers. I plan to encourage teacher reflection and engagement, either individually or collectively, with dispositions essential to the profession.[68] I hope such a text will create professional development opportunities for teachers to pause, reflect, and dialogue about dispositions and their role in professional practice; by doing so, all teachers can build dispositional self-awareness and practice a pedagogy of care.

Since Noddings first named care as a choice to serve and engage,[69] educators have continued to ponder how best to care. Consequently, I advocate that preservice programs earnestly consider how to demonstrate care and love students in deeper ways. This consideration of dispositions becomes all the more significant for Christian educators pondering a Christian ethic of care. Additionally, I hope school districts and teacher leaders can make efforts to strengthen the professional experience and collectively commit to recognize, shepherd, and grow professional dispositions in real-time active practice together. Can we extend the conversation and prioritize nurturing, developing teachers to flourish alongside students? I'm genuinely committed to care for new teachers so they can then care for their students. I wholeheartedly believe the continued investment in each and every teacher's dispositional journey is worth the time. Will you join me on this journey?

APPENDIX A: PERSONAL INTERVIEW AND FOCUS GROUP QUESTIONS

1. What year did you earn your teaching credential?
2. How long have you been teaching?
3. Are you currently teaching in public or private school?
4. What grade level(s)?
5. Please name previous positions and/or grade levels.
6. In your own words, define professional teaching dispositions.

---

67. Bryant, "Empathy as a Christian Calling."
68. Hill-Jackson et al., *What Makes a Star Teacher*; Paris, *Teach from the Heart*; Srinivasan, *Teach, Breathe, Learn*.
69. Noddings, *Caring: A Relational Approach*.

7. Do dispositions inform how you approach and teach? If yes, please give an example. If no, please explain.
8. In your opinion, name the dispositions that you feel are important to teaching and your classroom.
9. Please name and describe specific examples/times when you demonstrated specific dispositions in your teaching.
10. In your opinion, do the dispositions you named influence students? If so, please give a specific example.
11. In your opinion, do these dispositions influence student attitudes about learning? Please explain.
12. In your opinion, do these dispositions influence your attitude toward teaching and the profession? Please explain.
13. Describe the preservice program preparation you received regarding dispositions and teaching.
14. Did dispositions play a role in how you learned to teach? Why or why not? Do dispositions play a role in your daily work? Please explain.
15. If dispositions play a role, please name an example(s) from your daily work.
16. Do dispositions play a role with colleagues?
17. Do you intentionally work to cultivate dispositions in your daily work?
18. Do you feel supported as a teacher in your current teaching position? Please explain.
19. Do you have anything else to share or add?

APPENDIX B

Dispositions

The Department of Education is committed to the **mission** of the college, the profession of teaching, the state of California, and most importantly students' **personal and professional growth** within the context of a **Christian worldview**.

Dispositions, as defined by the Council for the Accreditation of Educator Preparation (CAEP), are the habits of professional action and moral commitments that underlie an educator's performance (2016).

Education Faculty are committed to nurturing professional dispositions in education students. Although there are a multitude of professional dispositions for teachers, particular emphasis is placed on building awareness and developing the following dispositions:

Lifelong Learner

Displays curiosity and passion for learning and transferring enthusiasm to learning to others.
"Search for wisdom as a hidden treasure."
Prov 2:4

Reflective Practitioner

Displays a willingness to think flexibly, adapt, and develop habits for growth and self-awareness.
"I applied my heart to what I observed and learned a lesson from what I saw."
Prov 24:32

Compassionate Professional

Displays sympathy, empathy, and responsiveness to others' needs.
"Clothe yourselves with compassion, kindness, humility, gentleness and patience."
Col 3:12

Grateful Servant

Displays a humble, appreciative, and professional demeanor dedicated to the service of others.
"Whatever you do in word and deed, do all in the name of the Lord Jesus, giving thanks to God."
Col 3:18

Statement of Commitment

Education students, along with Education Faculty, commit to seek and demonstrate the above dispositions in credential classes, coursework, fieldwork experiences, and in student teaching. The dispositions are introduced early and are sustained in assignments, lessons, collegial exchanges, reflections, and self-assessments. The program tracks and examines evidence of the dispositions primarily in the e-portfolio assessment.

Candidate Signature _____

Date _____

Faculty Advisor Signature_____

Date _____

BIBLIOGRAPHY

Aguilar, Elena. *The Art of Coaching Teams: Building Resilient Communities that Transform Schools.* San Francisco: Jossey-Bass, 2016.

Bercaw, Lynn A., et al. "Mirror Images: Teacher Candidates' Perceptions of Disposition Development." *Action in Teacher Education* 34 (2012) 514–25.

Bialka, Christa. "Beyond Knowledge and Skills: Best Practices for Attending to Dispositions in Teacher Education Programs." *Issues in Teacher Education* 25 (2016) 3–21.

Bryant, Danielle. "Empathy as a Christian Calling." *International Christian Community of Teacher Educators Journal* 13 (2018) 1–6. https://digitalcommons.georgefox.edu/icctej/vol13/iss2/4.

California Commission on Teacher Credentialing. "General Education Induction Program Preconditions and Program Standards." http://www.ctc.ca.gov/educator-prep/standards/GEd-preconditions-program-stds-12-2015.pdf.

———. "Teacher Performance Expectations." http://www.ctc.ca.gov/educator-prep/standards/adopted-TPEs-2016.pdf.

Choi, Hee-sook, et al. "Assessment of Teacher Candidate Dispositions: Evidence of Reliability and Validity." *Teacher Education Quarterly* 43 (2016) 71–89.

Claxton, Guy, et al. "Hard Thinking about Soft Skills." *Educational Leadership* 73 (2016) 60–64.

Conderman, Greg, and David A. Walker. "Assessing Dispositions in Teacher Preparation Programs: Are Candidates and Faculty Seeing the Same Thing?" *The Teacher Educator* 50 (2015) 215–31.

Costa, Arthur L., and Bena Kallick. *Dispositions: Reframing Teaching and Learning.* Thousand Oaks, CA: Corwin, 2014.

Council for the Accreditation of Educator Preparation Standards. "D." *Glossary A-Z.* http://caepnet.org/glossary?letter=D.

———. "Vision, Mission, and Goals." (2016). http://caepnet.org/about/vision-mission-goals.

Creswell, John W. *Qualitative Inquiry and Research Design: Choosing among Five Approaches.* Thousand Oaks, CA: Sage, 2013.

Cronon, William. "Only Connect: The Goal of a Liberal Education." *Liberal Education* 85 (1999) 6–13.

Cummins, Lauren, and Bridget Asempapa. "Fostering Teacher Candidate Dispositions in Teacher Education Programs." *Journal of the Scholarship of Teaching and Learning* 13 (2013) 99–119.

DaRos-Voseles, Denise, and Linda Moss. "The Role of Dispositions in the Education of Future Teachers." *Young Children* 62 (2007) 90–96.

Day, Christopher. *A Passion for Teaching.* New York: Routledge Falmer, 2004.
Dewey, John. *Democracy and Education.* New York: Free Press, 1916.
———. *Experience and Education.* New York: Touchstone, 1938.
Dweck, Carol S. *Mindset, the New Psychology of Success.* New York: Penguin Random House, 2006.
———. "Recognizing and Overcoming False Growth Mindset." www.edutopia.org/blog/recognizing-overcoming-false-growth-mindset-carole-dweck.
Educators Rising. "Educators Rising Standards." https://www.educatorsrising.org/uploads/people/Educators-Rising-Standards.pdf.
Evans-Palmer, Teri. "Building Dispositions and Self-Efficacy in PreService Art Teachers." *Studies in Art Education* 57 (2016) 265-78.
Farrell, Thomas S. C. "Teacher You are Stupid! Cultivating a Reflective Disposition." *Teaching as a Second Language Electronic Journal* 18 (2014) 1-10.
Francis, Dawn. "The Reflective Journal: A Window to PreService Teachers' Practical Knowledge." *Teaching and Teacher Education* 11 (1995) 229-41.
Giovannelli, Marietta. "Relationship between Reflective Disposition Toward Teaching and Effective Teaching." *The Journal of Educational Research* 96 (2003) 293-309.
Hayward, Michelle O. "Got Grit? Leading and Teaching for Success." *Association of Middle Level Education Magazine* 3 (2015) 24-26.
Hill-Jackson, Valerie, et al. *What Makes a Star Teacher: 7 Dispositions that Support Student Learning.* Alexandria, VA: ACSD, 2019.
Holmes, Arthur F. *The Idea of a Christian College.* Grand Rapids: Eerdmans, 1975.
Hughes, Michelle C. "One PreService Program's Dispositional Development Revealed." PhD diss., George Fox University, 2014.
Johnson, Lisa E., et al. "Let the Theory be Your Guide: Assessing the Moral Work of Teaching." In *The Moral Work of Teaching,* edited by Matthew N. Sanger and Richard Osguthorpe, 92–112. New York: Teachers College Press, 2013.
Korthagen, Fred A. J., et al. *Teaching and Learning from Within: A Core Reflection Approach to Quality and Inspiration in Education.* New York: Routledge, 2013.
Levin, Barbara B., and Lynn Schrum. *Every Teacher a Leader: Developing the Needed Dispositions and Skills for Teacher Leadership.* Thousand Oaks, CA: Corwin, 2017.
McKibben, Sarah. "Grit and the Greater Good: A Conversation with Angela Duckworth." *Educational Leadership* 76 (2018) 40-45.
Meidl, Tynisha, and Beth Baumann. "Extreme Make Over: Disposition Development of PreService Teachers." *Journal of Community Engagement and Scholarship* 8 (2015) 90-97.
National Council for Accreditation of Teacher Education. "Standards for Professional Development Schools." http://www.ncate.org/Standards/tabid/107/Default.aspx.
Noddings, Nel. *Caring: A Relational Approach to Ethics and Moral Education.* Berkeley: University of California Press, 1984.
Paris, Janell. *Teach from the Heart: Pedagogy as Spiritual Practice.* Eugene, OR: Cascade, 2016.
Ravitch, D. *The Death and Life of the Great American School System: How Testing and Choice are Undermining Education.* 3rd ed. New York: Basic, 2016.
Risko, Victoria J., et al. "Preparing Teachers for Reflective Practice: Intentions, Contradictions, and Possibilities." *Language Arts* 80 (2002) 134-44.
Sanger, Matthew N., and Richard D. Osguthorpe. *The Moral Work of Teaching and Teacher Education.* New York: Teachers College Press, 2013.

Schussler, Deborah L. "Defining Dispositions: Wading through Murky Waters." *The Teacher Educator* 41 (2006) 251–68.

Schussler, Deborah L., and Lea Knarr. "Building Awareness of Dispositions: Enhancing Moral Sensibilities in Teaching." *Journal of Moral Education* 42 (2013) 71–87.

Schussler, Deborah L., and Peter Murrell. "Quality Teaching as Moral Practice: Cultivating Practical Wisdom." In *Quality and Change in Education,* edited by John Chi-Kin Lee and Christopher Day, 277–91. Basel, Switzerland: Springer International, 2016.

Schussler, Deborah L., et al. "Swimming in Deep Waters." http://democracyeducationjournal.org/home/vol20/Iss2/5.

Schwartz, Katrina. "What's Your Learning Disposition? How to Foster Students' Mindsets." https://ww2.kqed.org/mindshift/2014/03/25/whats-your-learning-disposition-how-to-foster-students-mindsets/.

Shively, James, and Thomas Misco. "But How Do I Know about Their Attitudes and Beliefs?" *The Clearing House* 83 (2010) 9–14.

Smith, R. Lee, and Denise Skarbeck. *Professional Teacher Dispositions: Additions to the Mainstream.* Lanham, MD: R and L Education, 2013.

Smylie, Mark A., and Joseph F. Murphy. "The Call for Caring School Leaders." *Principal* 95 (2016) 16–19.

Srinivasan, Meena. *Teach, Breathe, Learn: Mindfulness In and Out of the Classroom.* Berkeley: Parallax, 2014.

Thiell, Aaron. "Adapt and Evolve." *Principal* 95 (2015) 8–11.

Thornton, Holly. "A Case Analysis of Middle Level Teacher Preparation and Long-Term Teacher Dispositions." *Research in Middle Level Education* 37 (2013) 1–19.

Titone, Connie, et al. "Cultivating Student Teachers' Disposition and Ability to Construct Knowledge." *Action in Teacher Education* 19 (1998) 76–87.

Tomlinson, Carol Ann. "The Caring Teacher's Manifesto." *Educational Leadership* 72 (2015) 90–91.

Toshalis, Eric. "Correcting Our Connecting." *Educational Leadership* 74 (2016) 16–20.

Wake, Donna, and Gary Bunn. "Teacher Candidate Dispositions: Perspectives of Professional Expectations." *The Teacher Educator* 51 (2016) 33–54.

Wilkerson, Judy R., and William S. Lang. *Assessing Teacher Dispositions.* Thousand Oaks, CA: Corwin 2007.

Wormeli, Rick. "The Seven Habits of Highly Affective Teachers." *Educational Leadership* 73 (2015) 10–15.

Chapter 9

SELF AND SOUL CARE
Spiritual Practices to Sustain Teaching

Stephanie Talley

Our coffee cups were empty. The Saturday breakfast crowd was gone, and the room was quiet. We had been discussing Trixie's first year of teaching. As both her former professor and current visitor/researcher in her classroom, I had a front row view of her teaching. Most of our conversation that day centered around the difficult work of teaching, though our discussion had taken many twists and turns. We laughed and cried—not at all unusual for a novice teacher sitting with her mentor. When we finished, the recorder was turned off. The interactive interview that was a part of my dissertation research was over, but then Trixie gave me one more nugget. As newlyweds, she and her husband were in a weekly small group that was part of their faith community. This group consisted of young professionals, all newly married, who were also all walking into their adult lives. Trixie noted how significant this group of people had been to her during her first year of teaching. I nodded, listening while I packed my bag. And then I heard the words that stopped me in my tracks. She said, "You know, it's funny that ya'll talked a lot to us in the program about how our faith informs our practices in the classroom. You never mentioned how important faith would be to keep you going." I was stunned. How is it that at a faith-based institution, where we make faith integration a priority in teacher education, we discussed faith to inform your practices, yet failed to mention how faith sustains your practices? Trixie's statement has hounded me for four years—I find myself revisiting this statement constantly.

As a faith-informed teacher educator, my mind often wanders back to this conversation. In fact, I would consider it one of the major discoveries of my dissertation and my journey as a teacher educator. While the idea of an ethic of care has permeated pedagogical conversations in departments of education, both secular and faith-based, for three decades,[1] Trixie's statement that day reframed the issue for me and caused a deeper examination. How are the ideas of faith and self-care intertwined? Noddings introduced the term "ethic of care" into the lexicon of education.[2] She suggests the roles of both the caregiver and the care receiver and the reciprocal relationship between the two are fundamental in the care cycle. In this way, the actions of the cared-for are as significant as the actions of the person giving the care. Both parties must contribute to the relationship. While the care relationship may not always be equal, it must always be reciprocal. All ethical decisions flow out of this mutuality. In contrast to ethics of reason and justice, care ethics is needs-based, not rights-based.[3] Quite simply, I give each student what they need as opposed to giving each student the same thing. Grounded in relationship and characterized by the ability to listen to and assess students' needs discerningly, teachers make careful decisions based on individual situations. As moral agents of care, ". . . carers listen to the expressed need, feel something as a result, and respond sensitively—not always positively—to the need expressed."[4] All responses to expressed needs are designed to preserve the integrity of the relationship. This has served as the foundation for my teaching in every classroom I have entered. However, it was not until I was a doctoral candidate that I encountered Noddings's assertion that education ". . . might be best organized around centers of care: care for self, for intimate others, for associates and acquaintances, for distant others, for nonhuman animals, for plants and physical environment, for the human-made world of objects and instruments, and for ideas."[5] I noticed that foremost on this list was "care for self," but it was not until Trixie's words that day that I fully comprehended the significance of Noddings's words.

Whether faith based or secular, most institutions address the principle of the ethic of care both explicitly and implicitly. Current trends in

---

1. Noddings and Brooks, *Teaching Controversial Issues*.
2. Noddings, *Philosophy of Education*.
3. Noddings and Brooks, *Teaching Controversial Issues*.
4. Noddings and Brooks, *Teaching Controversial Issues*, 15.
5. Noddings, *Challenge to Care in Schools*, xiii.

education and best practices taught in most teacher preparation programs, such as differentiation,[6] personalized learning,[7] and restorative discipline,[8] are grounded in the idea of decisions being made on the basis of individual needs, not rights, which is one of the tenets of care ethics. At a Christian university, our faith should permeate these conversations. The conversations and instruction surrounding an ethic of care must be explicit, intentional and clearly connected to faith. My experiences with the members of The International Christian Community for Teacher Education (ICCTE), and other professional organizations, provide evidence that this is happening in teacher preparation programs.

Still, my mind keeps going back to my conversation with Trixie on that day in the coffee shop. Are Christian teacher educators talking to preservice teachers about faith as sustenance and as care for their soul? Faith is the medium that informs my acts of self-care. Yes, my faith informs my practices: my relationships with colleagues, my curricular decisions, my approach to classroom management and discipline, and the hospitality I extend to students and their families. However, what is more significant is that my faith sustains these practices.

As a literacy specialist, the analogy that comes to mind is one of a reader and their book choices. Of course, my abilities as a reader inform my book choices. I choose books I can read and read well. Yet, it is the choices, the quality of literature, and the power of the stories that sustain me as a reader. They nurture my love of reading and my life as a reader. The relationship between the two is symbiotic. One cannot exist without the other. Teacher educators must prepare our preservice teachers to the best of our abilities in content and curriculum, but we must also inform them about this faith-care symbiosis. Just as stories sustain me as a reader, the acts of self-care that are part of my faith practices sustain me as a teacher.

FAITH TO SUSTAIN TEACHING

Faith informs my practice; faith also sustains my practice. The great secret, hidden from the view of many, is that faith can only inform practice if you are actively sustaining your faith (and it you). Parker Palmer writes, "Teaching, like any truly human activity, emerges from one's inwardness, for better or worse. As I teach, I project the condition of my soul onto my students,

---

6. Tomlinson, *How to Differentiate Instruction*.
7. Marzano, "How Classroom Teachers Approach."
8. Hopkins, "Restorative Justice in Schools."

my subject, and our way of being together."[9] Faith is what sustains, protects, guards, instructs, and heals the condition of my soul. Trixie's words captured for me the true meaning of faith integration as a teacher educator. For me, faith integration isn't simply about a specific assignment, or praying for and with my students. True faith integration comes when I model for my students the connection between the care I give myself and my soul and the care I give my students.

Faith and Self-Care

Self-care is generally defined as activities that allow one to maintain a healthy and balanced lifestyle.[10] Activities such as healthy eating, restful sleeping, routine exercise, daily hydration, and socialization are all viewed as behaviors that promote overall wellness, both physically and emotionally. Successful people employ these practices to live healthy and productive lives. However, as Christians, our theology of self-care demands that the above practices are working towards our end goal—restoration. Viewed in this light, "self-care becomes an essential and formative practice in faithfulness to God that has the restoring effect of addressing the brokenness present in all."[11] Participating in restorative self-care rituals that contribute to our own health and well-being allows us to support others in their own wellness.[12] Teachers cannot enter the classrooms of our broken world and do the difficult work demanded if they are not physically, emotionally, and spiritually healthy. Gates maintains:

> Self-care is not indulging ourselves without regard for God and others, but recognizing our legitimate need to care for ourselves by seeking what ultimately benefits us and protecting ourselves from what ultimately harms us—even as we do the same for God and others.[13]

In Christian teacher education programs, self-care conversations must also turn to defining soul care. If Palmer's assertions are correct,[14] and

---

9. Palmer, *Courage to Teach*, 2.
10. Jeffries et al., "Toward a Culture of Self-Care."
11. Riedel et al., "Teaching Students to Care," 79.
12. Freytag, "Embodying and Modeling Healthy Self-Care"; Tan and Castillo, "Self-Care and Beyond."
13. Gates, "Self-Care," 17.
14. Palmer, *Courage to Teach*.

teachers project the condition of their souls onto their students, soul care becomes of paramount importance.

Finding Sabbath

An examination of the biblical concept of Sabbath is helpful. My friend, colleague, and Old Testament scholar Glenn Pemberton[15] describes Sabbath as the ultimate act of trust in God: trust that God's work will continue while you rest; trust that God will move through you in stillness; trust that "our lives are not defined by the production and consumption of commodity goods";[16] trust that everything is not up to us.[17] As teachers in an era of high-stakes testing and endless accountability measures, "the relentless focus on performance"[18] often leaves us feeling as if we have been reduced to a commodity. Remembering that our identity in Christ has no relationship to our ability to perform is perhaps the single greatest gift of Sabbath.

Sabbath as a spiritual discipline is the disposition to "Be still, and know that I am God" (Ps 46:10). Nouwen suggests that in the spiritual life, discipline means "the effort to create some space in which God can act."[19] Spiritual disciplines are life rhythms that allow you to live in healthy relationship with God, self, and others.[20] Spiritual disciplines include solitude, prayer, silence, corporate worship, fasting, meditating, and the reading of Scripture. Sabbath as a discipline is a good starting place for teachers. While Sabbath is often observed as an intentional day of rest, it is also a "disposition to cultivate and practice throughout the week."[21] In this way, it is not merely refraining from work, "it is taking up God's rest."[22]

Teachers are in desperate need of God's rest. The demands of the classroom are many. Teaching requires attention to curriculum planning; differentiation of lessons; classroom management; federal, state, and local mandates; high-stakes testing and accountability measures; paperwork; and the social, emotional, and cognitive needs of the students in our classrooms. Stopping to lean into the rest of Sabbath means we fully acknowledge that God is in control and we are not. The relief of this act cannot be overstated. In

---

15. Glenn Pemberton (professor, writer) in discussion with the author, June 2019.
16. Brueggemann, *Sabbath as Resistance*, xiv.
17. Freytag, "Embodying and Modeling Healthy Self-Care."
18. Matthias, *Cry of the Teacher's Soul*, 59.
19. Nouwen, "Solitude to Community to Ministry," 81.
20. Yankoski, *Sacred Year*.
21. Riedel et al., "Teaching Students to Care," 95.
22. Riedel et al., "Teaching Students to Care," 96.

the classroom, teachers are in a constant state of decision-making—teachers make hundreds of decisions daily. Sabbath provides an alternative.[23] I can let go of the fear that I have not done enough. I can be still. I can cease to make decisions, hit pause, and experience divine rest. I can listen.

A return to Sabbath also requires an embracing of boundaries. I have a dear friend who proclaims that boundaries are like hugs. In her mind, boundaries make you feel safe and warm, much as hugs do. Early in my career in higher education, I struggled with boundaries. This friend, then a colleague, helped me see the necessity of healthy boundaries in my life and work. Sabbath itself is a boundary. Sabbath as a practice is a time and a place and a space that is set aside for holy rest. In this time, we reconnect both with the Spirit of God and our own spirit. Extending this view, Sabbath can also be experienced when we allow ourselves to fully embrace the power of saying "no." Rebecca Addleman confesses that, as a Christian, her first idea of service was, "Say yes to everything."[24] This notion is problematic for Christian educators because teaching is a service profession. Teachers will never run out of opportunities to say "yes." In fact, in this profession, teachers are often rewarded for this very mindset. It is often a badge of honor to be able to say, "There is never enough time" or "My to-do list is always full." In this setting, establishing healthy boundaries is a constant struggle.[25] Yet, those boundaries can produce tremendous benefits.

First, by saying "no," I am admitting I cannot do it all and that my worth is not determined by my ability to do it all. My identity rests in the knowledge that I am a child of God. Nouwen states that with this at the forefront of our mind, we "can deal with an enormous amount of success as well as an enormous amount of failure without losing [our] identity, because [our] identity is that [we] are beloved."[26] For teachers, this concept can be freeing. While there is no doubt we need to work hard at teaching in the service of our students, acknowledging that I simply cannot do it all is healthy. This admission, and submission to God, also allows space for the Holy Spirit to work through me. Remembering our identity as beloved children of God allows us to acknowledge that as Christians, God does not love us because we are good. He makes us good because he loves us.[27]

Second, boundaries not only protect our own needs and interests, they protect others as well. Many times, we are swayed by the thinking that if we

23. Brueggemann, *Sabbath as Resistance*.
24. Addleman, "Service," 142.
25. Addleman, "Service."
26. Nouwen, "Solitude to Community to Ministry," 82.
27. Lewis, *Mere Christianity*.

don't do this good thing, it will not get done. At its core, this is arrogance. Believing that God's work will not continue if I say "no" places me in a dangerous position. God has raised people up to do his work for generations and he will continue to do so. While his purpose for my life is to join in this work, the work will continue regardless. Thoughtful and responsive boundaries recognize God's presence and allow him to do his good work in both my life and the lives of others.[28] In this way, I see myself as part of God's community. Community in this manner is a way of living and being in the world. Life in God's community allows the gifts of others to be honored and raised up.[29]

THE NECESSARY CONVERSATION

As I think back to the many first year teachers I have observed, I now realize this is what I want them to know most about the connection between faith and teaching practice. If they remember only one thing, I want them to remember that when you teach, you are projecting the condition of your soul onto your students.[30] Therefore, the caretaking of your soul is critical to sustainable teaching. It is as important as staying current in pedagogy. And, dare I say, perhaps more important. I have witnessed teachers with great skill and current pedagogy who have done harm to children. The reverse is also true. I have watched teachers whose pedagogy is a bit less innovative, but whose "inner landscape"[31] is vibrant, do amazing things with children. The best pedagogy in the world will not save your teaching if the condition of your soul is not healthy. For this reason, faith to nurture, protect, and sustain your inner landscape, your soul, becomes of critical importance. Content knowledge and pedagogy do matter. Teaching is a complex endeavor and teachers must be prepared to do the difficult work of teaching. Loving children is important, but it is not enough. My faith demands that I maintain the highest standards for my students in any classroom I enter. Preservice teachers must rigorously train to become teachers. However, I do want to clearly let my teacher candidates know that in addition to being experts in content and pedagogy, they must protect and guard the condition of their soul. If we lose the ability to reflect on the condition of our soul, our teaching cannot easily recover from the loss. Christian educators who lose

---

28. Freytag, "Embodying and Modeling Healthy Self-Care."
29. Nouwen, "Solitude to Community to Ministry."
30. Palmer, *Courage to Teach*.
31. Palmer, *Courage to Teach*, 5.

their spiritual mooring will find their classroom practices less effective, and their teaching will suffer.

This is the discussion I fear is lacking in departments of teacher education at faith-based institutions. Palmer states, "The growth of any craft depends on shared practice and honest dialogue among the people who do it."[32] In light of Trixie's comments at the coffee shop that day, I contemplate whether I, as a teacher educator, have honestly spoken with my colleagues and students about faith to sustain practice—faith to care for the condition of the soul. There is a connection between the care given to oneself and the care that can then be given to students.

During her first year as a teacher, Trixie utilized her faith to sustain in the challenges of marriage, teaching, and life, and this was evident in her interactive interviews and journaling.[33] Regrettably, she did not learn this in our teacher preparation program, even at a faith-based institution. While Trixie's time in our program did focus on how faith, or faith-based principles, can inform your chosen vocation, little to no time was spent on examining how spirituality gives sustenance to teaching. As a faculty member of the faith-based university Trixie attended, this revelation stunned me. Knowing that teaching is a stressful vocation, filled with a giving of oneself daily, I was shocked to realize that there had been little formal discussion of faith as sustenance in our program. The question as I now see it is this: As teacher educators at Christian colleges and universities, how do we prepare our preservice teachers to use their faith and spiritual practices to support the difficult work of teaching?

THE PATH FORWARD

If teaching is a spiritual endeavor, in that it allows those who teach to "answer the heart's longing to be connected with the largeness of life,"[34] Christian teacher education programs must begin to equip their students to ameliorate their stress through spiritual practices. While spiritual practices will look different for each individual due to personalities and faith traditions, attention must be given to the issue. Attending to the spiritual may include seeking solitude, meditating or meditative readings, walking along the beach or in the woods, keeping a journal, participating in a faith community, exploring hobbies, engaging in physical activities, or finding a friend or family member who will listen. Whatever it looks like for each

---

32. Palmer, *Courage to Teach*, 148.
33. Talley, "Under Construction."
34. Palmer, *Courage to Teach*, 5.

individual, it must be done. Teachers, and teacher educators, must be attuned to our inner being, the part inside of us all that longs to be connected to the largeness of life.

The Bible provides many illustrations in both the Old and New Testaments of God's people renewing their spirits and reconnecting to their faith. Examining the life of Jesus in the New Testament, believers can find several examples: Jesus spent time alone, he spent time with friends, he spent time in quiet and prayer. In Mark 6, when things were so busy that the disciples had not eaten or rested in some time, Jesus urged them, "Come with me by yourselves to a quiet place and get some rest" (Mark 6:31). The text then states the disciples went away by boat to find solitude. In the narrative of Jesus' time with his disciples, this brief respite happened during one of the most hectic periods of traveling, preaching, and performing miracles. In the midst of his brief life on earth, while fulfilling his holy ministry, Jesus understood the need for renewal. Palmer reminds us that "self-care is never a selfish act—it is simply good stewardship of the only gift I have, the gift I was put on earth to offer to others."[35]

Simply put, you cannot give what you don't have. Currently, few, if any, teacher education programs provide students with any instruction on how to cope with the daily stresses of teaching.[36] Drawing from data collected from a sample of 1,000 teachers, Hartwick found if matters of spirituality are discussed at all in a teacher education program, they are discussed in terms of being called to teach.[37] Teacher education programs must work towards extending this dialogue.

First and foremost, teacher educators must model for our students the connection between care for the soul and its connection to teaching. This is no easy feat. It demands that we are mindful of paying attention to our inner landscape and making public, when appropriate, our private faith practices. Many of us depend on our faith and our faith communities to sustain our work. However, grappling with how to share and model this with our preservice teachers is challenging. How do teacher educators have this conversation with students and yet maintain their status as the "expert" in the room? Freytag wrestles with the same question.[38] She suggests the most caring thing one can do is model what it means to be a "genuine human

---

35. Palmer, *Let Your Life Speak*, 30.
36. Hartwick and Kang, "Spiritual Practices."
37. Hartwick, "Religious and Prayer Lives."
38. Freytag, "Embodying and Modeling Healthy Self-Care."

being who exemplifies appropriate vulnerability by humbly admitting that I do not always have the answers and I, too, need help."[39]

In our program, faculty are attempting to engage in these conversations with our preservice teachers. I confess our attempts at times seem feeble and faculty continue to grapple with how to have intentional conversations with preservice teachers about faith to sustain them in the difficult work of teaching. As with most things, students will learn best through our modeling in our own lives how faith sustains our practices. In my practice, I attempt to share pieces of my own faith journey with my students. Conversations with students happen in individual, small-group, and large-group settings. This type of conversation requires vulnerability on my part. I must be open and honest about how I use my faith practices (journaling, participating in a small group, practicing solitude, etc.) to sustain me in teaching and why I need to do so. The conversations must include disclosing my own doubts, fears, and struggles. Doing so also requires that I admit to my preservice teachers the true difficulties of teaching in schools today. Often, as teacher educators, we are reluctant to fully discuss the enormous challenges facing teachers today for fear that it will discourage new teachers from entering the field.[40] Practicing this type of vulnerability with our students seems counter-intuitive, but it serves our teaching well.[41] Good teaching is a "daily exercise in vulnerability."[42] In modeling this type of vulnerability, teacher educators are giving their preservice teachers permission to be vulnerable as well, and this is necessary to sustain good teaching. As teachers of faith, it is important for us to remember that when we only allow our students to see the perfect image of self we present to the world, "we unknowingly set unrealistic expectations for others; but when we show our neighbors that we also need help and support, our transparency gives them permission to safely expose their humanity as well."[43]

EXAMPLES FROM ONE PROGRAM

On a larger scale, our department has attempted to have this conversation in an event we schedule at the end of the semester of student teaching. After students have completed their final week of student teaching, we call them

---

39. Freytag, "Embodying and Modeling Healthy Self-Care," 4.
40. Talley, "Under Construction."
41. Freytag, "Embodying and Modeling Healthy Self-Care"; Matthias, *Cry of the Teacher's Soul*.
42. Palmer, *Courage to Teach*, 17.
43. Freytag, "Embodying and Modeling Healthy Self-Care," 4.

back into community on campus for an event we call Launch. Based on my conversation with Trixie and other findings in my dissertation research, our faculty realized that after the most formative experience of their teacher education program, student teaching, we were simply ending the semester with little, if any, time to reflect on the events of student teaching in a meaningful or formative manner. During Launch, faculty spend one or two days, depending on what time allows, guiding students in both individual and group reflection so they may understand and learn from their student teaching experiences as fully as possible. A good deal of this time is spent discussing the need for spiritual practices—reflecting and journaling, seeking solitude and Sabbath, and participating in a faith community—as means of sustaining their teaching. Specifically, in Launch, faculty examine school culture and discuss how to find and contribute to a healthy school culture. Discussions include topics such as the need for quality mentors and how and where to find them in both their professional and personal lives. Conversations pertaining to the setting of appropriate boundaries for oneself and the necessity of healthy boundaries to protect the ability to care for self and others are also included. Students reflect on their use of time during student teaching and assess how time can and should be dedicated to self-care. After having been in the trenches, the teacher candidates have a greater understanding of the significance of the issue and are hungry for the conversation. I regret that we are saving this conversation for the end of program; however, as teacher educators, we are navigating the tension between what our students need to know and when they are able to know it.

Another event that holds potential for my program is our New Teacher Institute. In North American schools, 40 to 50 percent of teachers leave the profession within the first five years.[44] To combat the problem, our program annually hosts a New Teacher Institute the second weekend in June. Over the course of a long weekend, we provide fifteen hours of high-quality professional development, along with meals and lodging, to graduates of our program from the previous five years. During this weekend, alumni of our program learn from professionals and have the opportunity to mentor each other and the faculty of our program. This is done in community with each other in the place where they first started their teaching journey. At the end of the weekend, we give each teacher two books to read. One is a professional resource; the other is a spiritual read. While in the past, the conversations pertaining to faith and spiritual practices have been incidental and largely happened during communal meals, coffee breaks, and private

---

44. Ingersoll and Smith, "Wrong Solution"; Maciejewski, "Supporting New Teachers."

conversations, recent years have included speakers who address spiritual practices and their connection to teaching. While this program does not directly impact preservice teachers, it does influence teachers in the critical novice or induction period and has implications for preservice teachers as well. In the future, inviting teacher candidates into dialogue with the novice teachers may provide a safe space for conversations pertaining to faith as sustenance in teaching. Engaging in conversations with their peers, preservice teachers may be able to better comprehend the need to proactively prepare for the stresses of classroom teaching. It is one thing for a professor to discuss this issue in a university setting; it is a different matter entirely for a teacher candidate to hear an alumnus close to their own age, who is currently in the classroom, verbalize the real trials and tribulations of teaching and articulate the need for faith-informed self-care to sustain their practice.

Small group events also provide fertile ground for conversations pertaining to faith and teaching. Being with students in small groups outside of classroom instructional time allows for deeper relationships to develop among peers and with faculty. Teacher education faculty at my university host a variety of small-group events. One secondary professor hosts book talks at his home twice a month on Sunday evenings. Students share a meal with the faculty member and his family and then share conversations pertaining to the book of choice for the semester. Many times, the book has a spiritual theme. Secondary students overwhelmingly mention these book talks as one of the most formative experiences of their time in our program. One of my colleagues and I host a Rookie Club for new teachers in our local schools. If you are a graduate of our program and have been teaching for less than five years, you are invited once a month for dinner and conversation in one of our homes. We have a meal, a pertinent topic to discuss, and door prizes. Often with these practicing novice teachers, the conversation turns to matters of faith and teaching. In fact, many novice teachers express that simply making the time to come to Rookies every month is an act of self-care. While this is a ripe opportunity to work with novice teachers in the critical induction period, it also holds great potential for impacting practices with preservice teachers. First, the faculty members present learn a great deal about what was done well in the program and what work remains. Second, by providing support to local educators, faculty are training a new generation of mentor teachers for preservice candidates in our program. And, as above, there is the potential to invite preservice teachers into conversation with the novice teachers. Frequently, the faculty in our program utilize these novice teachers as mentors for students in the program, guest speakers in our university classrooms, and colleagues in curriculum development and design.

All the above practices, both formal and informal, are grounded in deep personal connections with students. This type of intentional relationship is one of the foundations of modeling healthy self-care for students.[45] Teacher preparation programs must explore options outside of the university classroom so that faculty may form the type of deep relationships necessary for conversations pertaining to our doubts, fears, and struggles, and how we utilize our faith as a means for sustaining our practice in the midst of these forces.

CONCLUSION

Four years later and my coffee cup is empty again. I am back at the coffee shop, my secret writing hideaway. The questions today seem bigger than ever. Trixie's question is still on my mind. And there are new questions. Another former student texted weeks ago saying, "I'm at the point of questioning why I even do what I do and if I am really cut out to be a special education teacher. I hate being beat down and going home every day totally mentally and emotionally drained."[46] Weeks later, she informed me she had decided to leave teaching. I can't help but wonder what factors contributed to her decision to leave and if there was any way our teacher preparation program could have prepared her to be more resilient. In her text message, I heard deep frustration. Her words and story echo those of Matthias who warns that teacher educators must listen to the cries of teachers because, if not addressed, "burnout and attrition will inevitably happen."[47] My recent experiences confirm her words. Two stellar novice teachers have confided in me in recent months that they will be leaving the classroom. In my mind, command of the content and love for their students is not the problem. Fatigue, frustration, and burnout lie at the heart of the issue. Could they have more fully called upon their faith in order to sustain their teaching? As a faith-sustained teacher educator, I cannot afford to allow students to fail to make the connection between their work lives and their faith journey. Preservice teachers must see their spiritual life and their academic life as fully integrated[48] because, as future teachers, they cannot be personally committed if they are not spiritually invested—and neither can their professors.

---

45. Freytag, "Exploring Perceptions of Care"; Freytag, "Embodying and Modeling Healthy Self-Care."
46. Former student, text to the author, April 2018.
47. Matthias, *Cry of the Teacher's Soul*, xv.
48. Shotsberger, "Faith Integration."

BIBLIOGRAPHY

Addleman, Rebecca A. "Service." In *Faithful Education: Themes and Values for Teaching, Learning and Leading,* edited by Amy Lynn Dee and Gary Tiffin, 142–55. Eugene, OR: Wipf & Stock, 2012.

Brueggemann, Walter. *Sabbath as Resistance: Saying No to the Culture of Now.* Louisville: Westminster John Knox, 2014.

Freytag, Cathy E. "Embodying and Modeling Healthy Self-Care in Teacher Education." *International Christian Community of Teacher Educators Journal* 11 (2016). http://digitalcommons.georgefox.edu/icctej/vol11/iss1/3

———. "Exploring Perceptions of Care in Christian Teacher Education Communities: Toward a Faith-Informed Framework of Care." *International Christian Community of Teacher Educators Journal* 10 (2015). http://digitalcommons.georgefox.edu/icctej/vol10/iss1/4.

Gates, Jeffrey. "Self Care: A Christian Perspective." *Evangelical Review of Theology* 39 (2015) 4–17.

Hartwick, James M. M. "The Religious and Prayer Lives of Public School Teachers." In *Christianity, Education, and Modern Society,* edited by William Jeynes and Enedina Martinez, 129–60. Charlotte: Information Age, 2007.

Hartwick, James M. M. and Shin Ji Kang. "Spiritual Practices as a Means of Coping with and Ameliorating Stress to Reduce Teacher Attrition." *Journal of Research on Christian Education* 22 (2013) 165–88.

Hopkins, Belinda. "Restorative Justice in Schools." *Support for Learning,* 17 (2002) 144–49.

Ingersoll, Richard M., and Thomas Smith. "The Wrong Solution to the Teacher Shortage." *Educational Leadership* 60 (2003) 30–33.

Jeffries, Carolyn, et al. "Toward a Culture of Self-Care." https://www.insidehighered.com/views/2017/08/18/value-self-careprograms-campus-essay.

Lewis, C. S. *Mere Christianity.* New York: Harper Collins, 1952.

Maciejewski, Jennifer. "Supporting New Teachers: Are Induction Programs Worth the Cost?" *District Administration* 43 (2001) 48–52.

Marzano, Robert. "How Classroom Teachers Approach the Teaching of Thinking." *Theory into Practice* 32 (1993) 154–60.

Matthias, Laurie R. *The Cry of the Teacher's Soul.* Eugene, OR: Wipf & Stock, 2015.

Noddings, Nel. *The Challenge to Care in Schools: An Alternative Approach to Education.* New York: Teachers College Press, 1992.

———. *Philosophy of Education,* 2nd ed. New York: Teachers College Press, 1984.

Noddings, Nel, and Laurie Brooks. *Teaching Controversial Issues: The Case for Critical Thinking and Moral Commitment in the Classroom.* New York: Teachers College Press, 2017.

Nouwen, Henri J. M. "Moving from Solitude to Community to Ministry: Jesus Established the True Order for Spiritual Work." *Leadership* 16 (1995) 81–87.

Palmer, Parker. *The Courage to Teach: Exploring the Inner Landscape of a Teacher's Life.* San Francisco: John Wiley and Sons, 1998.

———. *Let Your Life Speak: Listening for the Voice of Vocation.* San Francisco: John Wiley and Sons, 2000.

Riedel, Kirsten D., et al. "Teaching Students to Care for Themselves." In *A Calling to Care: Nurturing College Students Toward Wholeness,* edited by Timothy Herrman and Kirsten Riedel, 77–102. Abilene, TX: Abilene Christian University Press, 2018.

Shotsberger, Paul. "Faith Integration: What Does it Really Look Like?" *International Christian Community of Teacher Education Journal* 12 (2018). http://digitalcomons.georgefox.edu/icctej/vol12/iss2/5.

Talley, Stephanie. "Under Construction: An Autoethnographic Study of a Novice Teacher and Her Professor." PhD diss., Texas Tech University, 2014.

Tan, Siang-Yang, and Melissa Castillo. "Self-Care and Beyond: A Brief Literature Review from a Christian Perspective." *Journal of Psychology and Christianity* 33 (2014) 90–95.

Tomlinson, Carol Ann. *How to Differentiate Instruction in Mixed-Ability Classrooms.* 2nd ed. Alexandria, VA: ASCD, 2001.

Yankoski, Michael. *The Sacred Year: Mapping the Soulscape of Spiritual Practice—How Contemplating Apples, Living in a Cave and Befriending a Dying Woman Revived My Life.* Nashville: W, 2014.

Chapter 10

CARING FOR NEW TEACHERS ONCE THEY LEAVE CAMPUS

Elaine Tinholt

When I began my teaching career, I was filled with excitement and anticipation of what lay ahead. I was hired for my first teaching position at the end of May and spent the remaining summer months preparing to meet my students. I studied the teacher manuals for the content areas I would be teaching my first graders in the fall. I met with fellow teachers, janitors, and secretaries. I spent time decorating my classroom, purging file cabinets of the various accumulated materials that had not been used in several years, and even stenciling an apple border along the top of my classroom walls.

Through much prayer and hard work during that summer, I felt my classroom and lesson plans were well-prepared for the beginning of school. However, there were some aspects of being a first-year teacher that I had not been able to plan for during my summer months. As I began teaching, I felt dismayed by my students' slow academic progress. When I met with my first-grade teaching team, we would debrief about our students' progress in relation to the content we had been covering. I continually struggled to understand why my students were not able to comprehend the material at the same pace as the other first-grade students. My students had sweet dispositions and kind hearts, but there was something different about my class compared to my colleagues' students.

By the end of the first six weeks, I mustered the courage to approach my principal and confess my concerns about the lack of progress my students were making. I broke down in tears, thinking my students' struggles were the direct result of my inability to teach. It was at this watershed moment when my principal informed me that my classroom was comprised of students who had indicated prekindergarten levels of maturity and learning skills on their entry assessments. These students had been put together in the same class and assigned to the "new teacher" because they were sweet and kind. Administration felt the new person on the team would be able to focus on teaching content without having to worry about serious behavior problems. This news, while shocking, actually relieved me tremendously. I was able to adjust my expectations and choose more appropriate instructional strategies based on the needs of my students. From that point forward, I was able to focus on meeting their needs and developing their skills instead of measuring their performance against other students in the first grade. We progressed throughout the year, just at a different pace than the other classes. I ended my first year with a positive outlook on the teaching profession, despite the rocky beginning. Had I not gone to my principal and sought advice, I would have continued to struggle to meet the needs of my students and questioned my effectiveness as an educator.

My principal and fellow teachers tried to care for me by giving me the easy students, but they failed to communicate the constraints I was working within and the ways it should impact my pedagogy. I was not prepared to walk that road alone and could have used a support system to help me navigate the various needs that existed within my class. This lack of care made a significant mark on my first year of teaching and helped me in my Christian walk to take notice of others. Throughout Scripture, God shows special concern for those in need. He gives specific declarations to care for the widow, the orphan, and the poor. In the book of James, followers of Christ are called to put their faith into motion by caring for those who are afflicted. God also calls us to seek justice for the oppressed and offer refuge for those in distress. Isaiah reminds us to take notice of those around us and seek to do what is within our ability to ease their afflictions. As a Christian educator working in a public school setting, I was sometimes given opportunities to walk alongside fellow teachers as they experienced the challenges associated with the profession.

Fast forward twenty years and now I can see how God used my first year of teaching to influence my current perspective as a college professor working with preservice teachers. The education profession is demanding, rigorous, and challenging. Teachers feel pressure to meet the needs of their students, the desires of the parents, the expectations of their principals, and the content standards required for the state in which they teach. These pressures can be compounded for first-year teachers who are adjusting to both the freedom and responsibility that come with being the full-time lead teacher in a classroom setting. A lack of support can lead to higher stress levels, which may lower the new teacher's job satisfaction level.[1] This situation could also lower a first-year teacher's perception of the care being offered during this challenging time. Increased stress levels can cause these young professionals to question their career choice, and sometimes end their teaching career altogether. When an educator chooses to leave the profession, the school must then face the challenge of finding and training another highly qualified teacher.[2]

National studies report that three out of ten teachers either move schools or leave the profession altogether by the end of the first year of teaching.[3] Gray and Taie conducted an analysis of the Beginning Teacher Longitudinal Survey, which showed 17 percent of teachers who started teaching in 2008 left the profession completely over a four-year time period.[4] Induction-level teachers also report feelings of being overwhelmed, and experiencing self-doubt, frustration, and isolation.[5] New teachers may abandon the profession due to these negative feelings and emotions. However, this situation may be avoided when a school community recognizes the needs of first-year teachers and seeks to offer care in tangible ways.

THE ROLE OF TEACHER PREPARATION PROGRAMS

At the Christian college where I teach, we care deeply for our students and strive to integrate a perspective of care into our programmatic decisions. We seek to help our teacher candidates view their calling in education as a means of serving God by caring for his creation. The beauty, wisdom, and knowledge revealed in math, literature, science, history, and the arts can guide us to be effective stewards of his creation. Our courses seek to bring a perspective of redemption to the classroom through differentiated instruction, which honors the student as being made in the image of God by caring for their individual learning needs. The classroom management strategies we teach seek to restore broken relationships and help students care for their neighbors by recognizing how their actions affect those around them.

1. Womack et al., "Teachers' Perceptions."
2. Perrachione et al., "Why Do They Stay?"
3. Smith and Ingersoll, "What are the Effects?"
4. Gray and Taie, "Public School Teacher Attrition."
5. Fry, "Analysis of an Unsuccessful Novice."

Educators are seen as models and facilitators of care in the K-12 setting by the way they engage students in active learning, approach curriculum from an integrated perspective, and foster relationships with students.

To help care for our teacher candidates and prepare them for the role of being an educator, they enter the teacher preparation program in a cohort model during the spring of their junior year. For three semesters, the candidates take courses together, work collaboratively on group projects, and support one another through peer feedback on certain assignments. Over time, the cohort begins to function as a learning community with shared experiences and goals. Our Education Department helps our candidates prepare for the final semester of Clinical Practice by hosting a Partnership Meeting prior to the start of the semester. Our college pays for substitute teachers to allow mentor teachers to come to campus for an entire day and spend time with their teacher candidates. The day-long meeting is spent discussing ideas to make the clinical practice experience beneficial for both the teacher candidate and the mentor teacher. This event offers all those involved in the clinical practice experience—teacher candidates, mentor teachers, and college supervisors—the opportunity to discuss what care looks like in the classroom setting. Throughout the clinical practice experience, the teacher candidate is offered support through eight to ten observations and post-observation conferences conducted by his or her college supervisor. The mentor teacher is also present each day to observe and offer feedback to the teacher candidate. In conjunction with Clinical Practice, seminar meetings are held on a weekly basis to allow the candidates to connect with their fellow classmates and discuss topics applicable to the clinical practice experience. During this phase of their professional development, the teacher candidates have multiple support structures in place, such as mentoring, ongoing feedback, and a community of fellow teacher candidates, to help care for them throughout the learning experience.

STRUCTURING HIGHER EDUCATION PRACTICES TO PREPARE NEW TEACHERS

When candidates graduate, and are hired as teachers, there is a drastic shift in support. The feedback they were accustomed to receiving is often lacking in their new school setting. As new teachers, they face challenges that are associated with inexperience in their chosen profession. Such issues include lack of resources, parent-teacher conferences, building relationships with colleagues, the dynamics of bureaucracy that can exist within an organization, and teaching state standards despite a lack of funding for materials to support effective learning strategies.[6] To help prepare new teachers for these challenges, higher education is encouraged to collaborate with school districts to inform teacher candidates of the demanding environments associated with education as a means of decreasing the risk of stress for first-year teachers and to help avoid possible burnout.[7]

Traditional preservice preparation consists of content-based courses, fieldwork experiences, and student teaching, all of which occur under the guidance of a higher education establishment. The components of content, theory, and practice are structured in ways to offer scaffolding for college students as they transition into teaching practitioners. Ronfeldt, Schwartz, and Jacob used the data offered in the national 2007–2008 Schools and Staffing Survey to conduct an analysis of the respondents' preservice preparation, retention, and perceptions of preparedness.[8] Based on the survey responses, teachers who completed more methods-related coursework and practice teaching felt better prepared and were more likely to stay in teaching. These findings are consistent with the prior research of Boe, et al., which utilized the 1999–2000 Schools and Staffing Survey.[9] The 1999–2000 survey data indicated teachers with extensive preparation in pedagogy and practice reported being better prepared to teach assigned subject matter. The data gained from two administrations of the Schools and Staffing Survey indicate two ways in which higher education can care for future educators: requiring more practice teaching, and increasing methods-related coursework.

PREPARING GRADUATES FOR THE CHALLENGES OF THE FIRST YEAR OF TEACHING

Reflecting on my first year of teaching, I can now recognize the types of support systems that were missing. At the time, I was just trying to meet my students' needs and learn the curriculum I was teaching. These tasks overwhelmed me and left little time to reflect on what I needed in the way of support. I was so busy caring for my students that I did not know I needed to seek care for myself. This care could have come from colleagues, administrators, mentors, or former professors. It would have been helpful to have another voice speaking into the situation, offering guidance and suggestions on how to cope with the stresses I was facing.

---

6. U.S. Department of Education, "Survival Guide for New Teachers."
7. Fitchett et al., "Examination of US First-Year Teachers' Risk."
8. Ronfeldt et al. "Does Preservice Preparation Matter?"
9. Boe et al., "Does Teacher Preparation Matter?"

College-based support for teacher graduates is recommended, and sometimes mandated, in various states.[10] Institutions of higher education have control when teacher candidates are under their direct supervision, taking specific courses, and participating in selected fieldwork experiences. During the clinical practice experience, colleges can choose the mentor teachers who work with teacher candidates. During this critical time of candidates' professional development, it is essential that they be placed with teachers who are skilled at mentoring young educators, through the means of caring relationships, and not just placed in a setting to develop their teaching skills.[11] College faculty can oversee and support the development of caring relationships through frequent observations and ongoing communication with both the teacher candidate and the mentor teacher. However, even the best preparation programs cannot foresee every challenge a first year teacher may face. There is a growing understanding among educational establishments that teaching is complex and that a significant portion of the knowledge needed for success has to be acquired on the job.[12]

Teacher preparation programs are given a short window of time to prepare candidates for the expectations associated with the career. Programs are expected to cover required content the teacher candidates will need to know, address appropriate pedagogy based on the developmental levels of students, equip teacher candidates with classroom management strategies, and instruct them on how to analyze student data and adjust their teaching practices based on the learning that is or is not occurring. Given the amount of information preparation programs must cover, it is easy to overlook the on-the-job challenges faced by first-year teachers, such as working in collaboration with other teachers, parents, and administrators, implementing management systems, and finding a balance between teaching and life outside of the school setting. As a means of caring for future educators, these challenges can become focus topics for seminar classes offered during a teacher candidate's final semester of college. Creating time within the clinical practice semester to host informative meetings can help future graduates consider the impact these issues will have on their teaching experience. It can also prepare them for the interview process by allowing them to think through key questions they may want to ask concerning the types of professional development opportunities and support they will be given during their first year of teaching. Preparing teacher candidates to navigate uncharted waters can help them avoid feeling overwhelmed during

10. Ingersoll, "Beginning Teacher Induction."
11. Fry, "Characteristics and Experiences."
12. Ingersoll, "Beginning Teacher Induction."

their first year of teaching and allow them to continue developing their teaching abilities.

HIGHER EDUCATION PARTNERSHIPS

Several higher education institutions are exploring creative partnerships with school districts to support early-career teachers. Huling, et al. reported on an innovative induction support program developed by the Texas State University System in partnership with thirty-seven school districts.[13] Through the program, recently retired teachers were hired to provide mentoring services for new teachers. Each retired teacher worked two and a half days per week observing and conferencing with an assigned eight to ten new teachers. The mentor teachers also attended evening meetings and trainings to support their own professional development in the mentoring process. The new teachers were enrolled in graduate courses at the participating universities. One requirement of the graduate course work was a biweekly seminar that focused on a wide range of issues encountered by teachers during their first year in the profession. Based on the five-year retention rate for three different cohorts that participated in the study, the teachers remained in the profession at a higher rate of 4 to 10 percent more than other teachers across the state who did not participate in the program. The higher retention rate suggests participation in a university-based induction program had a positive impact on new teacher retention over a five-year period. The higher retention rate may also indicate the positive effect care plays in a teacher's decision to remain in the profession.

These findings are similar to a study conducted by Carr and Evans.[14] In the study, Southeastern Louisiana University developed an induction program incorporating graduate-level courses. The first-year teachers are employed by the university through a twelve-month contract agreement with the participating school district. Participants are offered support by both an assigned mentor teacher and a faculty member from the university. Mentor teachers are employed by the local school districts and are assigned two to four new teachers, with the expectation they will spend six to eight hours weekly in each classroom. The mentors assess the new teacher's classroom instruction and model various teaching methods. University faculty members also meet weekly with the mentor teachers to discuss the practicum. Faculty members visit the new teachers' classrooms and any observed needs are addressed in the graduate courses being taught. Over a seven-year

---

13. Huling et al., "Supporting and Retaining Novice Teachers."
14. Carr and Evans, "Helping Beginning Teachers Remain."

span, of the seventy new teachers who participated in the program, sixty-three (90 percent) remained in teaching. This finding suggests that early support structures and university partnerships play a pivotal role in teacher retention.

Building supportive relationships can be viewed as a means of caring for both new teachers and the students they seek to serve. As teachers feel supported, they are able to focus less on self-preservation and more on caring for the academic, social, and emotional needs of their students. When teachers build relationships with students, they are able to establish a foundation to support successful pedagogical activities while creating a positive learning environment.[15]

SUPPORTING FIRST-YEAR TEACHERS

As Christian educators, the call to support and care for new teachers is even more poignant. Christ cared for those around him. He recognized people's needs and his ability to minister to them in their given situations. As believers and followers of Christ, we are called to offer to each other the presence of God in us, through our words and actions.[16] A Christian ethic of care can be demonstrated by being cognizant of the challenges new teachers face and offering supportive communication. In a college classroom setting, the student's ability to learn and ask for guidance can be negatively impacted by the environment the professor creates.[17] I believe the same can be said for the school settings where new teachers are employed. The school environment can be either inviting or forbidding, based on the interactions new teachers have with colleagues. New teachers are often hesitant to ask for help, unless they feel the source of potential assistance can be trusted. Revealing their inadequacies can be either freeing or humiliating, the result being dependent upon the response of the listener. As Christian educators in school settings, we can be Christ's hands to new teachers by embracing them, along with their challenges and frustrations.

---

15. Noddings, "Caring in Education."
16. Frank, "'Ethic of Care.'"
17. Ambrose et al., *How Learning Works*.

Novice Teachers Benefit from Reflective Practice and Seeking Advice

Novice teachers experience a professional transition during their first year of teaching. As college students, they were supported through interactions and observations conducted by college supervisors and mentor teachers. This process offers ongoing feedback during a developmental stage of professional growth. As a lead teacher, novice teachers may not have the same opportunity to receive this level of feedback concerning professional endeavors such as lesson planning, interacting with parents, and dealing with classroom management issues. Beginning teachers generally look to other teachers for solutions to problems they encounter.[18] It is during this time that new teachers can analyze their situations and draw upon the wisdom found in their own teaching community as a means of finding support. Novice teachers can help themselves by engaging in reflective practice and seeking advice, participating in collaboration with peers, and taking part in collective leadership opportunities.

Colleges and universities can prepare preservice teachers for this transitional time by encouraging them to engage in planning and reflection with their assigned mentor teachers during the clinical practice experience. One component could include an observation of a lesson conducted simultaneously by both the mentor teacher and the college supervisor. After the observation, the teacher candidate, mentor teacher, and college supervisor meet to discuss the observation. This dialogue opportunity can offer the teacher candidate a chance to engage in reflective practice and seek advice on how to improve in the areas of instructional strategies and student engagement. This process also allows teacher candidates to understand how this kind of conversation is a form of care and not just an assessment of their teaching abilities.

Reflective practice is based in real-life dilemmas, which allow new teachers to think deeply, problem-solve, and feel confident in their ability to meet the needs of their students.[19] Cherkowski defined reflective practice as an inquiry into the learning and teaching conditions of a school, with a focus on engaging in school improvement.[20] When a teacher engages in personal reflection and development with a focus on the well-being of self and others, colleagues and students also benefit from this process.

---

18. Smith, "Faculty Mentors in Teacher Induction."
19. Yost, "Reflection and Self-Efficacy."
20. Cherkowski, "Positive Teacher Leadership."

Research suggests that when teachers employ reflective practice to analyze student learning and assess the effectiveness of instructional strategies, their self-confidence can be enhanced.[21] Yost conducted a qualitative study concerning teacher reflection and self-efficacy.[22] Through the process of interviewing second-year teachers and observing their teaching performance, as well as interviewing principals who supervised the teachers, Yost found critical reflection was a problem-solving strategy that teachers employed to cope with the challenges associated with the first few years of teaching. In order for novice teachers to become successful, they need time to reflect on their practice and determine solutions for solving problems.

Successful professional experiences during the first years of teaching can enhance a new teacher's desire to remain in the profession.[23] Teachers report having a higher degree of job satisfaction when they feel like they are making a difference in the lives of students.[24] For success to occur, new teachers can identify key areas of their own teaching practices in which they need additional support. Suriano, et al. conducted a case study based on an induction support program being implemented in an elementary school.[25] The new teachers identified areas in which they wanted support, then a school-wide curriculum team, consisting of instructional coaches and curriculum administrators, planned how that support would be given. Sources of support included instructional coaching, assistance with classroom management and setup, instructional modeling, and individual teacher professional development plans. After implementation of the new program, the teacher attrition rate dropped from 60 percent to 10 percent. New teachers who returned credited their decision to the support they received from school leadership, experienced teachers, and supportive peer relationships. Receiving care from multiple sources positively affected the teachers' perceptions of their school environment. This study highlights the benefits related to teacher retention when new teachers are allowed to seek advice from the broader school community. Experiencing support from multiple sources can help new teachers understand how they are valued and cared for in their specific school setting.

Schools that support new teachers view relationships as central and at the core of all the work and learning that happens within the school environment. This perspective on school culture can foster well-being for

21. Kelley, "Why Induction Matters."
22. Yost, "Reflection and Self-Efficacy."
23. Fry, "Characteristics and Experiences."
24. Wang et al., "Self-Efficacy and Causal Attributions."
25. Suriano et al., "Here to Stay."

all.[26] Research suggests that communication and collaboration can support teacher retention. Smith and Ingersoll found that activities involving teacher collaboration, such as shared planning time or regularly scheduled discussions concerning instructional practices, reduced the risk of new teachers leaving a school by 43 percent.[27] Having collegial support can ease the transition new teachers experience as they grow in their chosen profession.[28]

Constructive Feedback

Institutions of higher education need to facilitate preservice teachers' developing ability to seek and receive constructive feedback, which can be an ongoing component of the formal observation process. Constructive feedback focuses on improving the observed teaching skills of preservice and novice educators. Many new teachers are provided with a mentor teacher to help them transform into the role of lead teacher during the induction phase. Mentors can establish a caring relationship by treating new teachers as respected colleagues and devoting time to providing constructive criticism of their teaching.[29] Through post-observation conversations, mentors can ask the novice teachers why they did something and then suggest ways to improve the teaching practice, as needed. Feedback on the use of strategies and collaboration on the implementation of the strategies also helps new teachers improve their instructional practices.[30] Standards and data-based conversations aid in new teacher development more than casual feedback that is not supported by evidence.[31] This time investment can extend care to new teachers as they navigate and master the challenges of the new profession.

Structuring and maintaining quality feedback assists novice teachers as they establish their own classroom protocols and teaching methods. Hannan, et al. conducted a qualitative case study analysis of a Feedback Management System constructed by the Building a Teaching Effectiveness Network (BTEN) organization.[32] The Feedback Management System included conversation protocols, observation cycles, surveys, and coordination meetings aimed at supporting novice teachers. Participating teachers worked with principals and support facilitators to develop goals for classroom practices.

26. Cherkowski, "Positive Teacher Leadership."
27. Smith and Ingersoll, "What are the Effects?"
28. Schuck et al., "Experiences of Early Career Teachers."
29. Algozzine et al., "Beginning Teachers' Perceptions."
30. Sowell, "Effective Practices for Mentoring."
31. Wiebke and Bardin, "New Teacher Support."
32. Hannan et al., "Using Improvement Science."

Based on follow-up conversations with the novice teacher, the support team would determine whether the new teacher was ready for an observation that would show evidence of meeting predetermined goals. After the observation, the observer and new teacher would have a follow-up conference to discuss whether the goals were met. The new teacher and support team would begin working together to develop new goals once the original goals were met. If the goals were not met, the new teacher would continue to work on that specific focus area. The ten schools that participated in the Feedback Management System reported that regular and targeted conversations appeared to support the development of positive relationships and encouraged new teachers' participation in the school environment. When new teachers are able to identify personal struggles and seek assistance from the broader community, they feel cared for and valued as contributing members of that community.

Induction Support Structures

When teachers participate in a collaborative culture in which they actively contribute to the decision-making process, they have the opportunity to assume new leadership roles.[33] Incorporating novice teachers in this process allows them to foster trusting relationships with colleagues, consider possible instructional initiatives that meet the needs of their students, and begin developing as teacher leaders through professional growth of their own skills and dispositions.

In order to successfully meet the expectations of being a lead teacher, novice teachers must implement strategies they learned through their teacher preparation program and during their student-teaching experience.[34] New teachers need different levels and methods of support during this initial period.[35] Based on qualitative data gathered from fifteen case studies conducted over a five-year period, Cochran-Smith, et al. reported that different teachers need different forms of support, both to improve their instructional practices and to increase the chances of remaining in a particular school setting.[36] When structured properly, induction support can help novice teachers apply what they have learned to their new setting, build confidence in their teaching abilities, and remove the stress associated with unknown expectations. Support structures for first-year teachers can

33. Nicholson et al., "Using a Teacher Leadership Network."
34. Fry, "Characteristics and Experiences."
35. Sowell, "Effective Practices for Mentoring."
36. Cochran-Smith et al., "Longitudinal Study of Teaching Practice."

include formalized introduction programs, implementation of a mentoring program, and mutually beneficial partnerships between school systems and universities. Caring for new teachers through multiple support systems also translates into caring for the students they serve.

The purpose of induction support is to offer scaffolding for new teachers as they develop the skills and dispositions needed to be successful in their chosen profession. How the induction support is structured may determine the overall effectiveness of the program. The Alliance for Excellent Education offers parameters for determining a comprehensive induction program.[37] The term "comprehensive induction" refers to multiple levels of support that are offered to new teachers during their first year in the profession. The components of a comprehensive induction program include high-quality mentoring from carefully selected teachers who teach in the same grade level or content area, implementation of regularly scheduled common planning time with grade-level or content-area peers, ongoing professional development focused on student learning, and the opportunity to network with other educators outside of their own school setting. The American Institute for Research reports similar findings by the New Teacher Center.[38] For successful implementation of an induction program, the New Teacher Center highlights the need to support participating staff and create a collaborative community to foster a novice teacher's professional development. Some of the specific conditions for success of a teacher induction program include leadership support for making the program sustainable, guidance for helping new teachers employ evidence-based instruction and how to use data to improve practice, opportunities to collaborate with and observe experienced teachers, and a positive instructional community climate and culture. These structures offer wrap-around support measures as a means of caring for new teachers while they develop their professional persona.

Certain support structures used during the induction phase of teaching have been shown to aid in teacher retention. Ronfeldt and McQueen reported on a quantitative study to determine if there was a measurable relationship between teacher induction supports and teacher migration and retention.[39] The structured induction supports that were measured included having an assigned mentor, participation in seminars, common planning time with peers, supportive communication with administration or department chairs, a reduced schedule for new teachers, and being provided with a teacher's aide. The data showed the more extensive the number of supports

---

37. Alliance for Excellent Education, "Tapping the Potential."
38. American Institute for Research, "Conditions for Success."
39. Ronfeldt and McQueen, "Does New Teacher Induction?"

that were offered, the less likely teachers were to leave the profession. When a first-year teacher was offered four to six support structures, the migration and attrition rates were four to five percentage points lower as compared to teachers who received fewer than four support structures. This finding suggests the importance of offering multiple levels of induction support during the first year of teaching.

During the first year of their profession, new teachers can experience the loneliness of a new setting, and in this particularly vulnerable time, they may lack supporting relationships to ensure their success. Mentoring programs can care for new teachers by offering systematic, intense mentoring in the first year as a means of support for developing their teaching skills, planning lessons, and problem-solving.[40] Based on an exploratory case study, Sowell found three elements necessary for the effective implementation of a mentoring program: First, the mentoring process begins by establishing a trusting relationship with the new teacher; next, the mentor teacher offers guidance to aid the new teacher in creating a positive classroom environment; finally, the mentor teacher offers support for the new teacher in the form of instructional strategies focused on the content and context of the classroom setting.[41] Through this systematic mentoring process, the new teacher is offered ongoing support to aid in student learning.

Through the use of a qualitative study, Fry also found similar benefits associated with providing mentors for new teachers.[42] In the study, first-year teachers were better supported when they were provided with caring, eager, and capable mentor teachers who had common planning times and taught in similar content areas or grade levels. Having the new teachers' classrooms in close proximity to their teaching peers was another key finding for fostering mentoring relationships. When teachers' classrooms are located in close proximity to their peers, it allows for new teachers to collaborate with others and avoid feelings of isolation. The implementation of common planning time with colleagues further supported new teacher development. Based on the results of her study, Fry also recommended encouraging new teachers to develop a support network that goes beyond their assigned mentors. Seeking advice from veteran teachers would be one way to foster relationships while gaining knowledge based on the prior experiences of others. Similar to Fry's results, Lozinak conducted a study in which participants' surveys, interviews, and observations were analyzed to determine patterns

---

40. Scherer, "Challenges of Supporting New Teachers."
41. Sowell, "Effective Practices for Mentoring."
42. Fry, "First-Year Teachers and Induction Support."

in the responses.[43] A common theme that emerged was providing a mentor in the same school to improve the induction process. Participants indicated that accessibility of the mentors to the mentees created a stronger sense of support. Participants also recommended that mentors/mentees should be at least in a similar grade or content area. This commonality allows mentors to offer specific support for instructional challenges, parent interactions, and content planning.

The New Teacher Center offers recommendations concerning how to approach the mentoring process.[44] First, a school or administrator should begin by implementing selectivity when choosing mentors who exhibit the qualities needed to build caring relationships. Mentor teachers should possess qualities such as evidence of effective teaching practices, strong interpersonal skills, respect from peers, and knowledge of professional development. Second, mentor teachers need to be offered ongoing professional development to refine the skills needed for coaching beginning teachers. Third, to ensure sustainability, it is recommended that a set time be established for weekly meetings between the mentor teacher and the new teacher. Ideally, 1.25–2.5 hours per week is recommended to allow for in-depth mentoring activities and discussion. Fourth, as a means of ongoing support, the mentoring experience should be extended to include the second year of teaching. During both the first and second year of the mentoring process, a common focus should be on guiding the new teacher in implementing instructional strategies to support student growth. As a means of caring for new teachers, they should be offered specific steps to help them improve their skills and abilities in relation to teaching practices. Based on an exploratory case study, Sowell reported positive outcomes of improving new teacher instructional strategies through the implementation of co-teaching, modeling, and planning teaching strategies with a mentor teacher.[45]

Supportive Communication with Administrators

Support and care for first-year teachers can come from multiple sources, including colleagues, family, parents, and the school community. However, research indicates one of the most influential sources of support for new teachers is the interactions they have with administrators. In a survey of 106 first-year teachers, Quinn and Andrews report that first-year teachers who feel they have supportive principals also perceive they are receiving support

43. Lozinak, "Mentor Matching Does Matter."
44. New Teacher Center, "High-Quality Mentoring and Induction Practices."
45. Sowell, "Effective Practices for Mentoring."

from their colleagues.[46] Based on the survey data, there is a significant correlation between the total support scores and principal support scores. The researchers concluded that principals who set an example of supporting first-year teachers develop a community perspective, which leads to staffs that are also supportive of those teachers. These supportive communities can reduce stress factors for new teachers and curb tendencies that lead to teacher attrition. Fitchett, et al. used the US National Center for Education Statistics Beginning Teachers Longitudinal study to classify new teachers according to their risk for stress.[47] Findings indicate teachers classified as at-risk for stress reported more burnout symptoms and less classroom control. The researchers highlighted the role of administrators in caring for new teachers by reducing the stress factors associated with the first year of teaching through spearheading initiatives that make use of professional induction programs.

Interactions with administrators can influence a new teacher's decision to remain at a school. Smith and Ingersoll found regular supportive communication with the school principal or other administrators was associated with reducing the likelihood of new teachers leaving the school.[48] Through an analysis of a more recent administration of the same survey, Ronfeldt and McQueen's research indicated receiving supportive communication from school leadership reduced the odds of migrating schools by nine percentage points.[49] Consistent with Smith and Ingersoll, the study's findings indicate in terms of migration, supportive communication persisted at significant levels across five years.[50] Therefore, supportive communication from principals was perceived as caring for new teachers and positively affected a teacher's decision to remain at a school.

Supportive Communication with Colleagues

To grow and develop as an educational practitioner, novice teachers also need the support and experience of veteran teachers.[51] Experienced teachers can aid novice teachers in structuring classroom routines, refining teaching practices, planning for instruction, and learning how to work alongside parents to guide students toward academic success. Working through the

46. Quinn and Andrews, "Struggles of First-Year Teachers."
47. Fitchett et al., "Examination of US First-Year Teachers' Risk."
48. Smith and Ingersoll, "What are the Effects?"
49. Ronfeldt and McQueen, "Does New Teacher Induction?"
50. Smith and Ingersoll, "What are the Effects?"
51. Rodgers and Skelton, "Professional Development and Mentoring."

challenges of first-year teaching with experienced educators allows new teachers to develop strong relationships with their colleagues.[52]

Developing a network of support through interactions with colleagues allows novice teachers to ask questions, seek guidance, and consider choices from multiple perspectives. Clandinin, et al. conducted a qualitative study in which forty induction-level teachers were interviewed concerning their personal experiences as they began their professional careers.[53] A thematic analysis of the interviews revealed the theme of support as a key finding. Through interactions with colleagues, new teachers recognized they were not alone in their challenges and developed a communication network with others. These communication supports ranged from collegial or collaborative interactions, formal or informal support, support from a teaching partner, and time with a principal. Participants stated they felt these support structures made a difference in the quality of their work. Boyd, et al. found the role of support was a common theme revealed in surveys of first-year teachers in New York City.[54] Based on the five survey questions dealing with staff relations, respondents were positive about building relationships with other staff members. The most positive response focused on getting good advice from other teachers in their schools when they have a teaching problem. These studies highlight the important role peer relationships play in caring for new teachers.

Perceptions of beginning teachers concerning the effectiveness of support structures offers guidance on what strategies are effective in developing educators. Positive outcomes are associated with other teachers making beginning teachers feel like part of the teaching community.[55] This relationship-building can begin with supportive communication to aid novice teachers as they navigate the profession, then develop into constructive critique focused on teacher and student growth.

PRACTICAL WAYS TO CARE FOR NOVICE TEACHERS

To cope with feelings of ambiguity, new teachers should be encouraged to become their own self-advocates by seeking out support systems through colleagues or administrators. Parker Palmer highlighted the need for teachers to reach out to their community of colleagues as a means of enhancing

---

52. Fry, "Characteristics and Experiences."
53. Clandinin et al., "Early Career Teacher Attrition."
54. Boyd et al., "Influence of School Administrators."
55. Algozzine et al., "Beginning Teachers' Perceptions."

both professional practice and personal growth.[56] Recognizing when and how to seek help may be hard at first, but it can be rewarding in the long run.

Preparation programs are encouraged to institute a formal follow-up to find out how the graduates are doing in their new jobs.[57] An electronic survey can be used to determine how well-prepared the graduates felt as they progressed through their first year of teaching. The information gained can then aid in determining if changes need to be made to the preparation programs so that candidates will be ready for the teaching field. Based on the survey results, institutions could offer webinars for certain areas of concern indicated by the graduates. The webinar topics could cover such issues as the use of assessment results for differentiation, navigating the nuances of working with administrators and parents, and ways to initiate collaborative communities to avoid feelings of isolation. To accommodate teachers' busy schedules, the webinars could be recorded and offered as a resource for teachers who were not able to participate in the initial event. Many of the challenges faced by first-year teachers result from learning what it means to be contributing members of their new community. Staying in touch with graduates is a form of care that institutions of higher education can offer during this time of transition and discovery.

During their college years, teacher candidates work closely alongside faculty members to learn the art and craft of teaching. Freytag found that teacher candidates felt cared for by faculty members when the faculty members were intentional about building personal relationships with students.[58] Intentionality begins with understanding the challenges faced by those who are choosing to go into the field of education. A means of caring for teacher candidates is to help them understand the challenges they will face in the classroom setting while also supporting the development of dispositional skills needed to weather those challenges. Once teacher candidates graduate, maintaining a relationship of care between faculty members and new teachers may require professors to initiate the process by serving as a point of contact. Often, first-year teachers are overwhelmed with their own duties and responsibilities, leaving little time for research in their content areas. College professors can offer support by sharing resources and information concerning current research on best practices. Establishing online support communities is another way to allow graduates to stay connected with each other and former professors. Colleges can create regional networks for

---

56. Palmer, *Courage to Teach*.
57. U.S. Department of Education, "Survival Guide for New Teachers."
58. Freytag, "Exploring Perceptions of Care."

graduates who are hired in the same school district. The network would be structured to pair alumni who are experienced teachers with first-year teachers who have been hired in the same school district. The two teachers would share a common foundation based on their college experience and training in pedagogy. This shared perspective could help foster a working relationship and allow the new teacher to be more open about struggles he or she may be facing. For graduates who teach locally, colleges could invite them back to speak to preservice teachers concerning the successes and challenges they faced during their first year. Such opportunities would allow graduates to offer wisdom to the upcoming teachers, while remaining connected to their alma mater.

CONCLUSION

Caring for new teachers first begins with noticing their needs. Some needs may be evident at the moment: teaching materials, guidance in learning new curriculum, becoming knowledgeable of school procedures and processes. However, other needs may arise over time: feelings of isolation, questions about parent/student dynamics, or issues related to classroom management. As college professors, administrators, and fellow teachers, we need to acknowledge the challenges faced by first-year teachers and then look for ways to walk alongside them as they move forward in their careers. As we think of ways to care for new teachers, we are also caring for the students they serve in their classrooms.

BIBLIOGRAPHY

Algozzine, Bob, et al. "Beginning Teachers' Perceptions of Their Induction Program Experiences." *The Clearing House* 80 (2007) 137–43.

Alliance for Excellent Education. "Tapping the Potential: Retaining and Developing High-Quality New Teachers." https://all4ed.org/reports-factsheets/tapping-the-potential-retaining-and-developing-high-quality-new-teachers/.

Ambrose, Susan A., et al. *How Learning Works: Seven Research-Based Principles for Smart Teaching*. San Francisco: Jossey-Bass, 2010.

American Institute for Research. "Conditions for Success in Teacher Induction." https://lincs.ed.gov/publications/te/conditions.pdf.

Boe, Ed, et al. "Does Teacher Preparation Matter for Beginning Teachers in Either Special or General Education?" *The Journal of Special Education* 41 (2007) 158–70.

Boyd, Donald, et al. "The Influence of School Administrators on Teacher Retention Decisions." *American Educational Research Journal* 48 (2011) 303–33.

Carr, Sonya C., and Elizabeth D. Evans. "Helping Beginning Teachers Remain in the Profession: A Successful Induction Program." *Teacher Education and Special Education* 29 (2006) 113–15.

Cherkowski, Sabre. "Positive Teacher Leadership: Building Mindsets and Capacities to Grow Well-being." *International Journal of Teacher Leadership* 9 (2018) 63–78.

Clandinin, D. J., et al. "Early Career Teacher Attrition: Intentions of Teachers Beginning." *Teaching Education* 26 (2015) 1–16.

Cochran-Smith, Marilyn, et al. "A Longitudinal Study of Teaching Practice and Early Career Decisions." *American Educational Research Journal* 49 (2012) 844–80.

Fitchett, Paul G., et al. "An Examination of US First-Year Teachers' Risk for Occupational Stress: Associations with Professional Preparation and Occupational Health." *Teachers and Teaching: Theory and Practice* 24 (2018) 99–118.

Frank, Kim. "The 'Ethic of Care' and the Christian Faith." *Educating with Reverence.* (2013). https://educatingwithreverence.com/2013/05/.

Freytag, Cathy E. "Exploring Perceptions of Care in Christian Teacher Education Communities: Toward a Faith-Informed Framework of Care." *International Christian Community of Teacher Educators Journal* 10 (2015). https://digitalcommons.georgefox.edu/cgi/viewcontent.cgi?article=1129&context=icctej

Fry, Sara W. "The Analysis of an Unsuccessful Novice Teacher's Induction Experiences: A Case Study Presented through Layered Account." *The Qualitative Report* 15 (2010) 1134–90.

———. "Characteristics and Experiences that Contribute to Novice Elementary Teachers' Success and Efficacy." *Teacher Education Quarterly* 1 (2009) 95–110.

———. "First-Year Teachers and Induction Support: Ups, Downs, and In-Between." *The Qualitative Report* 12 (2007) 216–37.

Gray, Lucinda, and Soheyla Taie. "Public School Teacher Attrition and Mobility in the First Five Years: Results from the First through Fifth Waves of the 2007–08 Beginning Teacher Longitudinal Study." https://nces.ed.gov/pubs2015/2015337.pdf.

Hannan, Maggie, et al. "Using Improvement Science to Better Support Beginning Teachers." *Journal of Teacher Education* 66 (2015) 494–508.

Huling, Leslie, et al. "Supporting and Retaining Novice Teachers." *Kappa Delta Pi Record* 48 (2012) 140–43.

Ingersoll, Richard M. "Beginning Teacher Induction: What the Data Tell Us." *Phi Delta Kappan* 93 (2012) 47–51.

Ingersoll, Richard M., and Thomas M. Smith. "Do Teacher Induction and Mentoring Matter?" *NASSP Bulletin* 88 (2004) 28–40.

Kelley, Linda M. "Why Induction Matters." *Journal of Teacher Education* 55 (2004) 438–48.

Lozinak, Kathleen. "Mentor Matching Does Matter." *The Delta Kappa Gamma Bulletin* 83 (2016) 12–23.

New Teacher Center. "High-Quality Mentoring and Induction Practices." *New Teacher Center Reflections* 10 (2008) 14–15.

Nicholson, Julie, et al. "The Affordances of Using a Teacher Leadership Network to Support Leadership." *Teacher Education Quarterly* 43.1 (Winter 2016) 29–50. https://files.eric.ed.gov/fulltext/ EJ1097616.pdf

Noddings, Nel. "Caring in Education." *The Encyclopedia of Informal Education* (2005). http://infed.org/mobi/caring-in-education/.

Palmer, Parker J. *The Courage to Teach.* San Francisco: Jossey-Bass, 1998.

Perrachione, Beverly A., et al. "Why Do They Stay? Elementary Teachers' Perceptions of Job Satisfaction and Retention." *Professional Educator* 32 (2008) 1–17.

Quinn, Robert J., and Byllie D. Andrews. "The Struggles of First-Year Teachers." *The Clearing House* 77 (2004) 164–68.

Rodgers, Christopher, and Jillian Skelton. "Professional Development and Mentoring in Support of Teacher Retention." *Journal on School Educational Technology* 9 (2014) 1–11.

Ronfeldt, Matthew, and Kiel McQueen. "Does New Teacher Induction Really Improve Retention?" *Journal of Teacher Education* 68 (2017) 394–410.

Ronfeldt, Matthew, et al. "Does Preservice Preparation Matter? Examining an Old Question in New Ways." *Teachers College Record* 116 (2014) 1–46.

Scherer, Marge. "The Challenges of Supporting New Teachers." *Educational Leadership* 69 (2012) 18–23.

Schuck, Sandy, et al. "The Experiences of Early Career Teachers: New Initiatives and Old Problems." *Professional Development in Education* 44 (2018) 209–21.

Smith, Emily R. "Faculty Mentors in Teacher Induction: Developing a Cross-Institutional Identity." *Journal of Educational Research* (2011) 316–29.

Smith, Thomas M., and Richard M. Ingersoll. "What are the Effects of Induction and Mentoring on Beginning Teacher Turnover?" *American Educational Research Journal* 41 (2004) 681–714.

Sowell, Martha. "Effective Practices for Mentoring Beginning Middle School Teachers: Mentor's Perspectives." *The Clearing House* 90 (2017) 129–34.

Suriano, Kirrianne Bird, et al. "Here to Stay: A Case Study in Supporting and Empowering Teachers." *Kappa Delta Pi Record* 54 (2018) 127–29.

U.S. Department of Education. "Survival Guide for New Teachers." https://www2.ed.gov/teachers/become/about/survivalguide/message.html

Wang, Hui, et al. "Self-Efficacy and Causal Attributions in Teachers: Effects on Burnout, Job Satisfaction, Illness, and Quitting Intentions." *Teaching and Teacher Education* 47 (2015) 120–30.

Wiebke, Kathy, and Joe Bardin. "New Teacher Support: A Comprehensive Induction Program Can Increase Teacher Retention and Improve Performance." *Journal of Staff Development* 30 (2009) 34–38.

Womack-Wynne, Carly, et al. "Teachers' Perceptions of the First-Year Experience and Mentoring." *International Journal of Educational Leadership Preparation* 6 (2011) 1–11.

Yost, Deborah S. "Reflection and Self-Efficacy: Enhancing the Retention of Qualified Teachers from a Teacher Education Perspective." *Teacher Education Quarterly* 33 (2006) 59–76.

www.ingramcontent.com/pod-product-compliance
Lightning Source LLC
Chambersburg PA
CBHW060608230426
43670CB00011B/2028